The Art of I

The Law of Attractic

MW00779070

Outstanding...I Loved It.

"Outstanding. Reading this beautiful book brings about inner peace while also teaching you how to live from inner peace. Heartfelt and healing. I loved it."

Dr. Joe Vitale
Star of *The Secret* and author of *Zero Limits* and *The Miracle*

~~~~~~~

Life Changing, Inspirational and Motivating!

"Life changing, inspirational, and motivating! Whether you're a martial artist or not, Dr. Bohdi Sanders' provides a clear and concise, easy-to-read, and practical guide to living a life of inner peace. He is not concerned with only one tradition or school of thought, but explores many different methods to encourage you to experiment and find the one that suits you and which best enhances your life.

Bohdi has done a great job capturing what it takes to help you live your life to the fullest. *The Art of Inner Peace* is full of insights, inspiration, and useful information on how to be a high achiever and live a life of inner peace. Your success in any area of your life will be guaranteed when you apply and practice the formula laid out in this amazing book. *The Art of Inner Peace* is a goldmine of information for personal development!"

Sifu Al Dacascos
Martial art grandmaster, champion, and founder of Kajukenbo WHKD,
author of the #1 bestseller, *LEGACY: Through the Eyes of the Warrior*,
and founder of the Dacascos Tactical System (DTS).

~~~~~~~

This Work is Genius!

"This work is genius! Ideal tool for seekers of personal empowerment with tips for overcoming challenges and misperceptions of ourselves and others, and in reminding us, as Bohdi Sanders does brilliantly, happiness is what we make of it – it is a door that opens from the inside."

Frank W. Dux
Martial arts legend whose life is depicted in the movie, *Bloodsport*.
Frank Dux holds 14 martial arts world records
and is the author of *The Secret Man*.

Bohdi has Written a Masterpiece!

"THE essential manual for living a peaceful, happy, and tranquil life...This book is the most essential, thorough, and complete manual to providing the secret to a more harmonious and authentic life. I cannot recommend it enough.

Victoria M. Gallagher
Bestselling author of *Practical Law of Attraction*

~~~~~~

Highly Recommended!

"I highly recommend *The Art of Inner Peace*. Dr. Bohdi Sanders uses easy to understand language to teach how to have total control over your mind. You will learn how to cleanse and reprogram your subconscious mind, including misinformation and negative programming. You will also learn how to actively control your thoughts. *The Art of Inner Peace* is a worthy addition to any library."

John Shearer, Mindfulness Master
Author of *Mindful Insights: A 52 Week Journey to Master Your Mind*

~~~~~~

Extremely Important for Today!

I have read a couple of books by Dr. Bohdi Sanders and have always been impressed by the simplicity and accessibility of the style and the depth of the topics covered. I believe, however, that this book contains the heart and mind of the wisdom the author developed in his own life.

This book covers a topic of extreme importance for today. It comes out during a time of global pandemic – people all around the world experiencing stress, fear, and chaos. Speaking of inner peace, for many, may seem irrelevant considering the issues we are dealing with, but it is exactly what we need the most.

I am grateful that Dr. Sanders has given us his experience and wisdom. I hope it will take root in my mind, as I hope more and more people will learn about it and find peace.

Rev. Stanislao Esposito
Roman Catholic priest and 2nd degree black belt in taekwondo

The Art
of
Inner Peace

The Art of Inner Peace
The Law of Attraction for Inner Peace

Library of Congress Cataloging-in-Publication Data
Sanders, Bohdi, 1962-
The Art of Inner Peace
ISBN – 978-1-937884-27-7

1. Self-Help. 2. Self-Improvement. 3. Inner Peace. 4. Peace.
5. The Law of Attraction 6.Title

Kaizen Quest Publishing

Table of Contents

Foreword...viii

Introduction..xi

Inner Peace Comes from Within..1

Your Thoughts Create Your Reality....................................13

Cleansing Your Subconscious Mind....................................27

Your Mind vs. Your Emotions..45

Correct Actions Lead to Inner Peace..................................55

Your Words are Powerful..71

Develop Good Habits and Stay Calm...................................81

Ban Fear and Worry from Your Life....................................89

Actively Choose Inner Peace...103

Don't Allow Others to Sidetrack You................................ 113

Mind Your Own Business... 129

Overcoming Obstacles and Anger......................................137

Be Patient and Practice Forgiveness..................................147

Practice Kindness and Compassion.................................... 155

Determine to be Happy and Grateful.................................. 163

Live Your Life Your Way.. 173

Live in the NOW.. 183

The 12 Laws of Karma and Inner Peace............................. 191

Your Inner Peace Roadmap... 205

Do It Anyway.. 219

If... 220

The Prayer of Saint Francis.. 221

Six Important Guidelines in Life.......................................222

About the Author..223

Foreword

You could say that I'm somewhat of a self-help book junkie. I have a profound love for personal development because it has literally changed my life in so many wonderful ways.

I used to be a burned-out financial consultant, and that is what led me to discover more about myself and find my true passion in life. I've been so blessed to get to create hundreds of meditative and hypnotic recordings, write books about the law of attraction, teach online courses, and publicly speak on the topic for the past 22 years.

When Bohdi approached me about his new book, *The Art of Inner Peace*, I felt honored to read it, especially since he mentioned that reading my book was the reason he felt inspired to contact me.

I immediately familiarized myself and became impressed with the body of his work over the past decade, and I felt even more privileged and delighted after seeing the remarkable catalogue of his writings.

In *The Art of Inner Peace*, Bohdi has taken his readers in a different direction from his traditional writing on the subject of martial arts and warrior philosophy. Make no mistake, this book is not only going to become the cherry on top of his existing philosophical teachings, but I believe it's going to transform lives in a whole new way, as well as help other self-help seekers with his insightful approach to peace.

What I love about this book is the whole premise of understanding that what we truly want in our lives is inner peace. Nothing outside of you can bring about that peace. Yet, we all go searching for those external things that we believe will make us happy. Additionally, we think our unhappiness stems from outer events, situations, and people who disappoint us and "control our emotions." Our habitual mindsets, coupled with so many negative influences in the world today, have people very intolerant. A change is needed, and *The Art of Inner Peace* could easily be the catalyst for such change.

The way I think about the mind and what I teach is very much in alignment with this outstanding book. With its blend of concepts based on traditional ideas and new thought philosophies, it leaves no stone unturned in guiding the reader toward a greater understanding of how the mind works to create inner peace. It is an art. That's a great way to describe inner peace because it is absolutely a skill. You can study it and learn to become a master of this craft.

My honest opinion is that this book is most appropriate and the exact right book to put on your priority list at this interesting time in history because it's essentially what is needed most right now. It is designed to help you live your best life, and it is going to get you through any difficulties you experience. Having read many books on this topic, I've never read one that is more comprehensive than *The Art of Inner Peace*. I trust that it shall become THE essential manual for living a peaceful, happy, and tranquil life and deserves prime real estate on any spiritual seeker's bookshelf.

As you curiously flip through the wisdom on each page, every aspect of how to think and reprogram yourself to live your life at a higher level unfolds.

Coming from the perspective of a Law of Attraction teacher, this book would only enhance the reader's understanding of how you have created your own disharmony, and more importantly, the exact processes for turning your life around so that you can actively cultivate a life of inner peace. All you need to do is decide to consistently follow the clearly written guide, and you will find that you can shape your own destiny.

Each chapter of this book brings you closer to having a life you love. It provides the background, understanding, instructions, and deep thoughts to ponder. This book is the most essential, thorough, and complete manual to providing the secret to a more harmonious and authentic life.

I cannot recommend it enough. Whether you are just beginning your journey to a more enlightened life or you are an advanced student of metaphysical studies, there is so much here for everyone who chooses to take the time to read and study the lessons outlined in this book. What Bohdi has written is a masterpiece, giving you a solid foundation to create a dream life of happiness and inner peace.

Victoria M. Gallagher

Bestselling author of *Practical Law of Attraction,*
Hypnotist and Creator of HypnoCloud Apps
Victoria can be reached on her website:
https://victoriamgallagher.com

Introduction

For several years, I struggled with successfully maintaining a tranquil spirit and peaceful mind. As a teacher in very rough schools and a martial artist trained for hard-core self-defense, I have often found myself dealing with people who were not honorable, trustworthy, or well-intentioned. I have had many negative experiences with people and have definitely seen the malicious and darker side of the human spirit.

In addition, once my philosophical books became popular, and I found myself in the public eye, I was attacked endlessly by haters and internet trolls whose sole purpose seemed to be to destroy my reputation and hurt my family with unfounded libel, slander, and defamation. I saw how malevolent and nasty some people in our world could be.

I am very much an introvert and have always been a loner for the most part; these negative personal experiences only served to push me further into my own little world. I enjoyed being alone and would rarely even take phone calls as I simply did not want to talk to people. I spent much of my time in my own head thinking about life and wisdom, training, reading, and writing. I was completely jaded and no longer trusted anyone.

Moreover, after six years of football, 37 years of martial arts, and almost 40 years of bodybuilding, I was having physical issues. I had seven surgeries, one after another over a period of four years, including an emergency surgery to remove a brain tumor. In addition, while recovering from my surgeries, I was rear-ended by a drunk driver, and I found myself strapped to a board and rushed to the hospital with back and neck injuries which added to my physical challenges.

As you can imagine, the stress of these things was not conducive to a positive outlook on life, much less inner peace. It got to the point that I was not even meditating anymore, as I had a very hard time quieting my mind. I was used to quieting my mind through training and meditating, but all of a sudden, I wasn't able to do either on a regular basis, which I found discouraging and demotivating.

At the same time, I was allowing the negative events in my life and the maliciousness of some people to cause me to have a negative outlook towards people in general. I became very cynical and found it hard to trust other people or to have positive feelings towards those I did not know well. Needless to say, I was not in a positive place as far as my feelings towards others or my own inner peace.

I had been pushing myself very hard and not only continued my writing but started my own publishing company. I wrote 15 books, hundreds of articles, ghostwrote a #1 bestseller, and published eight books for other authors, all in only 10 years. I also did all my own daily marketing and dozens of interviews. Dealing with all this and my injuries, surgeries, and normal family life left me completely burned out! I felt mentally drained.

It was time to make a change. I knew that I had to make some changes to rebalance my life and regain my inner peace. I took some time off to decide what direction I should go next and to spend time getting rebalanced. I immersed myself in my studies and reacquainted myself with many of my favorite authors and the writings of the ancient sages.

I did an intense study on forgiveness and why it is important to forgive even my worst enemies, which has always been something that I have struggled with. I renewed my mind, transformed my thinking, forgave those who had wronged me, and regained my inner peace. Suddenly, meditation was easy for me again, and I started practicing many of the holistic arts that I had allowed to fade away while I was so busy building my business and recovering from one surgery after another.

Over the last seven years, I have dealt with more stress, surgeries, injuries, malicious people, deaths, and family challenges than I had during the rest of my life combined. But in the end, I came out victoriously. I regained my inner peace, and the things that used to anger or irritate me no longer bothered me very much at all. Where I used to get angry or irate when someone libeled or slandered me, I now simply shake my head, smile, and laugh.

I found that with real inner peace comes a different mindset, a mindfulness in which I recognize that I only control *my* thoughts and actions, no one else's. Now I accept life as it is, not as it should be or as I would like it to be. Small things make me happy, and it is hard for anyone to upset me. I play with my grandsons like an overgrown kid. I simply live my life my way and allow others to do the same.

Through some inner work and forgiveness, the cleansing of my mind, being mindful of my thoughts and words, and the other principles which I discuss in *The Art of Inner Peace*, I have overcome all of those challenges that were weighing me down. Once I got to this place in life, I knew what the topic of my next book was going to be – how to find and maintain lasting inner peace.

I took all of the challenges and negative experiences in my life, overcame them, and turned them into something positive. Not only did I use them as a learning experience, but I used those experiences, and the principles which helped me overcome them, to help others as well. That led me to write *The Art of Inner Peace*.

The Art of Inner Peace is about overcoming life's challenges and not allowing them to drag you down. It is about learning to live your life your way, no matter what anyone else thinks or says about it. It is about being happy and not allowing the opinions or actions of others to interfere with your inner peace.

In *The Art of Inner Peace,* I provide you with all the principles that you need to develop and maintain your inner peace. If you integrate the principles in this book into your daily life, they will transform your life in more ways than you can imagine.

Once you read *The Art of Inner Peace*, you will be able to clearly see many of the things which have been holding you back in life. Some of the science I share in this book will completely shock you, as it did me when I was doing the research. There are so many ways that we disrupt our own inner peace without even knowing it!

The Art of Inner Peace will help you avoid many of these mistakes and pitfalls by making you mindful of them. It will also provide you with many techniques and helpful advice on how to reverse the damage those mistakes may have caused in your life. This is a self-help book that truly puts you in charge of your life!

Designing the cover for *The Art of Inner Peace* was a process in and of itself. I had many ideas that would have made a very nice book cover, but somehow none of them adequately expressed the content of this book. While meditating on it, a vision of a simple lotus flower continued to appear in my mind.

I found that the lotus flower was the perfect symbol for *The Art of Inner Peace*. The lotus flower has many different symbolisms, and each one fits in perfectly with the principles of inner peace.

The ancient Egyptians saw lotus flowers as being symbolic of creation, rebirth, strength, and power. In Christianity, the lotus is seen as a representation of purity and the creation of the universe. Some have associated the lotus flower with Jesus, as the lotus rises from the muddy darkness for three days before it blooms.

Lotus flowers also have symbolic meanings in Hinduism, Sikhism, and Buddhism. In Hinduism, the lotus symbolizes the part of the soul that motivates one to overcome his struggles and strive for spiritual enlightenment. In Sikhism, it is a symbol for how one should live his life. Sikhs use the lotus flower as an analogy for remaining pure and staying unaffected by the evils and darkness of an impure world.

In Buddhism, the symbolism of the lotus flower is a representation of life itself. The lotus flower's roots grow deep in the mud. Buddhists see the mud as suffering, challenges, and obstacles that everyone faces during their life. To them, the lotus symbolizes overcoming and rising above these obstacles, which is a perfect analogy for maintaining your inner peace.

Lotus flowers also represent spiritual awakening, purity, and faithfulness in Buddhism. The fact that the lotus flower emerges from the mud to become a beautiful flower represents a human being rising from all the negativity and challenges in life to achieve wisdom, purity, self-regeneration, enlightenment, and rebirth. Buddhism teaches that every individual has the potential to rise from the murky darkness and become perfect and enlightened.

To the Buddhist, different color lotus flowers represent different things. The blue lotus symbolizes the spirit's victory over earthly knowledge and wisdom. White lotuses symbolize peace and purity. Red flowers represent love and compassion. Purple flowers represent the Noble Eightfold Path, which is one of the essential teachings of Buddhism. And the gold lotus flower symbolizes true spiritual enlightenment.

The lotus flower blooms slowly, one petal at a time. This symbolizes the gradual steps that it takes to reach inner peace and spiritual enlightenment. Even though it grows deep in the darkness and mud, it rises above those challenges and becomes a thing of beauty. It detaches itself from the water and the muddy environment in which it is born and rises above those things which would hold it back in its quest to reach light or enlightenment.

It symbolizes new beginnings, wisdom, the purity of the human soul, and a new life, which is what you will find if you patiently follow the principles set forth in *The Art of Inner Peace*. I felt led to use the symbol of the lotus flower to embody the kind of life that awaits you once you come to a place of inner peace and tranquility.

I hope that you thoroughly enjoy your study of the principles of inner peace and that you will find this book helpful on your journey. If you adhere to these principles, your life will change in ways that you can't even imagine. Your life is a journey – find the path that captures your heart and follow it to the end!

In order to write about life, first you must live it.
Ernest Hemingway

The Art
of
Inner Peace

Chapter 1
Inner Peace Comes from Within

Inner peace is beyond victory or defeat.
Bhagavad Gita

People look for happiness, tranquility, and contentment in many places, searching for that ever-elusive inner peace, which we all desire at a deeper level, to provide peaceful satisfaction in their life. But what exactly is this inner peace which people so desperately want and need? Where does it come from, and how does one find it?

Inner peace is defined as a state of mind where calmness and satisfaction exist, with all other unwanted factors being constant. It is being mentally and spiritually at peace, no matter what is happening around you. It is a way of life where one maintains a calm mental state in the face of disharmony or stress.

Living a life of inner peace does not mean living a life where there are no challenges, troubles, or stress, but rather that, in the midst of those trying times, one is able to maintain his or her state of calmness and not be affected by those external influences.

Many people are confused about what inner peace truly means. They see perpetual inner peace as only being available to monks who live in an isolated environment, such as a Buddhist temple or a monastery, but that is misguided thinking. Inner peace is not the absence of stress or problems, but the ability to preserve a peaceful mind and successfully deal with whatever comes your way.

When we were born, we effortlessly enjoyed inner peace. The only concerns we had were having a full stomach, being loved, and sleeping peacefully. But we soon learned from our environment and those around us that our inner peace could be easily disrupted. Stress, troubles, desires, and conflicts have a way of robbing us of our inner peace if we do not know how to maintain it in our lives.

And maintaining our inner peace does not come naturally; it is something that you have to cultivate. It is not a natural response to someone who is screaming at you or to someone who is trying to disrupt your life in some way. Our natural, human response when someone is verbally attacking us or trying to undermine our life is to respond in kind. But that doesn't keep you calm amidst the storm. If anything, it gets you more riled up and causes your mind to continue replaying the incident for days or weeks after the fact.

You must actively cultivate inner peace in your life; it doesn't magically appear out of the blue. Think of it this way; if you want to have a garden which provides you with fresh vegetables throughout the summer, you must first understand how to garden; you must know something about the principles of gardening.

If you don't understand the principles behind gardening, even if you get the right seeds and plants, and plant them in good soil, they will not produce the harvest you want. If you want the benefits from the seeds you have planted, you must cultivate that garden; you have to work at it. The same principle applies to developing inner peace in your life. It is not a matter of simply reading a couple of books and deciding to live a peaceful life. You must take action and discipline yourself to live the kind of life you want.

Making a firm decision not to allow anything to disrupt your inner peace is simply the starting point, but there is much more to it than that. To be successful at any art, you must first understand the core principles behind that art. Desiring to succeed in your art is merely the first step; then the work starts.

Since I have been a martial artist for over 37 years at the time I am writing this book, I will use martial arts as an example. When you first desire to learn martial arts or to earn a black belt, that is only the first step towards your goal. Desiring something is not the same thing as having it or earning it.

This is true with everything in life, whether earning a college degree, a black belt, or becoming a good golfer. Whatever you want to accomplish in life, you must first have a burning desire to accomplish it and to bring it to fruition.

Desiring to possess the skills of a black belt is essential, but your desire alone will not produce results; you have to consistently put in the work and the effort to achieve your objective. You don't develop the skills of a black belt overnight. It is a process that can take years, and even then, earning your black belt is merely the first step in a long, ongoing process of mastering your art.

The same principle applies to mastering the art of inner peace. First, you must have a strong desire to live a life of inner peace, and then you must learn the principles of developing your inner peace. Next, you have to consistently integrate those principles into your life and then maintain the inner peace that you have cultivated. It is not easy, but it is worth the effort.

Eleanor Roosevelt once stated, "It isn't enough to talk about peace. One must believe in it. And it isn't enough to believe in it. One must work at it." Many people talk the talk, but few walk the walk. You will see a lot of people talk about inner peace, and they truly believe what they are saying, but very few of them are willing to put in the work to consistently maintain that inner peace in their own lives.

Reading about inner peace and believing that inner peace is a good thing and necessary to your health is great, but neither of those is going to change your life. If you sincerely want to change your life, you have to start with your mind; you have to actually apply the principles of inner peace in your life. Only then will you consistently see the benefits of living a life of inner peace and tranquility on an ongoing basis.

Inner peace is a day-to-day, and sometimes a minute-to-minute, challenge. It is a result of overcoming a multitude of trying events, judgments, and challenging people. Achieving inner peace is not something you accomplish once and then sit back on your laurels; it is an ongoing process of learning to master your mind and emotions. And it takes dedicated effort, at least in the beginning. That is why so few people are successful at maintaining their inner peace; they are not willing to *consistently* put in the effort.

Many people start martial arts classes, both children and adults. But very few of those people are willing to put in the consistent effort to become a black belt, and even fewer go on to become masters of their martial art. Fewer than 2% of the people who start martial arts classes continue to earn a black belt. And it is estimated that only one out of 1,000 go on to master his or her art.

Norman Vincent Peale said, "The life of inner peace, being harmonious and without stress, is the easiest type of existence." If it is so easy, why aren't a lot more people living a life of inner peace? The answer is that they give up before they achieve a life of inner harmony because they allow life's stresses and challenges to sidetrack them.

Nothing is easy in the beginning. Everything worth doing in life has a learning curve to overcome before it becomes second nature in your life. Take the art of meditation for example. Science has proven the tremendous benefits of meditation; there is no doubt about how much meditation can help those who are willing to consistently integrate this practice into their daily lives. But very few people have the discipline to meditate daily, even when they know that it is good for them.

Why is that? The answer is that they allow other things to sidetrack them. They get too busy, too stressed, or they are simply not in the mood. Many people who start meditating do so consistently for a couple of weeks or more, then gradually allow life to get in the way.

They start to skip their meditation for one reason or another, and soon they find that they have forgotten about meditating altogether. One missed day turns into three, three days soon turns into a week, and a week soon turns into a month. Before you know it, you forget

3

about the benefits that meditation was having in your life, and the thought of meditating rarely crosses your mind.

If you are not careful, the same thing will happen when you are first learning the art of inner peace. You start out excited about the prospects of living a life of inner peace and tranquility, and you keep it fresh on your mind. When some person at the grocery store is rude to you, your mind says, "No! I am not going to allow this person to disrupt my inner peace!" So you smile and say, "Have a nice day," and go on your way feeling good about yourself.

But, as you get back into your regular routine, if you are not mindful and keep your goal of living a life of peace fresh on your mind, you start to forget about maintaining your inner peace. And the next thing you know, someone snaps at you, and you snap back, and then you are upset about it for the rest of the day. You just allowed the actions of someone else to disrupt your inner peace.

This can happen before you know it. That is why you must keep your intention of maintaining your inner peace fresh on your mind, at least until it becomes second nature to you. And to do this, you must first understand the principles of inner peace and integrate them into your life throughout each day.

You must put them into practice day after day until you start to cleanse your mind and change your thought process. You must do some house cleaning, starting with removing many of the unproductive beliefs and negative thoughts which you have been entertaining over the years.

Maintaining your inner peace is a process, just like earning your black belt. When you first start training in a dojo, you have to learn certain things which are totally foreign to you, and you have to unlearn some of the things which you have been doing wrong for years. When you have done something over and over for years, it becomes ingrained in both your mind and your physical body. It takes time and effort to break those bad habits and to replace them with new habits that are more advantageous for you.

Most of us have many bad mental habits that we have developed over the years as a defense mechanism we use in dealing with stress, rude people, or people we are in a relationship with such as friends, family, and our significant others. And many of those habits are contrary to maintaining inner peace in our lives.

Dr. Wayne Dyer taught that "Peace is the result of retraining your mind to process life as it is, rather than as you think it should be." This is an important point. Since inner peace resides in your mind, you must retrain your mind to see things differently. You must let go of your expectations. Stop expecting life to be as you think it should

4

be and start accepting life as it is. Stop expecting other people to behave as you think they should, and simply accept them as they are.

You cannot live a life of inner peace when you are constantly upset by external things, whether it is events in your life or other people in your life. You have to realize that the only thing you truly control in life is your mind, your attitude, your choices, and your actions. You can decide to be calm and happy no matter what else is happening in your life. It is your choice. You, and only you, get to choose how you will respond to every situation in life.

The key to living a life of inner peace is remembering that inner peace comes from within and that nothing outside you can disrupt your inner peace unless *you allow it to*. You are the commander of your life. Even if you have not been taking charge up until this point, you can change that immediately by making a firm decision to take charge of your life today! Hopefully, *The Art of Inner Peace* will help you in your quest to take control of your life once and for all.

> *We can never obtain peace in the outer world*
> *until we make peace within ourselves.*
> Dalai Lama

Once you decide to live a life of inner peace and to take charge of your own life, the next step is realizing that inner peace does in fact come from within. Inner peace is called "inner" peace for a reason – it resides in your mind. If you want inner peace, you have to develop it and maintain it internally because that is the only door inner peace comes through. Just like happiness, it does no good to search for inner peace anywhere outside yourself.

Furthermore, since inner peace resides in your mind, and since you are the only person who controls your mind, you are indeed in control of your own inner peace. You get to choose your response to every situation in your life, and therefore, you can choose to live a life of inner peace regardless of what is happening around you.

There is nowhere you can go that is more peaceful than your own mind once you cleanse it and learn how to control it. And because inner peace resides in your mind, you have the opportunity to take your inner peace with you wherever you go, no matter what else is happening in your life. Once you learn to control your thoughts, your inner peace is absolutely under your control.

The great Persian poet, Rumi, knew this as well. He wrote, "Remember, the entrance to the sanctuary is inside you." The word "sanctuary" means a place of refuge or safety and is synonymous with the word "immunity."

5

Your sanctuary is inside you. This means that you have a place to go to keep yourself safe and immune from the stresses of life, trying situations, and frustrating people. It is your mind which can give you immunity from everything that life has to throw at you. But you have to learn the combination to the lock on the door of this sanctuary so you can enter it anytime you want. You have the power if you are willing to learn how to use and control it.

Both Rumi and Jesus taught that the Universe, or the Kingdom of God, is within you. We have an awesome power available to us. You are much more powerful than you can imagine. We have been blessed with this remarkable power, but we were not given a user manual or instructions on how to use it. Once you figure out how to use your mind to develop and maintain your inner peace, nothing can phase you because you will be invulnerable to negative, external influences.

After you have put the principles in *The Art of Inner Peace* to work in your life, you will be able to consistently live a life of peace, if you are willing to consciously take control of your thoughts, which I will discuss in the next few chapters.

Science is continuing to prove that our minds are much more powerful than we ever realized. As John Milton stated, "The mind is its own place and in itself, can make a Heaven of Hell, or a Hell of Heaven." This means that you have the power to choose how you see every situation in your life. When you change how you choose to look at a situation, you ultimately change what that situation means to you. Therefore, you are able to change *your* reality.

My father passed away while I was working on this book. While it is always sad when someone you love passes away, especially when you feel he or she died too young, you can change your feelings about death. You absolutely have that power.

Now, I could allow myself to dwell on low-energy, sad thoughts such as, "I should have called my dad more often. I will never get to talk to him again. I wish we would have been closer. How he died was unfair. I am going to miss him so much, etc." These kinds of thoughts would do nothing more than cause me to feel sad, upset, and depressed about the death of my father. And these are the types of thoughts that most people have when a loved one passes away.

But you do have the power to see the death of a loved one in a different light. Instead of those sad, negative thoughts, you could choose to have happier thoughts like, "Oh, he must be so happy now! He is with his parents and grandparents. He was excited to see Heaven and be with God, and now he is there forever with no more pain or sadness, just pure joy. Wow, I am so happy for him. It must be amazing!"

6

Now, when you read those two completely different ways of thinking about the death of a loved one, it is obvious that your thoughts concerning that situation control how you feel about it. It all depends on how you choose to think about the situation. And make no mistake about it, you do *choose* how you see every situation in life; you *choose* what thoughts you will and won't dwell on.

You have total control over your mind. Actually, let me rephrase that. You have total control over your mind once you learn how to cleanse and reprogram your subconscious mind of the misinformation and negative programming and learn how to actively control your thoughts.

Since inner peace comes from within your mind, it depends on the thoughts you choose to dwell on and how you choose to see the events of the world. Inner peace is something that no one can take away from you. You can choose to allow your inner peace to be unsettled, but no one can take it from you without your permission.

Let me make an important point here. When I say that inner peace depends on how you choose to see the events of the world, I am not talking about refusing to acknowledge things for what they are. That is simply deceiving yourself. I am talking about seeing things as they truly are, but *choosing* not to be affected by those things in spite of what they are.

For example, Abraham Lincoln asked an audience how many legs a dog has if you count the tail as a leg. Well, as you would expect, most people in the audience answered, "five." When they did, President Lincoln told them that they were wrong, stating "The correct answer is four. The fact that you called the tail a leg does not make it a leg."

Choosing not to see the truth is not the path to inner peace; it is the path of self-deception. While turning a blind eye to the truth in certain situations may be a more blissful way to live, it can also be a very precarious way to live. Yes, ignorance is bliss, but it is also perilous. There is no true benefit in deceiving yourself. Ultimately, you must be mature enough to see things as they are, but not allow those things to disrupt your inner peace.

This level of maturity only comes from being able to control your mind and thoughts. Many either refuse to see the truth or see the truth, but cannot control their thoughts concerning what they observe, so their view of the truth triggers their unconscious emotional responses and disrupts their inner peace.

Our emotions are controlled by our thoughts, and those thoughts cause us to do things such as lose our temper and yell at someone who has pushed our buttons. If you don't take control of your

7

emotions, your inner peace will be sporadic. Once you learn to control your mind, you can also control your emotions.

To maintain your inner peace and calm during a stressful event, you first must be able to control your thoughts. You cannot control your emotional response to outside events until you learn to control your thoughts and beliefs concerning those events. And those thoughts and beliefs have been ingrained in your subconscious mind for many years.

If you want to see real, lasting changes in your life, you first have to make some changes deep inside your subconscious mind. You have to start by cleansing and reprogramming your subconscious mind. That consists of removing the negative thoughts and beliefs which you have held for years or even decades, and replacing them with thoughts and beliefs which support inner peace. Once you do this, you will start to see changes in your life.

When I was working on my doctorate in natural health, one of the premises that was common throughout my studies was that your body heals from the inside out. This means that you first have to change the environment inside your body before you will see the changes on the outside of your body.

The same principle applies when it comes to developing your inner peace. Things must get right on the inside before they can be right on the outside. Healing starts from the inside and then manifests itself on the outside. For example, when you are sick and the doctor gives you medicine, you take that medicine internally. It will start to work on the infection or issue inside your body, even if you don't immediately start to feel better.

Although the medicine starts to work internally when you take it, it may be several days before you begin to feel the physical results. The same principle applies to living a life of inner peace. You have to do the internal work to cleanse your subconscious mind and take charge of your thoughts before you can experience that inner peace in your life. Only when your inner life is balanced will you begin to see the results of inner peace in your words and actions.

Many people are constantly looking for something outside themselves to provide them with the inner peace that they are searching for, but what they are looking for has been inside them the whole time. Your mind is the ultimate source of inner peace, and once you master your subconscious and conscious mind, you will find the inner peace you have been looking for.

Our modern society has become used to having whatever they want very quickly and easily. We have fast-food restaurants where you order what you want and get your food without ever having to get

8

out of your own car. We can shop online without ever leaving our homes and have what we buy delivered to us the very next day. We can watch whatever we want on television anytime we want to see it. With just a few clicks of a computer mouse, we can access all the information we could ever want immediately on the internet. We enjoy getting what we want and getting it fast.

People have been spoiled in our modern society and are not accustomed to having to slow down and put in the mental work to get what they want. But when it comes to developing inner peace, cleansing your mind, and controlling your thought process, you must be patient and be willing to put in the work. Not everything comes quickly or easily in life.

Many want the benefits of living a life of inner peace without taking the time to put in the work and effort that must be done in order to consistently live that life of tranquility. There are no shortcuts to living a life of inner peace; you must be willing to apply the principles of inner peace to enjoy the benefits of it. It takes determination, patience, and effort.

When you decide to plant a garden because you want to enjoy fresh vegetables, you must first prepare the soil. You have to till the ground, remove any weeds, add some good compost or rich garden soil, and then you are ready to start planting. It takes a good bit of work to prepare your garden before you are even ready to plant your seeds.

If you simply went out and threw some seeds on the ground without preparing the soil first, you would never see the benefits of having a rewarding garden. Most of them would not grow at all. And even if by some miracle some of the seeds started to grow, it would not be long before the weeds crowded the young plants out, and you would never enjoy the vegetables that you wanted.

It takes preparation and cultivation to grow a successful garden. Even after the seeds grow into mature plants, you still must maintain your garden for it to produce results. You have to keep the weeds out, fertilize it, and water it. If you don't continue to give it the care and attention it needs, it will quickly wilt and die. It takes continual care for your garden to produce a bountiful crop. You don't stop caring for it once the plants start to grow, and you can see the results of your initial work.

The same principle applies to maintaining your inner peace. Inner peace must be constantly maintained, even after you have confidently cultivated it in your life. You must "fertilize and water it" with the techniques and principles in this book. There are no shortcuts to developing your inner peace; take the time and apply the principles.

9

You must start to prepare the soil of your mind in order to have lasting benefits. You do this by removing negative thoughts and beliefs from your subconscious mind, reprogramming your subconscious mind, and then learning to consistently control your thoughts. I will discuss how to do this in the next chapter. Essentially, we will start preparing your internal environment in order to plant the seeds of your inner peace.

Peace comes from within.
Do not seek it without.
Buddha

Thoughts to Ponder

To be calm is the highest achievement of the self.
Zen proverb

At the center of your being you have the answer;
you know who you are and you know what you want.
Lao Tzu

Promise yourself to be so strong that
nothing can disturb your peace of mind.
Christian D. Larson

Inner peace is when you do
what's right and let go of the rest.
Maxime Lagacé

Nothing can bring you peace but yourself.
Ralph Waldo Emerson

Inner peace is beyond victory or defeat.
Bhagavad Gita

It isn't enough to talk about peace. One must believe in it.
And it isn't enough to believe in it. One must work at it.
Eleanor Roosevelt

The life of inner peace, being harmonious and
without stress, is the easiest type of existence.
Norman Vincent Peale

Peace is the result of retraining your mind to process
life as it is, rather than as you think it should be.
Wayne Dyer

We can never obtain peace in the outer world
until we make peace within ourselves.
Dalai Lama

Peace of mind is that mental condition
in which you have accepted the worst.
Lin Yutang

Thoughts to Ponder

Peace comes from within.
Do not seek it without.
Buddha

True power is within, and it is available now.
Eckhart Tolle

Direct your eye inward, and you'll find a thousand
regions of your mind yet undiscovered.
Henry David Thoreau

Each individual is responsible for his own evolution.
Lao Tzu

What we achieve inwardly will change our outer reality.
Plutarch

The answer lies within ourselves. If we can't find peace
and happiness there, it's not going to come from the outside.
Tenzin Palmo

The inward journey is about finding your own fullness,
something that no one else can take away.
Deepak Chopra

When we are unable to find tranquility within
ourselves, it is useless to seek it elsewhere.
La Rochefoucauld

Man conquers the world by conquering himself.
Zeno of Citium

You have a treasure within you that is infinitely
greater than anything the world can offer.
Eckhart Tolle

Every breath we take, every step we make,
can be filled with peace, joy, and serenity.
Thich Nhat Hanh

Chapter 2
Your Thoughts Create Your Reality

Human beings, by changing the inner attitude of their minds,
can change the outer aspects of their lives.
William James

The thoughts that you dwell on determine your life; what you think, you become. This may sound overly simplified to you, but it is true nonetheless. Your thoughts are much more powerful than you have been led to believe. This is not some New Age mumbo-jumbo or mystical theory; it is a fact.

Think about it. Anything that you have ever accomplished in your life started with a thought. You planted a seed by thinking a specific thought, and then you nourished that seed by continuing to focus your thoughts on what you wanted. Soon, those thoughts led to actions, and your actions manifested those thoughts in your life. The thoughts which you *consistently* focus and meditate on dictate the direction your life will take.

This is not only true when it comes to accomplishing your goals but is also true in the negative sense. If you are allowing yourself to consistently entertain negative, low-energy thoughts such as hate, anger, jealousy, envy, and resentfulness, then you will manifest more of those things in your life.

What you think about expands. This has been proven to be true. Now, you may be thinking that you tried making positive affirmations and meditating on what you wanted to manifest, but it did not work. Even if your attempts at manifesting what you want in your life have not worked in the past, the principles which you will learn in this book will give you the tools and knowledge that you need to be successful this time around.

Saying your thoughts are not powerful and that they have no effect on your life because you tried to manifest something and it did not work is self-deception. Most people who make such statements did not even stay on track for a month. Some may have tried it for two or three months and then quit, and others only made a half-hearted attempt for a few weeks before quitting.

These principles are not magic. You don't work on changing your thoughts for a few weeks, meditate on and off for a while, and focus on the principles in this book whenever you happen to think about them and expect great results. That is a blab-it-and-grab-it mentality, and inner peace does not work that way. Developing your inner peace

13

and changing your internal thoughts is a process, and it takes time and dedication.

Think about it like this. If you were interested in developing great martial arts skills like Chuck Norris or Bruce Lee, do you think that is going to happen after you start training for a couple of months or even a year and then quit? Of course not!

Those men did not develop those skills overnight, and neither will you. They consistently focused their minds on developing their skills for years and years. They trained their minds, put their thoughts into action physically, mentally, and spiritually, and then consistently stayed on their path until their thoughts and goals became reality.

Bodybuilding would be another great example. If you wanted to become a professional bodybuilder, do you think you could do that in just a few months or even a year? Absolutely not! Bodybuilders work on their bodies for hours every day, and it still takes more than a year or two for them to get where they want to be.

You don't become a lawyer in a month or two. You don't become a professional dancer in a month or two. You don't become great at golf after a month or two. Why would you expect to manifest your goal of inner peace, or anything else, after "trying" for only a short period of time? That is just erroneous thinking.

You cannot manifest anything in your life with a half-hearted effort. Saying that you *tried* to control your thoughts and manifest your goal for a month or two, and nothing happened so you quit, indicates that you were never completely serious about it to start with. What did you expect?

Your life is what it is now because you have spent years entertaining certain thoughts and beliefs until they have become ingrained into your subconscious mind. And your subconscious mind worked to reinforce the beliefs that you fed it. You will not completely reverse years of negative thinking and misguided beliefs in a month or two of focused work.

That is not the way your thoughts work. While it is true that what you consistently focus your thoughts on will manifest in your life, it does not happen automatically or overnight. And that is a very good thing for us. Just think of the nightmare your life would be if every thought you had quickly came to fruition!

The fact is, manifesting what you want and making lasting changes in your life is a slow process, at least most of the time. Your thoughts become your desires; your desires lead to your actions; your actions change your life, and the changes in your life lead to continued changes in your thoughts. It is a never-ending cycle that starts with your thoughts and cycles back to your thoughts.

What you think about expands, so it is vitally important that you think about things that you *want* in your life, not about those things you don't want in your life. You must avoid entertaining any thoughts which weaken you or which bring negativity or strife into your life. When you start changing your thoughts, you will begin to see changes in your life.

If you want more inner peace in your life, you must consistently think peaceful, tranquil thoughts. As you start to think calm and peaceful thoughts, the desire to live a life filled with inner peace will grow. Then as your desire for inner peace grows, you will start to see your actions fall in line with those thoughts and desires. The more you act on those thoughts and desires, the more inner peace you will manifest in your life, and the more you will ingrain a lifestyle of inner peace into your subconscious and conscious mind.

Moreover, if you are not currently living a life filled with inner peace, then your thoughts must be wrong on some level. If you were thinking calm, peaceful thoughts, you would be living a life filled with inner peace. Anytime you are not manifesting what you want in your life, it is time to examine your thoughts and make some changes. Once you change your thoughts, you will see changes in your life. As Norman Vincent Peale taught, "Change your thoughts, and you change your world."

You change your conscious thoughts just like you change anything else in your life – by consistent practice. You will never be able to stop random thoughts from appearing in your mind, but you can change the thoughts that you allow to *remain* in your mind. When a negative thought appears in your mind, cancel it. Just say to yourself, "No, I will not allow that thought." Then replace it with a positive, constructive thought.

The more you stop negative, low-energy thoughts, and replace them with positive, higher energy thoughts, the faster you will take control of your conscious mind. You must be consistent with this practice until it becomes second nature for you; you must make it a habit.

If you don't take control of your thoughts, it will be impossible for you to consistently live a life of inner peace. If you have a great day and think nothing but calm, peaceful thoughts all day long, and then allow something to totally disrupt your inner peace the next day, entertaining all the negative thoughts which come with that stress, anger, fear, etc., you are taking one step forward and one step back, and accomplishing very little.

Consider another bodybuilding example. It takes much more to build the muscle mass of a professional bodybuilder than lifting

15

heavy weights and training. A bodybuilder must make sure that he is getting the proper nutrition and taking in enough calories to support his muscle mass. If he eats right one day and then stuffs himself with junk food and garbage the next day, he is making it very hard to reach his goal.

When you take one step forward and one step back, you end up right where you started. Controlling your thoughts one day and then allowing your thoughts to run wild the next will not lead to lasting changes in your life. You must be consistent in controlling your thoughts until it becomes your norm. Only then will you be able to consistently live a life of inner peace.

Living a life of inner peace requires you to control your conscious thoughts because, in addition to your subconscious thoughts, it is your conscious thoughts that determine how you respond to people and situations in your everyday life. If your mind is polluted with thoughts of anger, hate, jealousy, resentment, fear, etc., then your responses to the situations in your life will come from those low-energy thoughts and emotions.

Your thoughts are made up of both familiarity and emotion. This means that your thoughts come from both your background knowledge and the emotions which you have become accustomed to allowing in your life. Background knowledge is prior knowledge that you have obtained from different experiences, education, or events in your life, and can be skewed if your experiences have been negative.

For example, if you have had a negative experience every time you have dealt with people from a certain race or culture, you may see that race or culture in a negative light because of your personal experiences. Your background knowledge would be skewed because your subconscious mind generalizes and connects negative thoughts from your past experiences with people from that race or culture. This can cause you to have a warped view of reality.

If that experience has been overwhelmingly negative, then your emotions connected with those thoughts will be negative as well. While you may mentally understand that not every person from a certain race or culture is the same, those negative experiences have been embedded into your subconscious mind and will continue to skew your thoughts until those beliefs are deleted and replaced with a true assessment of your background knowledge.

Your mind will automatically gravitate to the thoughts with which it is familiar, and when you add emotion to those thoughts, they become very powerful. It is your emotions which charge your thoughts with energy and put things in motion. Your emotions and beliefs are what make your thoughts powerful.

16

To live a life of inner peace, you must remove every thought of personal condemnation. Condemn the wrong action if you must, but not the person who committed it. This may be a complex concept to wrap your head around, but it is imperative to your inner peace. Condemning the person instead of the action will almost always cause thoughts of anger, hatred, revenge, and other low-energy thoughts.

This is especially true if you are in the habit of condemning others and following that condemnation with emotions filled with anger, disgust, hatred, revenge, and punishment. Remember, your thoughts are made up of both familiarity and emotion. Your mind will always revert back to the thoughts that it is in the habit of entertaining. And if you add strong emotions to those thoughts, it further reinforces them in your subconscious mind.

You must change the way you think in order to change the results that your thoughts produce. If your mind is constantly troubled by low-energy thoughts, then it will be almost impossible to live a life of inner peace and tranquility.

To consistently live a life of inner peace, you must focus on calm, peaceful, loving thoughts. Remember, you must focus your thoughts on what you want, not on what you don't want. When you find your thoughts wandering and focusing on what you don't want (low-energy thoughts), stop yourself and ask, "What do I really want? Are these thoughts helping me move closer to my goal or preventing me from achieving my goal?"

Simplify your thought life! You don't have to have an opinion on everything in this world. I recall a scene in the movie *Crocodile Dundee*, where Crocodile Dundee was asked what he thought about the arms race. Dundee responded, "None of my business." It did not bother him at all because he did not consider it his business, and he did not allow his thoughts to dwell on it.

Dundee's lady friend was totally shocked that he was not concerned about the arms race, stating, "How can you not have an opinion on the arms race!" People seem to think that they must have an opinion on everything as if it makes them appear educated or intellectual. I have news for you; you don't have to have an opinion on everything in the world. Simplify your life and stop concerning yourself with things that you have no control over.

Many of the things in this world that add stress to your life and disrupt your inner peace are things which you can do nothing about. If you can do nothing about them, why waste your mental energy or disrupt your inner peace by dwelling on them. Does thinking about things such as the arms race or what some countries may do with their nuclear weapons foster inner peace or increase your stress?

17

It would be more advantageous to you and your inner peace if you adopted the attitude of Crocodile Dundee and simply saw things which you can do nothing about as none of your business and move on. Focus on *your* life and *your* self-improvement!

Science tells us that we have somewhere between 6,000-60,000 thoughts per day, depending on the study. Many of those thoughts are not conducive to inner peace. To consistently live a life of inner peace, you must be selective about the thoughts you entertain. Don't entertain thoughts that have no purpose and that do not help you achieve your objectives. You must make it a habit to be aware of your thoughts and control them.

Scientists have proven that your thoughts can either weaken or strengthen you. This is easily proven with a simple muscle test. Hold your arm straight out and have someone push down on it to give you a baseline. Now think a peaceful, loving thought while he pushes down on your arm. Then think a hateful, angry, resentful thought and have him push down on your arm again. Feel the difference?

If simply thinking certain thoughts can weaken your muscles, as in the muscle test above, just think about what they are doing to other parts of your body and mind. This doesn't only work with the human body, but with other things as well.

Masaru Emoto did experiments on how human consciousness, and even certain words, could affect the molecular structure of water. In his book, *Messages from Water*, he showed how different words and messages changed the structure of ice crystals. Positive words such as "love" made the molecular structures more beautiful, while negative words such as "hate" distorted the molecular structure of the ice crystals.

Consider the fact that water makes up about 75% of the human body. If simple words can affect the molecular structure of water, then think how important it is for you to take control of your thoughts, rid yourself of negative, self-defeating thoughts, and replace them with positive, self-affirming beliefs.

David Hawkins, in his book *Power vs Force*, states that around 87% of people are functioning at an energy level that weakens them. How can you possibly live a positive life of happiness and inner peace if you are constantly weakening yourself through negative, low-energy thoughts? You must change the energy of your thoughts if you are ever going to be able to consistently maintain your inner peace and tranquility!

Another fact to consider is that if you think about something for even a period of time as short as 17-20 seconds, your mind will start to focus more on the same type of thoughts. You have started the ball rolling, and you will begin to vibrate at that frequency. Remember, what you think about will increase in your life! I know I repeat that often, but there is a reason for that – it is vital that you understand how important this concept is to your inner peace.

It is crucially important to your goal of living a life of inner peace to actively create the life that you want to live by controlling your mind and your thoughts. Your thoughts create your reality, so design your reality as you want it to be.

Living a life of inner peace does not come automatically; you must cultivate it by being the master of your mind. If you cannot control your thoughts, you cannot control your emotions; if you cannot control your emotions, inner peace will continue to elude you. You must control your thoughts in order to control your emotions and live a life of inner peace.

In addition, it is not merely your conscious thoughts that you must change. You have spent years feeding certain thoughts and beliefs to your subconscious mind. Subsequently, they have become embedded in your subconscious and are accepted as truth by your subconscious mind.

If you try to control your thoughts without first dealing with all the negativity and false beliefs which have been embedded into your subconscious mind, you are fighting an uphill battle. You must address the issues of your subconscious mind first.

The Subconscious Mind

It is a psychological law that whatever we desire to accomplish we must impress upon the subjective or subconscious mind.
Orson Swett Marden

Your subconscious mind is much more powerful than you ever considered, if you have even thought about it at all. Most people have never really given the subconscious mind much thought. In fact, most people have never thought about it at all outside the possible exception of those who have dabbled in subliminal meditation CDs. But your subconscious mind plays a major role in the success or failure of your quest to develop and maintain your inner peace.

The science of psychology has now conclusively proven that most of our struggles come from the depths of our subconscious mind and that our subconscious mind contains vast amounts of information that affect our behavior. All the information which we have learned in various forms since our birth is still contained somewhere in our subconscious mind.

19

Imagine your subconscious mind as a computer hard drive. You may not know how to access every piece of information in your computer's hard drive, but you know that it is still in there somewhere. The same thing applies to your subconscious. Everything you have ever learned over the years, and every belief that you have had about yourself and life in general, is still programmed deep into your subconscious mind.

Moreover, all of that information is affecting your life today in one way or another, even if you are not aware of it. The most up-to-date scientific evidence suggests that 95% of your brain activity is unconscious, which means it is coming from your subconscious mind. This includes your habits, creativity, emotions, personality, beliefs, values, long-term memory, and more.

The science of Epigenetics, the study of changes in organisms caused by modification of gene expression rather than alteration of the genetic code itself, has proven that your subconscious mind can even change your physical body. Your mind has an effect, either positive or negative, on your DNA. Remember I stated that your mind is much more powerful than you think. When you learn to control your mind, you can change your whole life! And now science is starting to prove that this is absolutely true.

The thoughts buried deep in your subconscious mind define your world views, even if you are not aware of them. Those thoughts guide your beliefs, your morals, your view of the world, your view of yourself, and ultimately, whether or not you consistently live a life of inner peace. Therefore, in order to change your view of the world, your view of yourself, and your negative thoughts and beliefs, you must do some work on a subconscious level.

If you want to change a negative thought pattern or belief that is holding you back or disrupting your inner peace, you must start by working to change your core beliefs. You have to work on cleansing your subconscious mind. With the exercises presented in *The Art of Inner Peace*, you can change those thought patterns and replace them with positive thoughts that help you to maintain your inner peace no matter what is happening outside yourself.

Every word and thought is recorded in the "hard drive" of your subconscious mind. If you habitually speak badly about yourself, other people, or life in general, those words are now embedded into your subconscious mind. Your subconscious mind accepts those thoughts as truth. Furthermore, those beliefs, which you have strengthened by repetitive reinforcement through your words and thoughts, are now dictating your behavior, even though you are not consciously aware of it.

We are all familiar with the concept of "your life flashing before your eyes" when there is a close call with death. Many people who have had near-death experiences recalled that they saw everything in their life flash before their eyes as if they were watching a movie. How could that even be possible? The answer is because everything is recorded in your subconscious mind, even though you do not know how to access it.

Your subconscious mind is pulling the strings behind the scenes. It has been programmed over the years by your thoughts and words, by what you have read and seen, as well as, by what you have been taught. Because of that, it is now regulating everything you say and do to consistently fit in with your programmed core beliefs.

The subconscious mind does not care whether or not you have programmed it to see life negatively or positively. Like a computer, you can program it as you please; it simply accepts and uses the data (thoughts and words) that you program into it.

Emmet Fox, the Irish "New Thought" spiritual leader, had incredible insight into the workings of the subconscious mind and was far ahead of his time. He stated, "Before an idea can work in our lives, it must be accepted by the subconscious mind. When the idea is accepted by the subconscious, it *must* work in our lives...We make mental laws for ourselves and then we have to live under them."

Fox went on to say, "Every word you say and every thought you think are recorded in the subconscious mind. The Apostle Paul stated that 'We are transformed by the renewing of our minds.' Maybe we should take our subconscious recording more seriously and do some deleting and making a new recording."

Now, there's an important concept! If your subconscious mind can be programmed, much like a computer, then you also have the power to deprogram it. This means that you can get rid of the negative, unhelpful information which you have programmed into your subconscious mind over the years, and replace it with information that better serves your new self-concept and who you want to be now. *The Art of Inner Peace* gives you the "code" to do just that.

The unproductive beliefs which have been accepted by your subconscious mind must be removed before you can function without those beliefs disrupting your life. If you have consistently repeated that you can't speak in public, guess what, your subconscious mind takes that as the gospel truth and causes your life to conform to that belief. If you have repeated over and over again that you will never allow anyone to get away with being rude to you or that you will never forgive someone who betrays you, then your subconscious makes sure that your actions conform to that internal dialogue.

21

These are just two examples of the multitude of negative information that can be programmed into your subconscious mind. It would be beneficial to pause here and make a list of all the negative self-talk and negative views of the world that you have fed into your subconscious mind over the years. You will want to delete those beliefs and replace them with positive convictions which better suit the life you now want to live. Take a few minutes and list as many of these as you can.

You might be thinking that you no longer believe some of these negative thoughts, so they can't be affecting your life. But if you have never done the work to change or replace those negative thoughts, they are still there. Your subconscious mind is still trying to make your life fit into that mold. Don't worry; I am going to give you several techniques to help you change this.

Your mind will always find a way to justify everything you do or feel – every habit, every reaction, and every feeling or emotion. Your conscious mind will fight back when you try to change its long-held beliefs. This is because your subconscious mind is working behind the scenes to make sure that your mind, your words, and your actions fit the self-concept and core beliefs that you have programmed it to believe. Your subconscious believes the core truths and beliefs that you have consistently affirmed over the years.

The longer a core belief has been ingrained (programmed) in your subconscious mind, the more resistance you will experience and the harder it will be to change it. The good news is that the subconscious mind can absolutely be changed and transformed to believe what you want it to believe.

Look at it like this. A computer can get viruses because some bad information was somehow programmed into it. But your computer can be cleaned, and the viruses can be removed from the hard drive. After the viruses are removed, it works much better. It is faster and has more space for the information that you want to program into it. The information which was causing problems has been removed.

Your subconscious mind works in much the same way. You can use certain techniques to delete or change the negative information and beliefs that you allowed to be programmed into it. It is not a fast process, but it absolutely can be done.

Don't expect your subconscious mind to change overnight. You have spent years programming it with all of the information, beliefs, and values that it now contains. It will take some time to deprogram it and replace that information with beliefs and values which better serve you today. You must be patient and persistent in your mission to reprogram your subconscious mind.

22

I was very interested in bodybuilding for many years. Building and shaping your muscles takes a lot of work and does not happen overnight. You have to do the work and spend many hours training to build your muscle mass. You have to be more careful about what you put into your body and give it the proper nutrition and rest to see your desired results.

If you train consistently, provide your body the proper nutrition and fuel, and give it plenty of rest and recovery time, you will start to notice changes in your strength and appearance after a month or so. After six months, you will see many more changes. Your body will respond to your new habits.

But to maintain your gains, you have to continue the routine, making it a part of your overall lifestyle. If you stop and go back to your old eating habits and discontinue your training, you will gradually lose what you have worked so hard for.

The same principle applies to changing your subconscious mind. Once you decide to change your thoughts and words, and reprogram your subconscious mind, you have to be consistent. You may not see changes right away, but work on it consistently for 30-40 days, and you will see changes in your life.

Science has proven that it takes a minimum of 30 days to change a habit. And when you change any habit, you need to replace it with a more advantageous habit. Remember, the Universe abhors a void. Something will always take the place of any habit that you remove. You want to make sure that you replace your negative habits, or in this case, your negative thoughts, with positive habits (positive, constructive thoughts).

It would make no sense to have all the viruses removed, and then bring it back home and upload the same viruses on your computer again. When you start deleting the negative programming from your mind, you must replace it with the kind of thoughts that support the life you want to live. Replace the negative thoughts and beliefs with positive, self-affirming thoughts and beliefs.

There is one more thing you must understand before we get into the techniques to change your subconscious mind. The subconscious mind does not work in terms of negatives. This means that you can't tell your mind *not* to think of something. For example, if I tell you not to think of a shark, what is the first thing that you see in your mind's eye? Right, a shark.

Don't tell yourself, "I will not be negative anymore." It is much better to tell yourself, "I *will be* positive. I *am* a positive person." If I tell you not to think of a shark, the first thing you see in your mind's eye is a shark. But, if I tell you to think of a red ball, you no longer focus on a shark. Your mind's eye now sees a red ball. Feed your mind what you want it to focus on, not what you don't want it to focus on. That is a fine line, but an important point to remember.

Now it's time to get to work. In the next chapter, I will give you several techniques to reprogram your subconscious mind and to help you on your journey to living a life of calm tranquility.

Before an idea can work in our lives, it must be
accepted by the subconscious mind. When the idea is
accepted by the subconscious mind, it must work in our lives.
Emmet Fox

Thoughts to Ponder

You create your universe as you go along.
Winston Churchill

Whatever you think upon grows. Whatever you allow
to occupy your mind you magnify in your own life.
Emmet Fox

It is true that the subliminal in man is the largest part
of his nature and has in it the secret of the unseen
dynamisms which explain his surface activities.
Sri Aurobindo

Change your thoughts, and you change your world.
Norman Vincent Peale

Change the way you look at things,
and the things you look at change.
Wayne Dyer

We cannot solve our problems with the
same thinking we used when we created them.
Albert Einstein

Progress is impossible without change, and those who
cannot change their minds cannot change anything.
George Bernard Shaw

Although difficult, change is always possible.
What holds us back from making the changes we
desire are our own limiting thoughts and actions.
Satsuki Kiryuin

You only have control over three things in your life, the thoughts
you think, the images you visualize, and the actions you take.
Jack Canfield

Deep within, there is something profoundly known,
not consciously, but subconsciously. A quiet truth, that
is not a version of something, but an original knowing.
T. F. Hodge

Thoughts to Ponder

To shift your life in a desired direction,
you must powerfully shift your subconscious.
Kevin Michel

Except for your thoughts, there is
nothing absolutely in our power.
Rene Descartes

Your subconscious is a powerful and mysterious force
which can either hold you back or help you move forward.
Without its cooperation, your best goals will go unrealized;
with its help, you are unbeatable.
Jenny Davidow

Think good, and good follows. Think evil, and evil follows.
You are what you think all day long.
Joseph Murphy

Thoughts lead to purposes;
purposes go forth in action;
action forms habits;
habits decide character;
and character fixes our destiny.
Tyron Edwards

You are not a helpless victim of your own thoughts,
but rather a master of your mind.
Louise Hay

Thoughts are energy.
And you can make your world or break
your world by your thinking.
Susan L. Taylor

The best cure for the body is a quiet mind.
Napoleon Bonaparte

There is no thought in any mind,
but it quickly tends to convert itself into power.
Ralph Waldo Emerson

Chapter 3
Cleansing Your Subconscious Mind

Without meditation it is not possible
to control and master the mind.
Sri Satya Sai Baba

I have given you a quick overview of the subconscious mind and its importance to your life and inner peace. As I stated, in order to consistently maintain your inner peace, you need to cleanse and reprogram your subconscious mind. Now let's discuss how you can actually do that and make those changes to your subconscious mind.

There are several different techniques that can be used to remove the negative programming of your subconscious mind and replace it with positive, self-affirming beliefs. Let's get started and take control of your mind once and for all.

Meditation

Science has proven the many benefits of meditation, not just when it comes to your subconscious mind, but to your life in general. Meditation reduces stress, helps control anxiety, promotes emotional health, enhances self-awareness, improves sleep, helps control pain, decreases blood pressure, helps offset the effects of aging on the brain, improves concentration, helps fight depression, sharpens your attention span, helps addiction recovery, increases compassion, reduces your biases, and is helpful in reprogramming your subconscious mind. Whew, that is quite a list of benefits!

I can tell you from personal experience that I can always tell a difference in my stress level, my inner peace, and my overall attitude when I am meditating regularly compared to when I have allowed myself to neglect my meditation. It is like night and day. Meditation is one of the most crucial aspects of changing your subconscious mind, taking control over your mental state, and consistently maintaining your inner peace.

According to scientific studies, you have somewhere between 6,000-60,000 thoughts per day, as I stated earlier. The newest study was done by a team of psychology experts at Queen's University in Canada. They concluded that the average person has around 6,200 thoughts per day. But a study done in 2017 by the National Science Foundation concluded that the average person has 12,000-60,000 thoughts per day. Either way, that is a lot of thoughts every single day of your life. And many of those thoughts are simply mental chatter that add nothing of value to your life.

In addition, the National Science Foundation concluded that, of those thousands of thoughts, 80% of them are actually negative thoughts, and 95% of them are repetitive thoughts. Think about that for a minute. If 80% of your thoughts are negative and 95% of those negative thoughts are repetitive, that is a massive amount of negative programming that you are feeding into your subconscious mind!

In order to cleanse and make changes to your subconscious mind and have any chance of consistently maintaining your inner peace, you absolutely have to change that. There is no way you can maintain your inner peace and live a happy life if you are continually allowing your mind to dwell on negative thoughts 80% of the time, and repeating 95% of those negative thoughts over and over throughout the day.

Meditation is a powerful way to quiet your mind and give it a break from all of these repetitive thoughts. Regular meditation is a practice that can restore your inner harmony and mental energy. Consistent meditation is a vital aspect of maintaining your inner peace. The more you meditate, the more peaceful your life will become.

The Indian spiritual master, Sai Baba, stated "Without meditation, it is not possible to control and master the mind." If you cannot control your mind, then it is impossible to consistently live a life of inner peace and tranquility. There will always be someone or some situation that will disrupt your inner peace if you are unable to control your mind and emotions. Therefore, meditation is a must if you are to have any chance of living a life of inner peace.

J. Donald Walters, recognized as one of the world's foremost authorities on meditation, stated, "The more regularly and the more deeply you meditate, the sooner you will find yourself acting always from a center of peace." And Baba Ram Dass, the American spiritual teacher and psychologist, stated "Meditation and concentration are the way to a life of serenity."

Using meditation as a tool to control your mind, maintain your inner peace, and live a more serene life, is a practice that is taught throughout the world and in most religions. There is a reason for this – it works!

You don't need extensive instructions to meditate. In fact, it should come naturally to everyone. What could be easier than relaxing and sitting quietly? But since almost all of us have spent years not controlling our minds and allowing our thoughts to run wild and unchecked, it is not as easy as it should be. The first step is to learn to quiet your mind.

At first, you may find it hard to quiet your mind and sit silently, even for just a few minutes. But the more you practice, the easier it will become. Soon you will find that you look forward to your meditation time and the peace it brings to your life.

The good news is that modern science and technology have developed a way that makes it easier for you to learn the art of meditation. It is called binaural beats. Binaural beats is a form of sound wave therapy, and it really works. I have been using meditative CDs with binaural beats and different brain wave frequencies for years. And even if you have no experience meditating, these will put you into a deep meditative state.

Binaural beats work by sending a different tone, in a different frequency, to each ear. (Note: You do have to use headphones when using binaural beats to meditate.) Studies show that meditating with binaural beats can positively affect your behavior and sleep cycle, decrease your anxiety, increase your concentration, reduce stress, increase focus, improve confidence, improve long-term memory, enhance your mood, and help you reach a much deeper state of meditation.

There are five different frequencies used in binaural beats meditational CDs.

- **Delta Waves:** Waves which operate at a frequency of 0.5–4 Hz. Delta waves are associated with a deeper stage of sleep.

- **Theta Waves:** Waves which operate at a frequency of 4–7 Hz. These contribute to improved meditation, creativity, and sleep in the rapid eye movement (REM) phase.

- **Alpha Waves:** Waves which operate at a frequency of 7–13 Hz. These provide relaxation and a feeling of peace.

- **Beta Waves:** Waves which operate at a frequency of 13–30 Hz. These help promote concentration and alertness.

- **Gamma Waves:** Waves which operate at a range of 30–50 Hz. These frequencies promote maintenance of alertness while a person is awake.

As I stated, I have used binaural beats during meditation for years and can attest to the fact that they absolutely work. I am able to get into a much deeper meditation when using these types of meditation CDs than I do without them.

I have even had some of my students use binaural CDs during meditation, and they went into an extraordinarily deep meditative state. So much so, that at the end of the meditation, I had to actually bring them out of their deep meditation. And these were people who had never meditated before.

There are several companies which make binaural beats meditation CDs. Personally, I use a company called Brain Sync. I have found their CDs to be exceptional. They not only provide meditational CDs with binaural beats, but they also have CDs with guided meditations and subliminal messages.

I do recommend that you learn to meditate both with and without binaural beats. Find a quiet place in your home where you will not be disturbed, and sit with your back straight and your feet on the floor. I sit with my hands together, palms up, right hand over my left hand. Then quiet your mind, release your thoughts, and relax.

It is not necessary for you to get too technical as far as what kind of meditation that you do or to be overly strict about how you position your hands or feet. The most important thing at this stage is for you to learn to quiet your mind.

There are several different kinds of meditation. You may want to start with one of the guided meditations from Brain Sync, as guided meditations are a great way to learn to meditate. Don't try to force yourself to meditate for a specific amount of time. You will know when you are finished. If the guided meditation is 30 minutes, and you finish at 20 minutes, then stop.

The key to seeing results with your meditation is consistency. If you only meditate for a week, then stop for two weeks, then meditate for a couple of days, and then stop, you won't see great results. Consistency is vital. The more you practice, the easier it becomes, and the better results you will experience.

Once you start feeling the results of your meditation, you will start looking forward to it. The results will be there, even if you are not aware of them at first. After you get into the habit of meditating daily, if you want to do an easy test to see if your meditation is helping, just stop it for a few days and see if you can tell a difference. Most likely, you will be able to feel a big difference in your peace of mind, stress levels, and overall attitude.

Also, there are many relaxing music videos and CDs which integrate binaural beats with different frequencies to put you in a relaxed state and while elevating your energy. Certain frequencies are used to bring about specific energetic vibrations.

I find it helpful and relaxing to play these as background music while I am working on my computer or writing. There are dozens of these on YouTube, which you can access for free and play on your phone or computer while working or relaxing. I find that these can put you in an alternative state and help combat stress, anger, and frustration.

You can find them in many different frequencies meant to help with different issues. Find the ones which work best for you and use them to help maintain a peaceful, relaxed atmosphere while you work. This is a great way to help you maintain your inner peace.

In addition, you may also want to add some subliminal messages to your meditation time. These are messages that your subconscious mind can hear, but your conscious mind cannot. This is an easy way to reprogram your subconscious mind and can even be done as you go to sleep. Although the science behind subliminal messages is not conclusive, you might want to give these CD's a try and see if they work for you. One thing is for sure – they won't hurt anything, so what do you have to lose? This is a good supplement to your positive affirmations, which I will discuss next.

There is an old Peruvian proverb which states, "The tree of silence yields the fruit of inner peace." If you want to develop and maintain your inner peace, start by meditating daily. Make it a habit, and you will absolutely see positive results.

Positive Affirmations

Repeating positive affirmations about the changes you want to bring about in your life can be a very helpful tool to change your subconscious mind. An affirmation is simply making positive statements about how you want your life to be. You can look at positive affirmations as a blueprint for the life you want to create. You decide what you want in your life, and then you use positive affirmations as a way of reprogramming both your subconscious and conscious mind.

Many people get confused when it comes to making positive affirmations. Reciting positive affirmations is not about lying to yourself or saying things that aren't true in the hope that they will magically materialize if you say them often enough. This is a misconception. There is a difference between affirming what you want in life and merely lying to yourself.

Saying fifty times a day that you are the richest man in the world is simply a lie. It is not going to make you the richest man in the world. In contrast, stating that you are extremely blessed and live a life full

31

of all the best things that life has to offer will actually help you make those changes. The words you use matter.

No matter how many times you state that you are the richest man in the world, you know at both a conscious and subconscious level that this is untrue. Your subconscious mind will not accept that affirmation because it is obviously not your reality. Making ridiculous affirmations like that is simply wasting your time.

On the other hand, if you state that you are living a blessed life every day and that your life is filled with everything good, your subconscious mind will start to accept that as truth, and you will start to see positive changes in your life. You must construct your affirmations in such a way that your subconscious mind will accept them as truth.

Science has proven that positive thoughts are hundreds of times more powerful than negative thoughts, which is a good thing when you consider how most people speak about themselves. This gives you the power to change all the negative beliefs and thoughts that you have been programming into your subconscious mind for years or even decades. And to top it off, it is very easy to do, although it may feel awkward at the beginning.

The first step is to decide what you want for your life and what kind of person you want to be. Then make a list of affirmations that support your objectives. Make sure that you have worded your affirmations in a positive and believable way. Remember, your words matter, especially when it comes to affirmations. Then you simply set aside some time each day, two or three times a day is better, and recite your affirmations to yourself.

In order to make your affirmations even more powerful, you should get your emotions involved. Say your affirmations with feeling. Get excited about the changes you are making in your life and express that excitement through your voice as you recite your affirmations. Adding positive emotions and enthusiasm to your affirmations will supercharge them and take them to another level. If you do this, you will see results much faster.

Another practice that will boost your results is to say your affirmations while looking at yourself in a mirror. This will feel awkward at first, and you might even find this practice kind of hard to do until you get used to it. But it is a powerful tool and will make your affirmations more effective.

In addition, you can write your affirmations on your tablet, phone, computer, etc. This way, they stay fresh in your mind throughout the day whenever you see them. Say them as you are driving, sitting in traffic, or just taking a break from work. The more you affirm the life you want to live, the more you will be transforming your subconscious mind and bringing it in line with how you want to live your life.

I would also encourage you to say your affirmations after you meditate and before going to sleep at night, as your mind is relaxed and more open to accepting your declarations at that time. It only takes a few minutes, and the payoff is substancial. Try it and you will see the difference!

Doing your affirmations before going to sleep allows you to program your mind as you drift off to sleep. This is a powerful tool as these positive statements will be the last things you think about before going to sleep. Another way to amplify your affirmations is to visualize them as you speak.

Visualization

It helps if you can visualize what you want and who you want to be. When you add visualization to your affirmations, you amplify them. Actually see yourself living the life that you want to live, full of peace and tranquility. The process of visualization is like playing a movie in your mind's eye. When I say your "mind's eye," I am simply referring to seeing things in your mind, like I talked about earlier when I discussed seeing a shark or a red ball in your mind.

Your mind does not see words; it sees pictures. For example, if you want to develop and maintain inner peace, it is good to have a mental image of what inner peace looks like to you. Visualize that whenever you are repeating your affirmations on inner peace.

If you want to live in a nice house on a lake, visualize your house on a lake. Go into details about how it looks. Create the boat dock, the yard, the trees, the house, etc. The more detail you can visualize, the more authentic it becomes to your subconscious mind. Visualize you and your family enjoying the lake, relaxing in the house, playing in the yard, sitting by the fire pit, etc.

Suppose I say picture a dog in your mind. Do you see the letters that spell out the word "dog," or do you simply see a dog? Of course you see a dog. When you are reading a book, you don't picture words in your mind; you see images. This is how your mind works. That is visualization.

Visualization is a very powerful tool to help you develop and maintain your inner peace and change those negative images in your subconscious mind. In fact, an experiment was done with basketball players to see if visualization actually helped them on the court, and the results were nothing less than amazing.

The study divided the participants into players who physically practiced shooting free throws, and players who only visualized shooting free throws, but did not actually practice with the basketball. The players who actually practiced with a basketball improved their skills by 24%. What was unexpected was that the players who only visualized shooting free throws improved their skills by 23%, almost the same improvement as those who physically practiced with a ball. That is pretty remarkable!

If visualization can make those kinds of improvements with athletes, just think of how much it can help you control your mind. Your mind is much more powerful than you know, and once you learn to control it, you will be amazed at the results.

What is important when it comes to visualization is that you get as much detail into your visualization as possible. Include not only the visual piece but also the sounds, smells, and feelings. See it as if you are truly there.

For example, if you were visualizing shooting free throws with a basketball, see yourself walking up to the line, feel the shape and texture of the basketball. See the hoop, the net, and the backboard. Hear yourself bounce the ball. Feel the ball come off your fingers. See it traveling through the air perfectly. See the trajectory of the ball as you shoot and hear the swish of the net. See yourself follow through and hear the crowd cheer. Details, details, details!

So, how would you use visualization to help reprogram your subconscious mind? You can customize it any way you want. It is totally up to you. You could visualize yourself actually programming your subconscious mind, deleting the negative, non-helpful information, and replacing it with the positive information that you want to establish, much like reprogramming a computer. You could visualize yourself scrubbing the negative beliefs from your mind and then replacing them with beautiful images that better support your tranquility. Do whatever feels right to you.

The same thing goes for developing and maintaining your inner peace. See yourself living a peaceful, calm life and enjoying every moment stress-free and happy. See yourself walking away from the rude person in the store, feeling great that you did not allow him to disrupt your inner peace.

Visualize different situations which would normally disrupt your inner peace, and see yourself handling each of those situations peacefully with tact, class, and a big smile. Make a mental movie of each situation and always see yourself peacefully handling everything that is thrown at you. Always see yourself being successful, calm, and having a sense of inner peace.

Visualization works, and it is easy to do. All you have to do is discipline yourself to take the time to integrate it into your life. Remember it is very powerful when used in combination with your positive affirmations. Additionally, it can also be used during your meditation.

Vision Boards

A vision board is kind of like visualization, except you are actually looking at the pictures of what you want. Cut out photos of what you want and who you want to be, and place them on a board that you see throughout the day. This keeps prioritizes your goals and helps you visualize what you want in your life and what kind of person you want to be.

You can even turn your phone, tablet, or computer into a vision board by making a collage on your device or putting the pictures on your screen saver. I have a vision board on my computer which has 30-40 photos rotating on my screen saver. I take time throughout the day to stop and focus on these photos, picturing how great it is going to be living the life I see in the peaceful, beautiful photos.

The key to making a vision board is not just adding a bunch of photos of things you want, but adding photos that elicit an emotional response when you look at them. You have to add emotion and feeling to your desires in order to supercharge them. You want to feel butterflies in your chest when you look at your board and think about your goals.

My vision board showcases photos of a nice home on a beautiful lake with a boat dock and a nice big yard. When I see them, it makes me excited thinking of how nice it is going to be living there. I can't wait to tie my boat up to the dock, fish in the lake, and sit by the fire pit overlooking the beautiful lake. I can imagine my grandsons playing on the dock, diving into the lake, and having a great time.

You can use the same process to maintain your inner peace. Place beautiful, peaceful beach scenes or mountain scenes on your board or photos of your happy family. Maybe add some photos of people doing yoga or meditating peacefully, or some beautiful sunsets. You can use whatever creates a calm, peaceful mood for you. Personalize it as you need to in order to make it moving and meaningful for you.

Try making your vision board on your computer's screen saver, and you will see it daily. Keep your goal of living a calm, peaceful life constantly in front of you, so it is fresh on your mind. Using your phone as a part of your vision board allows you to take it with you everywhere you go. The more you focus your mind on your vision for your life, the faster you will reprogram your subconscious mind with the positive images that excite you.

Spend Time in Nature

You may be wondering what spending time in nature has to do with your mind or inner peace. The fact is, spending time in nature has been proven to be beneficial for your mental health. Clinical studies have shown that spending time in nature reduces cognitive fatigue and stress and can even help with depression and anxiety. It has also been proven to improve short-term memory, working memory, problem-solving skills, increase creativity, and increase feelings of positive well-being. And it can relax your mind and make it more receptive to the positive changes that you want. All of this makes spending time in nature very beneficial for you.

Even simply listening to the sounds of nature has been shown to reduce stress hormones up to 800% and to activate DNA segments that are responsible for healing and repairing the body. As far back as Roman and Greek times, people knew of the benefits of nature. Seneca stated, "We should take wandering outdoor walks, so that the mind might be nourished and refreshed by the open air and deep breathing." The Greek physician, Hippocrates, who gave us the Hippocratic Oath, stated, "Nature itself is the best physician." The benefits of spending time in nature are unquestionable.

Communing with nature has obvious health benefits, but what does it have to do with reprogramming your subconscious mind? If you are increasing your feelings of positive well-being, decreasing your stress levels, improving your problem-solving abilities and creativity, and decreasing your anxiety, it will be much easier for you to make changes to your subconscious mind.

It is hard to remove negative thoughts and beliefs from your subconscious mind if you are constantly stressed and anxious. When the stresses and worries of life are overwhelming for you, your focus is simply on surviving, not reprogramming your subconscious mind or maintaining your inner peace. You have to remove as much of that stress as possible from your life in order to be able to focus on developing your inner peace.

This is where spending time in nature is beneficial for you. It helps to put things in perspective; it relaxes your mind and helps you remove your stress and worries. Nature can calm your mind and quiet your troubled thoughts. Once you get your stress under control, it is much easier to do the work that is necessary to maintain your inner peace. Try it, and you will see the difference.

Breathwork

Another great way to decrease your stress and prepare your mind for meditation, affirmations, or visualization is through breathwork. There are many different breathing techniques that you can use to oxygenize your body and calm your mind. The one which I teach my students, and that law enforcement officers use to maintain their mental calm during stressful times, is called autogenic breathing.

Autogenic breathing is very simple. You breathe in deeply for four seconds, hold that breath for six seconds, then breathe out slowly for four more seconds. You can do this as many times as it takes to calm your mind. This oxygenates your body as well as calming your mind and can be done any time you need to compose yourself.

This technique will help calm you down during stressful situations and is a great tool to maintain your inner peace. I am sure you have heard the saying, when you are angry, you should count to 10 before you respond. Autogenic breathing works along the same principle, except it actually does more than give you time to think; it quiets your mind so you can think *clearly* before responding.

Autogenic breathing is also helpful in relaxing your mind when you are ready to go to sleep at night. Do a few cycles of autogenic breathing and clear your mind for a good night's sleep. And once you have relaxed your mind, it is a good time to do your visualization exercises and/or affirmations, as they stay fresh in your brain as you go to sleep for the night.

There is another breathing exercise that I like to do as well, as taught by Wim Hof. You simply lie on your back and breathe deeply in and out 30-40 times without stopping. After your last exhale, take one more breath in and hold it as long as you can, then exhale. Take another deep breath and hold it as long as you can. This is one cycle. Hof recommends doing three cycles. This both calms your mind and really oxygenizes your body. You will actually feel a little light-headed after doing this, but it is very healthy and feels great.

There are a couple of other breathing techniques that I mainly use either before or after meditating. The first is alternate nostril breathing. To do this, you simply put your thumb and index finger on the sides of your nostrils. First, use your thumb to push on the side of your right nostril and breathe in through your left nostril. Then close your left nostril and breathe out through your right nostril.

After breathing out through your right nostril, keep your left nostril closed and breathe in through your right nostril. Then close your right nostril and open your left nostril, and breathe out. Keep alternating your breathing like this for a couple of minutes.

The last breathing exercise I practice is one I learned while training to become a Reiki master. It is called Breath of Fire or Dragon's Breath and is part of Kundalini yoga or Kundalini meditation. This one is the most difficult, at least for me, but the more you practice, the easier it becomes.

To perform the Breath of Fire or Dragon's Breath, breathe in deeply through your nostrils three times, and then quickly and forcibly breathe in and out for several minutes. After several minutes, stop, take a deep breath in, and hold it for several seconds before exhaling. This is a great practice to do before your meditation. Like Wim Hof's breathing technique, you will feel a bit light-headed once you are done with this exercise, so make sure you are sitting or lying down when you practice this one.

Science has proven that these breathing exercises will relieve stress, enhance concentration, increase mindfulness, enhance lung function, and promote a feeling of well-being. If you perform one of these exercises before your meditation, visualization, or affirmation work, it will help increase their effectiveness and help replace the negative thoughts and beliefs in your subconscious mind with positive thoughts.

Stop Complaining

Most people never stop to consider that, not only is complaining a waste of time, but it is bad for your physical and mental health. Science has proven that complaining increases your cortisol levels, otherwise known as your stress hormone. The more you complain, the higher your level of cortisol. Essentially, when you complain, you are doing nothing more than stressing yourself out for no reason.

Higher levels of cortisol in your body can lead to several health problems, including depression, sleep issues (which can lead to even more health problems and more depression), higher blood pressure, digestive issues, and even an increased risk of heart disease.

Scientific studies have proven that complaining also makes you more likely to think negative thoughts, which obviously are not conducive to maintaining your inner peace. Basically, the more you complain, the more you train your mind to think negatively.

You are essentially wiring the synapses in your brain to react negatively to whatever you are complaining about. The more you think negatively, the more you increase further negative thinking, which is the exact opposite of what you are trying to do by reprogramming your subconscious mind. Thus, complaining is hindering your progress towards living a life of inner peace.

Furthermore, complaining has been proven to damage your memory by shrinking your hippocampus, the part of your brain that is responsible for your cognitive function. This also negatively affects your ability to adapt and handle other stressful situations in a positive manner. Unfortunately, this can happen very quickly. Just a few days of being stressed out and complaining can actually lead to long-term damage to your brain!

Complaining can also be addictive. The more you complain, the more likely it is that you will continue to complain. Like I said previously, negative thinking will lead to more negative thinking. And your complaining can also spread to the people around you. People are very easily influenced. You will find that the more you complain, the more those around you will jump on the bandwagon and start complaining as well.

To top it all off, psychiatric studies have shown that complaining can actually shorten your lifespan! These studies showed that optimists live longer than pessimists. When you consider all of the negative side effects of complaining, there is simply no reason to complain about anything in your life. If you can do something about the situation, then do it; if you can't do anything about the situation, then move on and be happy.

How do you stop complaining? You simply make a firm commitment to refuse to complain about anything, period. Every time you notice yourself complaining, take a deep, cleansing breath and remind yourself that complaining does nothing to help the situation. Also, complaining does not have to be verbal. You must rid yourself of mentally complaining also. Remember, it is not just your words that matter, but your thoughts as well.

Reduce Time Spent Watching the News

One action that will help you stop complaining is to cut back on watching the news. I say to "cut back" on watching the news instead of completely stopping because it is wise to know what is happening in the world for many reasons. Ignorance may be bliss, but it is not wise.

If you have investments, you need to know when something is happening that will affect your investment strategies. You also need to know what is happening in order to keep your family safe and to be prepared in case of natural disasters or emergencies. So to completely stop watching the news, as many New Age teachers suggest, is simply unwise, although fasting from the news completely for short periods could be beneficial.

One major problem with watching too much news is that our news media today does not give us honest news. The news is mostly negative, fear-based, and biased. What passes for news today is closer to political propaganda than news. You will rarely see any news that is uplifting, positive, or simply straightforward and fact-based.

In my opinion, the news media is one of the biggest problems in the world today. They are continually dividing people against each other, spreading hate, racial tensions, and more often than not, feeding people half-truths or, in many cases, complete lies. But the media is a necessary evil because, as I stated, it is wise to know what is happening in the world. Just remember you have to filter through it to get to the truth.

I find that financial news shows give more accurate world news than other news media. And to get any unbiased world news, you must seek out alternative sources, not simply listen to whatever news shows your cable television airs.

You cannot maintain your inner peace when you are constantly allowing yourself to be bombarded by negative or false information meant to elicit fear, anger, and negative responses from you. Remember, you are trying to remove the negative thoughts and limiting beliefs from your subconscious mind, not feed your subconscious more of them.

If you find that the news is adding to your stress or negativity, then find a different news show to watch. Find an honest, reliable source of world news, and stop watching or reading any news which is constantly dumping biased, anger-inducing garbage into your mind. And even then, limit your viewing time to only what you need to stay informed about what is happening in the world. Your main goal is to maintain your inner peace; make sure nothing interferes with that goal.

Scratching the DVD

Another powerful technique that I use to remove negative thoughts or beliefs is something I call Scratching the DVD. I have used this technique to help people get over even the most traumatic life events. It is very useful in removing negative memories from your mind or even changing unproductive beliefs.

To use this technique, you simply see the negative event which has affected you, and implanted negative thoughts and beliefs into your subconscious, as a movie being played on a DVD.

You create a mental movie of the traumatic event or negative circumstance in your life. Then play it back in your mind as if it is

40

being played on a DVD player. Watch it and allow it to bring back the negative emotions connected to the event. Really feel the emotions, the anger, and the pain as if you are going through the event all over again.

Then take a sharp nail and mentally scratch the DVD as deep as you possibly can. Really go after it! Actually see the deep scratches go across the movie as it is playing, scratching the event out of your life. Scratch the whole thing so deeply that it is unplayable. Damage it so badly that no matter how much you want to watch it again, it will not play. Destroy it!

This may sound silly, but it does work. The next time something triggers your memories of the event, see it as if someone gave you another DVD of the event, take out your nail, and as you remember the details of the incident, scratch the DVD so badly that it will not play.

You can also imagine that you see the event as pictures in a book. As you see the pictures mentally, take out a pen and scribble on the pictures so much that they are no longer visible to you. Or mentally see yourself ripping the pictures out of the book and burning them, totally destroying those memories and the negative thoughts which accompany them.

But don't just destroy the old movie and stop there; you must actually *change* the movie. After you have destroyed the old DVD, make a whole new movie where the events and outcomes are positive. You are the director of your new movie, so make it in such a way that it removes any lingering negative feelings. Make it positive and life-affirming for you. You can also make it humorous or completely ridiculous – whatever works for you.

Then play that movie back in your mind. Feel the happy, peaceful emotions that come from watching your new movie. Smile when you watch it, knowing that the old event no longer has any power over you. Your thoughts and imagination are powerful – use them to your advantage!

This technique helps you remove these thoughts and memories from your subconscious mind. It will most likely take more than once for this technique to work, but it will work if you apply it patiently.

I find it helpful to do this during my meditation when my mind is relaxed. This is a completely different kind of meditation than your normal meditation. You are not simply quieting your mind, but meditating with a different purpose – to remove the negative thoughts and memories from a specific event in your life. This kind of meditation is more of an active visualization than a quiet meditation. Try it and see if it works for you.

I have given you several techniques and exercises which will help you cleanse your subconscious mind and begin to replace the negative thoughts and beliefs which no longer serve you. Some results will happen quickly, and others will take more time, but if you consistently work on cleansing your subconscious mind and ridding it of old thoughts and beliefs which hold you back, you will see the results. And remember, don't just delete the old programming; clean your hard drive and then reprogram it with new, positive thoughts which support your inner peace.

The techniques and exercises in this chapter are each very powerful on their own, but when you integrate all of them into your life, you will see results much faster. Also, the more often you practice them, the faster you will see positive results.

While it may seem like these exercises will take a lot of time, they can actually be done fairly quickly. Consider how much time you waste sitting in traffic, on social media, or staring at the television. Your affirmations, visualization, and breathing techniques can be done while sitting in traffic. You can perform your visualization exercises and look at your vision board while waiting for meetings or in the waiting room at the doctor's office, etc.

You have more than enough time to integrate these exercises into your life; you simply need to motivate and discipline yourself to make the changes you need in order to develop and maintain your inner peace.

If you truly want to live a life of inner peace, you have to take the time to do some house cleaning. When you have allowed your house to become a complete mess, it takes a while to clean it up; but once it is clean, it is much easier to maintain it and keep it clean and uncluttered.

The same principle applies to your subconscious mind. Once you do some house cleaning, it is much easier to control your thoughts and live the kind of life you want. And it will be much easier to maintain your inner peace and tranquility.

The tree of silence yields the fruit of inner peace.
Peruvian proverb

42

Thoughts to Ponder

Regular meditation not only restores our inner
harmony and vital energy, but provides us
with an actual experience of the peace we seek.
Diane Dreher

If you believe, you will receive
whatever you ask for in prayer.
Jesus

Everything in nature invites us constantly to be what we are.
Gretel Ehrlich

Meditation is a vital way to purify and quiet
the mind, thus rejuvenating the body.
Deepak Chopra

You can build any quality into your mentality
by meditating on that quality every day.
Emmet Fox

Meditation and concentration are
the way to a life of serenity.
Baba Ram Dass

To understand the immeasurable, the mind
must be extraordinarily quiet, still.
Jiddu Krishnamurti

Visualize the most amazing life imaginable to you.
Close your eyes and see it clearly.
Then hold the vision for as long as you can.
Now place the vision in God's hands and consider it done.
Marianne Williamson

When you visualize, then you materialize.
Denis Waitley

Visualize what you want to do before you do it. Visualization is so
powerful that when you know what you want, you will get it.
Audrey Flack

Thoughts to Ponder

You affect your subconscious mind by verbal repetition.
W. Clement Stone

Once the subconscious mind accepts an idea, it begins to execute it.
Joseph Murphy

If you do not run your subconscious mind yourself,
someone else will run it for you.
Florence Scovel Shinn

It is a psychological law that whatever we desire to accomplish
we must impress upon the subjective or subconscious mind.
Orison Swett Marden

The reason man may become the master of his own destiny is
because he has the power to influence his own subconscious mind.
Napoleon Hill

Act with purpose, courage, confidence, competence and intelligence
until these qualities 'lock in' to your subconscious mind.
Brian Tracy

In order to reprogram the subconscious mind, you need to relax the
body. Release the tension...Get to a state of openness and receptivity.
Louise Hay

The subconscious mind makes no distinction between constructive
and destructive thought impulses. It works with the material we
feed it, through our thought impulses. The subconscious mind
will translate into reality a thought driven by fear, just as readily
as it will translate into reality a thought driven by courage or faith.
Napoleon Hill

The subconscious mind cannot tell the difference
between what's real and what's imagined.
Bob Proctor

Whatever your conscious mind assumes and believes to be true,
your subconscious mind will accept and bring to pass.
Joseph Murphy

Chapter 4
Your Mind vs. Your Emotions

Control your mind and remain undisturbed.
That is the secret of perfect peace.
Sai Baba

One of the biggest hurdles to living a life of inner peace is getting control of your emotions, which always starts with controlling your mind. If you can't control your emotions, consistently living a life of inner peace is a pipe dream. There will always be some rude person out there to push your buttons or some event or situation which will disrupt your inner peace if you allow it to.

Consider a sailboat with no rudder. The captain of the sailboat may have the best intentions of reaching his desired destination, but without a rudder to control the boat, he simply goes wherever the wind may blow him. He is just along for the ride and has no control over his boat or his life. He is at the mercy of his external environment.

This same principle applies to your emotions. If you aren't able to control your emotions, you will be blown off course by any event, situation, or person who is able to agitate your mind and thus, control your emotions. You have to train your mind to be stronger than your emotions, or you will lose this battle every time.

The more you learn to control your thoughts, the easier it will be to control your emotions. And controlling your emotions is vital to your inner peace. You either control your emotions, or your emotions will control you.

Ultimately, your emotions come from your beliefs. If you believe something is supposed to make you sad, upset, or angry, then you allow yourself to be sad, upset, or angry when that situation or event occurs. That belief has been implanted into your subconscious mind for years, so much so that you have trained yourself to react automatically to certain situations and events in specific ways.

For example, if you are in the habit of getting angry every time some inconsiderate person cuts you off while you are driving, you respond that way almost automatically without giving it a second thought. You may not even be aware of your reaction to rude drivers anymore, as it has become second nature to you. The other driver cuts you off, you get angry, spew a few curse words, flip him the bird, and then continue with your drive, and you never even stopped to think about it. These negative emotional reactions have been ingrained into

45

your subconscious mind and have become a part of your nature and a deep-rooted habit.

Much of our reactions to the situations in our lives are preprogrammed. We have reacted in a certain way so many times, for so long, that we simply react in the same way without thinking, and it never crosses our mind that we don't have to react that way.

Think about this. When you first start driving a car, you have to think about everything you do. When you see a stop sign, you think, "I have to gradually brake and come to a stop." When you are going to turn, you think to yourself, "I need to slow down, turn on my signal light, and make sure I don't cut the corner to close." You nervously think about every part of driving the car.

But after you have been driving for years, all of those things become second nature; you do them all without even consciously thinking about them most of the time. You have trained yourself how to respond to other drivers hitting their brakes, what to do when you are turning, how to turn on the windshield wipers, how to stay in your lane, etc. You no longer have to think about doing these things; you simply do them almost like you are on autopilot.

That is how most people react to the events in their lives. They have trained their emotions to be on autopilot most of the time, and thus, they react without thinking. They react to each situation in life with the same emotional reaction that they have had for years.

If someone is rude to them, they get angry and respond rudely in turn. If someone dies, they get sad, depressed, and cry. If a friend betrays them, they feel hurt and angry. They allow themselves to be mastered by their emotions instead of mastering their emotions, just like the captain who allows the wind to randomly guide his boat instead of using the rudder to control where he goes.

The mind is the rudder of your emotions. Once you start to take control of your thoughts and do some work on your subconscious mind, you will be able to choose your emotions instead of allowing your emotions to operate on autopilot. And have no doubts about it – you absolutely can control your emotions. As W. Clement Stone taught, "When we direct our thoughts properly, we can control our emotions."

If you have a strong belief embedded in your subconscious mind, then certain emotions will be connected to that belief. When you change that belief, you also change the emotion that you have associated with it.

To live a life of inner peace, you must discipline your mind, control your emotions and stop using self-serving justifications to justify your lack of discipline. Nobody can *make* you angry; you *choose* to be angry. Nobody can *make* you sad; you *choose* to be sad. You have the power to choose your response to every situation in your life, but first, you must learn to control your mind. Your mind is the control panel for your emotions and ultimately, your actions.

You can choose to feel good in every situation, no matter how bad the situation may be. If you lose your job, you have a choice of how you will see that situation. If you think thoughts like, "I loved that job. I will never find a job I love as much as that one. All of my friends work there. What is this going to do to my finances? My life is such a mess!" Then what emotions do you think those thoughts will evoke? You are going to be sad, upset, depressed, and distraught.

On the other hand, what if you choose to think, "I guess it is time for me to move on and do something different. What a great opportunity this is! I bet I am going to find an even better job since I have so much experience in my field now. This is going to be exciting. I can't wait to see how cool my next job is going to be!" What emotions do you think those thoughts will evoke? Most likely, excitement, anticipation, and peaceful, happy thoughts.

Nothing changed about your job either way; you still lost your old job and will have to find a new direction for your life. But because you changed the way you think about the situation, you have changed the emotions associated with this situation. It all starts with controlling your mind.

The majority of the time, the issue is that we don't want to deal with the change that comes our way. Not many people enjoy job hunting or going for interviews. It may not be how you want to spend your time, but it is certainly not the end of the world. Your life is not over because your routine is interrupted.

Human beings are creatures of habit. We like our comfort, and we like to know what we are going to be doing tomorrow, next week, next year, etc. And because of this, we don't like unexpected changes; our minds turn many situations into bigger problems than they actually are. The solution is to learn to control your mind, which in turn controls your emotions.

Your mind is a powerful tool. You get to decide how you will respond to every situation in life, but you must take control of your thoughts in order to do so. Always question your emotions before you act on them. Many times our emotions are not in line with reality. And, as with the example above, the reality of a situation can depend on how you perceive that situation. I will once again remind you of what John Milton taught, "The mind is its own place, and in itself can make Heaven of Hell, or Hell of Heaven." You get to choose how you perceive every event or situation in your life.

47

Once you learn how to control your mind, nothing can disturb your inner peace unless *you give it permission to do so*. Your mind is controlled by you, unless you make the decision, consciously or unconsciously, not to control it. Your mind is your sanctuary; it is the only place where you have total control.

Your thoughts cannot be taken away from you, and you cannot be forced to think or believe one thing or another. Only you control your thoughts; you get to choose. Therefore, you have no one else to blame for your emotions, no matter what they may be. You have no one else to blame if you are not living a life of inner peace. If your mind is entertaining stressful, angry, hateful, fearful, unhealthy thoughts, it is because *you are choosing those thoughts*.

It is perfectly fine to feel good in every situation, even the sad, heartbreaking ones. Society dictates that we should feel sad or angry in certain situations, but you can choose to feel good and be happy no matter what. You are the master of your life; you, and only you, get to choose how you will respond to every situation in life. Stop allowing societal norms to choose your emotions for you and take control of your own life. Choose to be happy; choose to live a tranquil, peaceful life no matter what is happening around you.

You have to become so secure in who and what you are that nothing can disrupt your inner peace. Once you truly understand that you have the power to choose to be happy and at peace, regardless of what is happening around you, no opinion, no rejection, and no personal attack can affect you.

Epictetus, the Stoic philosopher, stated, "Men are disturbed not by things that happen, but by their opinions of the things that happen." Think about that. It is not the event or situation that upsets you or disturbs your mind, but what you *think* about it.

Your thoughts lead to certain emotions, and those emotions lead to certain actions. When you change your thoughts, you change your emotions, and as a result, your actions will change as well. It is not what happens to you that matters, but what you *think* about what happens to you.

When you get to the point that you are living consciously, you do not react mindlessly to the people and events in your life; you *respond* to them. When you react, you put your emotions in charge instead of your mind, and your reactions are limited and fairly predictable, depending on your long-held beliefs. When you respond, your mind is in charge, and your choices are limitless.

Once you take control of your mind, you have the power to maintain peace and tranquility in your life, no matter what is happening around you. Maintain a quiet, rational mind and choose

48

inner peace. Never allow your emotions to control your responses. Be the master of your mind instead of mastered by your mind.

When you learn to control your mind, your emotions will fall in line, and then you will be able to choose inner peace in every situation. Remember, things have to get right on the inside before they can get right on the outside. You can't expect your actions to be consistently right until you correct your subconscious mind. Learn to control your conscious mind and bring your emotions under control. After you have learned to control your mind and emotions, the next step is to rid yourself of all the negative energy that you have allowed into your life.

Let Go of Negative Energy

If you attach to the negative behavior of others,
it brings you down to their level.
Guru Singh

I have already touched on low-energy thoughts in previous chapters, but I believe that we need to get a little deeper into this topic. Low-energy thoughts such as anger, hate, shame, guilt, regret, resentfulness, and fear weaken you. Higher energy thoughts such as love, harmony, kindness, and peace strengthen you. Remember, the thoughts you entertain will manifest in your life one way or another.

Negative energy will continue to appear in your life until you remove that energy completely from your mind. When you start to change your life, if you haven't addressed your old patterns of negative thinking and negative reactions, the same old triggers will provoke you again and again, throwing you back into the same negative pattern that you have experienced over the years. You must recondition your mind to get rid of the habitual negative thoughts which you have allowed to permeate your consciousness in the past.

Dr. Wayne Dyer, one of my favorite teachers, taught, "When you're at peace, you radiate a different kind of energy than when you are stressed or depressed. The more peaceful you become, the easier you can deflect the negative energies of those you encounter. This is like having an invisible shield around you that nothing can penetrate unless it's at a higher spiritual energy than your shield."

Peace vibrates at a higher energy than anger, hatred, guilt, shame, jealousy, fear, etc. Therefore, once you have trained your mind to maintain thoughts of peace and tranquility, you will better be able to control how you respond to anyone who is allowing negative energy to control their behavior.

49

It is vital that you refuse to allow negative energy to reside in your mind, as it will always affect your emotions and responses. Simply refuse to entertain those negative thoughts. You may not be able to completely stop those thoughts from appearing in your mind from time to time, but you always have the power to refuse to allow them to remain there.

Refuse to participate in, or listen to, any conversation which is focused on complaining, whining, griping, or tearing down other people. Stop making negative statements such as, "I am getting sick," "I am really tired and hurting," or "I don't feel well."

Remember, when you feed those negative words and thoughts into your subconscious mind, your subconscious mind accepts them as true and goes to work to cause everything else to fall in line with that truth. So essentially, when you make those negative statements, your subconscious mind makes sure that those negative things begin to materialize in your life.

I previously discussed using affirmations to cleanse and replace the negative beliefs in your subconscious mind. When you are making negative statements like the ones above, you are basically making negative affirmations and doing the opposite of what you need to be doing to change your subconscious mind. You are feeding negative thoughts directly to your subconscious mind in a very personal and powerful way.

Let's go back to our analogy that cleansing your subconscious mind is like cleaning your computer, removing the viruses, and reprogramming it with the content that you now want in your life. Those negative statements are the equivalent of clicking on an infected website or email, which puts a virus on your computer and causes it to work less efficiently. If you are not careful and are constantly doing this, sooner or later your computer will crash.

When you make any statement starting with the words "I am," you are making a very powerful affirmation. If you recall, in the Bible when Moses was speaking with God, and Moses asked, "Suppose I go to the Israelites and say to them, 'The God of your fathers has sent me to you,' and they ask me, 'What is His name?' What should I tell them?" God responded, "I AM WHO I AM. This is what you are to say to the Israelites: 'I AM has sent me to you.'"

Starting any affirmation with the words "I am" is a very powerful statement. It is much more powerful than a simple affirmation about living a life of inner peace. Consider the difference between stating, "I *will* live a life of inner peace," and "I *am* peaceful, tranquil, and calm at all times." The first indicates a time in the future, while the second affirmation states what you are right now.

50

I understand how hard it is to stop making negative statements, especially if you are in the habit of speaking negatively to yourself or others. This is especially true if your body actually is hurting, you are tired, or you don't feel well. It will take time and effort to break this habit because you have probably trained yourself to talk like this since you were a young child. But all these statements do is reinforce the negative programming and negative energy in your mind.

As you begin to stop yourself from making detrimental statements filled with negative energy, your mind will fight against you. Your mind will say, "Yeah, but these things are true. All I am doing is stating the truth. I am getting sick. I am tired, achy, and don't feel well. What is wrong with stating the truth?" That is your subconscious mind justifying the thoughts it has been programmed with for decades. This is a good example of why you need to cleanse and reprogram your subconscious mind.

While it may be true that you are not feeling well and are tired and hurting, what good does it do you to reinforce those feelings by affirming them to your subconscious mind? Remember, when you are speaking, your subconscious mind takes what you say as the truth and believes that you want more of those things in your life.

Do you really want more sickness, tiredness, and pain in your life? Of course not! So stop reinforcing those things with the words that you speak. You can feel bad or tired without stating that fact over and over throughout the day. Instead, try to replace those negative statements, whining, and complaining with positive affirmations as I have already discussed.

An important aspect of choosing inner peace is being careful about what you feed your mind. You have to let go of all that negative energy. This includes what you watch on television or the internet, what kind of music you listen to, what you read, and the people you associate with during your life. All of these things will either strengthen or weaken you.

You are working to remove the negative, low-energy thoughts from your subconscious mind. If you are constantly filling your mind with low-energy, negative thoughts through other sources, you are canceling out much of the positive energy you are consciously feeding your mind through the exercises previously discussed.

What you want to do is replace all of the negative, low-energy thinking with positive, higher energy, peaceful thoughts. Refuse to allow negative, low-energy thoughts into your mind. You must replace your old habit of complaining and griping about the negative things in your life with positive thoughts about what you want in your life and what is good about your life.

51

Think back to the example of cultivating what you want in your garden. What you cultivate (think and speak about) in your life is what will grow and expand. If you want to have more inner peace, more health, and feel better, then start focusing on those things and quit feeding your mind negative, low-energy thoughts and words. Stop cultivating weeds in your garden!

Develop the habit of always looking at things in a positive light. The more you do this, the more inner peace you will experience. Positive energy will always cancel negative energy if you give it a chance.

During the Vietnam War, Mother Teresa was asked to join a march against the war. She replied, "No, I won't. But when you have a march for peace, I'll be there." This is a great example of refusing to be *against* something, but being *for* something instead. There is a completely different energy when you support something instead of being against something.

When you are for something, you are usually positive, excited, and filled with hope; when you are against something, much of the time you are angry and upset about what is going on. Often there is only a subtle difference, but the energy is completely different.

Be above the negative energy of others. Refuse to allow their negativity to affect you. Instead, allow your positive energy to cancel their negative energy. In order to do this, you must constantly cultivate that positive energy in your life. If you are feeding your mind negative, low-energy thoughts and words, then that is how you will respond to the people and circumstances in your life. Moreover, that is what you will get more of in your life.

What you feed your mind matters and will ultimately determine what actions you take in every situation of your life, and what direction your life continues to take. In order for your actions to be right, you must first get your mind right. And in order to get your mind right, you must quit feeding it negative, low-energy thoughts, and replace those thoughts with positive convictions. Your mind is the master of your actions, and your actions are the building blocks of your life.

The action of one thing produces effects on another.
Lieh Tzu

Thoughts to Ponder

When we direct our thoughts properly, we can control our emotions.
W. Clement Stone

I can control my thoughts as necessary; then how can I be troubled?
What is outside my mind means nothing to it.
Marcus Aurelius

Until you make the unconscious conscious,
it will direct your life and you will call it fate.
C. G. Jung

Be master of the mind rather than mastered by the mind.
Zen Maxim

Quiet your mind; leave the world to its fate.
Swami Muktananda

Muddy water, let stand, becomes clear.
Lao Tzu

Only in quiet waters do things mirror themselves undistorted.
Only in a quiet mind is adequate perception of the world.
Hans Margolis

One's mind should not agonize over anything.
Kok Yim Ci Yuen

Do not let trifles disturb your tranquility of mind.
Ignore the inconsequential.
Grenville Kleiser

No one can make you feel inferior without your consent.
Eleanor Roosevelt

When his mind is tranquil, perfect joy comes to the man of discipline.
Bhagavad Gita

Let's not forget that the little emotions are the great captains
of our lives and we obey them without realizing it.
Vincent van Gogh

53

Thoughts to Ponder

Don't waste another minute dealing with a toxic, negative,
energy-draining person. Some people are wired for negativity.
They love being argumentative, combative, and abusive.
Run for your life as quickly as possible.
Les Brown

The results of many years of general negative thinking
are seldom corrected in a few days…You must keep up
the new way of thinking for a reasonable period, and
refuse to be discouraged by seeming failure at first.
Emmet Fox

Keep your face to the sunshine and you cannot see a shadow.
Helen Keller

To dwell upon negative things, no matter what the pretext,
is to manufacture still more trouble.
Emmet Fox

Empty your mind, be formless, shapeless – like water.
Now you put water into a cup, it becomes the cup, you put water into
a bottle, it becomes the bottle, you put it in a teapot, it becomes the
teapot. Now water can flow or it can crash. Be water, my friend.
Bruce Lee

The negative things in your mind – the fears, doubts, resentments –
are to be starved out of existence by refusing to feed them
with the attention upon which they live.
Emmet Fox

Holding on to negative emotions and not dealing
with them will keep you unconsciously attached to them.
Victoria M. Gallagher

The Law of Substitution means that the only way to get
rid of a certain thought is to substitute another one for it.
If you want to dismiss a negative thought, the only way to
do so is to think of something positive and constructive.
Emmet Fox

Chapter 5
Correct Actions Lead to Inner Peace

Every action we take, everything we do, is either a victory
or defeat in the struggle to become what we want to be.
Anne Byrne

I have spent a lot of time discussing your thoughts and your mind. As I mentioned, the main reason your mind is so important to your inner peace is because that is where your inner peace resides, but there is another reason – it is also where your actions originate. Peaceful thoughts lead to peaceful actions. If your thoughts are not producing calm, peaceful actions, then something is wrong with your thoughts.

Zoroaster, the founder of Zoroastrianism, taught the importance of good thoughts, good words, and good deeds. Before your actions can be right, both your thoughts and words must be right. If you have successfully cleansed and learned to control your mind, then your words and deeds will be right. Thoughts that are filled with inner peace produce calm, peaceful words and correct actions.

Your actions reveal your thoughts. If your actions are hateful, spiteful, and filled with anger and resentment, then you know that you still have work to do mentally. Remember what I stated earlier. Things have to get right on the *inside* before they can be right on the outside. I know I repeat that phrase a lot, but that is only because it is so important for you to grasp. Once you have truly reigned in your thoughts, your actions will naturally fall in line.

Always act rationally and with a calm, peaceful mind. Have a reason for everything you do; never act without first knowing what your objective is. So many people act without thinking, and after they have calmed down and considered their actions, they are filled with regret. They live their life on an emotional rollercoaster, allowing their emotions to dictate their actions instead of thinking rationally and calmly.

The majority of the time, when you allow your emotions to dictate your actions, you will regret it. It is all too easy to forget your aspirations of inner peace and to allow your frustrations and anger to take control. The prisons are full of people who allowed their actions to momentarily be controlled by a flash of anger or rage, only to immediately regret their actions after it is too late.

They allowed the negative energy embedded deep in their minds to temporarily take control, and that negative energy came with a high price, devastating consequences. Your words and actions can never be taken back. They can be apologized for and lamented, but once words have been spoken or an action has been taken, what is said and done can't be undone. You have no power to change the past; you only have the power to change what you think, say, and do in the present moment. If you never speak or act thoughtlessly, you can eliminate a lot of pain and regret from your life.

When some guy is rude to you in the parking lot, it is very easy to forget your goal of inner peace and to react with the same emotion he unleashed on you. Instead of reacting to someone who is trying to push your buttons, pause and consider your objective of living a life of inner peace. Then *respond* instead of reacting. This is another thought I will often repeat, as it is absolutely vital to your inner peace.

Every action is important, and everyone is responsible for his or her own actions and the consequences that accompany those actions. If your mind is right, your actions will be right; if your mind is still entertaining negative, low-energy thoughts, your actions will be inconsistent at best.

You can't constantly entertain thoughts of anger, hatred, jealousy, resentment, and fear and expect your actions to be based on love, inner peace, levelheadedness, calm rationality, and wisdom. This is why I have spent so much time focused on your subconscious mind and your thoughts in the first part of this book.

Let's revisit my gardening example. There is a process to growing vegetables. No matter how badly you may want fresh vegetables right away, gardening simply does not work that way. You have to prepare the soil, plant the seeds, work to cultivate the plants which grow from those seeds, keep your garden weeded, and then you are able to enjoy the fruits of your labor. You can't simply skip to the end and enjoy your vegetables before you do the work.

The same principle applies to your inner peace. You have to do the internal work before you see the results externally. This means that you have to get your mind right *before* your actions will be right. Even if you have prepared your mind by cleansing your subconscious mind of all the negative thoughts and beliefs that were holding you back, you still have work to do.

You must be selective about the thoughts and words you are feeding your mind on a daily basis. These are the water and fertilizer that you are giving your plants. Just like gardening, if you allow weeds (negative thoughts and words) a place in your garden, then you can't expect to produce the kind of results you want. You must keep your garden (your mind) weeded in order for it to produce the harvest (the actions) that you want.

56

If you allow weeds to freely grow in your garden, sooner or later, they will take over the garden completely. And it goes without saying that weeding your garden is not a one-time thing; you have to consistently remove the weeds as they appear.

The more you weed your garden, the fewer weeds you will have. But there will most likely never be a time when it is completely weed free. You have to actively stay alert to keep the weeds removed so they do not interfere with the plants that you are trying to cultivate.

Your garden is your mind, and the negative, low-energy thoughts are the weeds that you must constantly remove in order for your mind to produce peaceful thoughts and actions in your life. There will most likely never be a time that you will be completely free of those negative thoughts. Again, we cannot completely control what thoughts come into our minds, but we can control whether or not we allow those thoughts to remain in.

The more we eliminate those thoughts, and replace them with positive, higher energy thoughts, the less we will have to deal with them. And the fewer of these negative thoughts we allow into our mind, the easier it will be to consistently choose the right action to every situation in our life.

Every action you take is important because you are reinforcing those actions and responses in your mind. Always do what's right, as that reinforces your standards in your subconscious mind. Never lower your standards in order to fit in with the crowd or to please others. When you lower your standards, you are putting yourself and your inner peace second place, and you are also weakening the core principles by which you live.

Always do what you feel is right according to the standards that you live by and in accordance with your inner peace. Your spirit and your conscience will always let you know what the correct action is, and they will absolutely alert you if your actions have compromised your standards.

Don't *try* to act correctly; *act* correctly. As that old Jedi, Yoda, taught us, "Do or do not. There is no try." When you say that you will try, all you are doing is leaving yourself an out. If you want to live a life of inner peace, then do it. Don't be wishy-washy. Decide that you are going to live a life of inner peace, and then make it a reality; accept nothing less.

You can't consistently think thoughts of inner peace but act in a totally different way. It's a package deal. It is impossible to live a life of inner peace internally and still allow fear, anger, jealousy, and resentfulness to dictate your actions. Jesus taught, "A double minded man is unstable in all his ways." Your actions must follow your thoughts; there is no other way. If low-energy thoughts are dictating your actions, then you are not living a life of inner peace.

If you claim to have inner peace, but your actions stem from low-energy, negative thoughts, then you are simply fooling yourself. Your actions and thoughts will always be in agreement, as your actions always begin with your thoughts. Peaceful, calm thoughts will equate to peaceful, calm responses.

Someone who claims to have inner peace yet consistently reacts out of anger, fear, or resentfulness has not completely cleansed those low-energy, negative thoughts from his or her subconscious mind. As I stated, cleansing your subconscious mind is a process; it won't happen overnight.

Your actions are always giving you feedback concerning where you are on your journey to inner peace. You will always know that you have more work to do in cleansing your subconscious mind when your actions are not in line with the inner peace which you seek.

Don't get discouraged if you are in the process of cleansing your subconscious mind, changing your thoughts, and taking control over your mind, yet still continue to have challenges when it comes to your actions. Just remind yourself that your actions will fall in line once things get right on the inside. Just keep removing those unproductive, negative thoughts and beliefs until your mind becomes the beautiful garden that you want it to be.

When you fall short of your objective of inner peace, don't be too hard on yourself. Living a life of inner peace is an ongoing process; you will always have good days and bad days. Your goal is not to become perfect but to gradually have more and more good days and fewer bad days. The more you purify your mind, the fewer bad days you will have, and your actions will attest to your progress.

Just continue to do what's right to the best of your ability and let the chips fall where they may. When you catch yourself reacting instead of responding to someone who has pushed your buttons, make note of it and stop yourself. It is human to have bad days when everything has gone wrong, and you have no more patience left, and the next person who gets on your nerves receives a less than peaceful response.

There is an old Zen proverb which states, "Before enlightenment, chop wood, carry water. After enlightenment, chop wood, carry water." Even after you have cleansed your subconscious mind and are living a life of inner peace, you are still a human being. You will still be dealing with the same type of people, work, stress, and unplanned hassles in your life. You are still going to be "chopping wood and carrying water."

58

The difference is that you will be handling the people and situations differently than you did before, at least most of the time. You will still have days that try your inner peace and your patience, but they will be fewer and further between, and you will be better equipped to handle those days.

When you fall short of your objective, just remind yourself that every day is a new beginning. If some person or problem got under your skin the day before, put it behind you. The past is over; it no longer exists; start each day anew. Give yourself a break; even Jesus lost his temper, flipped over the money changers' tables, and took a whip and ran them out of the temple. We all have our good days and bad days.

Don't waste time justifying your actions to yourself or to other people. Every criminal in prison finds a way to justify his actions. The mind has a way of justifying everything that you do. That is because we have programmed our subconscious mind to make our actions fit into our personal belief system.

If you responded wrong, own it and determine that you will not respond that way next time. Remind yourself that you are doing the best you can and improving yourself each and every day; then put it behind you. Learn from each mistake or slip-up, and use it to strengthen your resolve and move you closer to the tranquility you are seeking.

You do not owe anyone any justifications for your actions. If you snapped at someone who did not deserve it, simply make a heartfelt apology, *once*, and move on. You don't have to apologize over and over again. If you were sincere and meant it the first time, that should suffice. Sincerely apologize, mean it, and then drop it. When you start justifying your actions, you are allowing your ego to take over. You did what you did; own it and move on.

Furthermore, you don't owe anyone an explanation for the actions you take to keep yourself on your path of inner peace. If you choose not to take part in gossip or an argument (which you should, as I will discuss later), you don't owe anyone a reason. You don't have to justify your actions to anyone, nor do you have to prove anything to anyone. You were not put on this earth to walk your path according to the dictates of other people.

It is your life to live as you see fit. When you start justifying your actions to others, you start to doubt yourself. Unless you have wronged someone, you don't owe anyone any apologies or justifications concerning how you decide to live your life. If you are constantly worried about pleasing everyone else, then you will have a hard time pleasing yourself, much less maintaining your inner peace.

Moreover, if everyone likes you, you probably will not completely like yourself. You cannot please everyone all the time, and you should not even try.

Just do what's right to the best of your ability, and your inner peace will remain intact. Those who like you will like you; those who don't, wish them well and move on. Inner peace comes from the inside, and if you know that you have done the best you can and have continued to live up to the standards you have set for yourself, then you should be at peace with your actions.

Don't Be Attached to Outcomes

Attachment is the source of all suffering.
Buddha

Don't be too attached to the outcomes of your actions; be at peace with doing the right thing. Even if you do everything perfectly, you can't control the outcome of your actions. There will always be unexpected twists and turns that may skew the results that you are hoping for.

Your job is to do the best that you can and leave the outcome to God. Just do your best in every situation, take pride and joy in doing what you do, and release all attachments to the outcome of your actions, knowing that you did the best you could. What more is there for you to do? You can't force things to turn out as you want them to; all you can do is your best in every situation.

Of course, we hope for our desired outcome to come to fruition, but ultimately, we cannot control the outcome, only our actions. What is important is that you always do what you believe to be right. Then your inner peace will remain intact, regardless of the final outcome. It is your intentions behind your actions that truly matters.

Consider a fruit tree. You may have a fruit tree on your property that you enjoy gathering fruit from each summer. You can prune that tree, water it, fertilize it, and protect it from birds and squirrels, but you still cannot force it to produce fruit. There may be a late frost that kills the flowers, or the tree may get some unforeseen disease that damages the fruit.

There is a multitude of things that are out of your control which may negatively affect the bountiful harvest that you are hoping for, but that should not stop you from doing what you can to nurture and care for your fruit tree. All you can do is your part and leave the rest to nature.

If you have a bad year and your fruit tree does not produce much fruit, you don't cut your fruit tree down and give up on it. You simply deal with it and hope for better results next year. Just because the tree does not produce fruit this year is no sign that it will not produce fruit the next year, and it certainly does not mean that you should stop taking care of your tree.

If you discontinue taking care of your tree because it does not produce fruit this year, you are only increasing the chances that you won't get fruit again next year. You must have faith that if you continue to do the right things, it will eventually work out in your favor. Giving up and throwing in the towel has never enabled anyone to reach his or her goal.

Being overly attached to the outcomes of your actions adds a source of stress to your life and can disrupt your inner peace. If you are constantly worried about whether or not your tree is going to produce fruit this year, you are disrupting your own inner peace for nothing. Your worry has never affected the outcome of your actions, and never will, but worrying does negatively affect your mind and your inner peace.

The Stoics taught that you should not only be okay with how things turn out, but that you should embrace whatever happens with a happy heart. Epictetus taught, "Don't hope that events will turn out the way you want, welcome events in whichever way they happen; this is the path to peace."

Many ancient sages taught that attachment, whether it is attachment to people, things, ideas, or to the outcomes of your actions, is the source of suffering. If you are not attached to the outcome of your actions, then those outcomes will not disrupt your inner peace. Just be content with having done the right thing and leave it at that. Things are as they are; accept the outcome of your actions and move on.

Being detached from the outcomes of your actions is very freeing. It will eliminate worry, fear, and stress, and will allow you to simply be content with doing the best that you can. If you are only concerned with making sure that your actions are right and not with the results of your actions, then what is there to worry about, to fear, or to cause you stress? You are free to simply act.

Another reason that you should not be concerned with the outcome of your actions is that you truly do not know whether a certain outcome is good or bad. You may think that this is a ridiculous statement. Of course you know whether an outcome is good or bad, right? But do you really? Consider the parable on the following page whenever you are tempted to judge the outcome of your actions.

Maybe, Maybe Not

During the Warring States period in China, a farmer lived with his only son and depended on him to help do the farm work. They had only one horse, which they loved, and which was vital to help with their farming. One day the horse ran away, and the farmer complained to the village elder that he didn't know how he was going to survive without his trusted horse. "What terrible luck this is," he exclaimed.

The elder replied, "Maybe, maybe not. We will see."

This angered the farmer, but he held his tongue and returned home, thinking the elder must be losing his senses. A few days later, the farmer's horse returned, leading a wild mare back to the farm. The farmer was delighted at his good luck and exclaimed to the village elder, "My luck has changed! What a blessing this is!"

Again, the village elder simply replied, "Maybe, maybe not. We will see."

Later that week, the farmer's son was trying to break the mare so it could be used in the fields. Suddenly the horse bucked, throwing the son to the ground and breaking his leg. Again, the farmer complained to the village elder, "This is terrible luck! I cannot tend to the fields myself, and this is my only son. I am ruined!"

The wise elder again seemed unmoved and stated, "Maybe, maybe not. We will see."

This time the farmer had had enough. He lost his temper and yelled at the elder, "What do you mean maybe? My son's leg is broken. My farm will be lost! This is the worst thing that could have happened to us, and you act as if it is nothing at all!"

The elder remained calm and unmoved. "Don't give up hope my friend; none of us can see the future. Everything happens as it should."

Three weeks later, the army from the farmer's province marched through the town, forcing every able-bodied young man to join the army and to march into battle. The farmer's son was not taken because of his broken leg, and he was unable to fight.

The other people in the village were excited that their sons would return heroes and exclaimed to the farmer, "It is bad luck that your son could not go to war and return as a hero as well."

The farmer started to feel disgraced but then recalled the lesson that the village elder had been trying to teach him and replied, "Maybe, maybe not. We will see."

Two weeks later, word came to the village that the entire army was defeated in an epic battle. Not one of the young men from the village had survived. The farmer's son was the only boy of age from the village that survived this tragedy. It was only then that the farmer understood the wisdom of the village elder.

~~~~~

What may seem like a terrible tragedy to you may in fact be a blessing, and what may seem like a blessing could turn out to be a tragedy. We simply cannot see the future and do not know whether something will turn out to be good or bad in the end. Just accept what is, and continue to do your best.

Every action you take produces an outcome. It may or may not be the outcome that you had hoped for, but in the end, it is not the outcome that truly matters. What matters is that you have done what you think is right to the best of your ability.

If you have done your best, there is no reason to second guess yourself or stress over something you should have done differently. Those thoughts are only for people who did not do their best and are filled with regret because they know that they had the chance to do better, but for whatever reason, they didn't.

If you want to permanently remove regret from your life, simply do the best you can all the time. No matter what it is that you are doing, whether it is a project that you are working on, a conversation with a friend, or performing your role in your family, if you always do the best you can, you will have nothing to regret.

Another thing to keep in mind when it comes to doing your best is that your best will fluctuate. There will be days when the best you can do is far below your actual "best." If you are sick, exhausted, or overwhelmed, and are functioning at a low level, your best will not be the same as it is on your best day.

Even though you are not at your peak performance level on those days, you can still do the best that you can do given the circumstances. Having down days is simply a part of being human. Even professional athletes do not perform at their peak every single day. Why would you expect to be able to do that?

You must be patient and forgiving with yourself. You will have days when the best you can do is to be silent and not snap at those around you. There will be days when you are just not functioning at a high level or just don't feel like yourself. Do the best you can with what you have to work with each and every day. That is the most that anyone can expect from another human being.

If you have done your best and things did not turn out as you wanted, that doesn't mean you have failed; it simply means that you produced a specific result or outcome. If you want a different result, go back and make the appropriate changes, and you will get a different result next time.

Don't get upset or down with yourself. Just remind yourself that you did the best that you could do given the time you had, the information you had, the tools you had to work with, the knowledge that you had, etc. The best you can do is the best that you can do; just make sure that you are *actually doing the best that you can do* and not deceiving yourself.

One last thing to consider about the outcomes of your actions is that, no matter what happens, always remain calm and centered. Don't allow what appears to be a negative outcome to disrupt your inner peace. Whatever happens, embrace it and be okay with it.

How many times have you done something and produced a result that you were stressed about, only to find out later that it wasn't that big of a deal after all? You allowed yourself to get upset and worried, which ruined your whole day or week, and maybe even made yourself sick worrying about it, all for nothing.

Don't let the outcomes of your actions bother you. Embrace them, learn from them, and continue to do the best that you can. Judge yourself not by the outcomes of your actions but by the intentions behind your actions. When your intentions are right and honorable, then your conscience is clear.

Maintain a Clear Conscience

The superior man will watch over himself when he is alone.
He examines his heart that there may be nothing wrong there,
and that he may have no cause of dissatisfaction with himself.
Confucius

When it comes to inner peace, your conscience plays a huge role. A clear conscience is a must in order to maintain inner peace. You cannot consistently enjoy inner peace if your conscience is continually convicting you about something you have done wrong, how you mistreated someone, how you rudely snapped at someone, or something else you have done. If you are out-of-line, your conscience will be sure to let you know about it.

So what exactly is your conscience? Your conscience is the part of your mind that helps you determine what is right and wrong. It keeps you from acting on urges and desires which go against your core beliefs, and causes you to feel guilty when you do something that you know you should not have done. It is the silent voice inside you which convicts you when you know you have not lived up to your

64

standards. Your conscience is your moral compass and helps keep you on the right track.

For example, if you go through the self-pay checkout line at the store and slip an item into your bag without paying for it, your conscience will continually remind you about it. You will feel it in your chest and in your mind. Throughout the day, you will hear the voice of your conscience saying, "That was wrong. You should have paid for that item. You know better than that. What were you thinking?"

Your conscience does not believe in letting things slide. It simply thinks in terms of right or wrong. If you do what is right, your conscience is at peace; if you do something that is wrong, your conscience will not let you rest until you set the matter right. This is why I say that you cannot consistently live in inner peace if your conscience is continually nagging at you about something you have done wrong.

Your conscience is your moral compass, and it gently, but consistently pushes you to stay on course. When you are on course, it quietly makes you feel good about your choices. When you veer off course, it needles you until you correct your mistake and get back on your true path. It should be obvious to you why you must preserve a clear conscience in order to maintain your inner peace.

This is another reason why you have to keep a close watch over your thoughts, words, and actions. If you want to maintain your inner peace, you must be dedicated to doing what's right. Now I know that many people will want to argue, "What's right is subjective. What one person may consider right, another may consider wrong. There is no right or wrong, only different perceptions."

Okay, let's look at that theory for a minute. Right and wrong are not subjective, although personal codes of ethics and cultural norms may vary. In addition, there may be certain actions or activities which some people consider right, and others consider wrong.

For example, your religion may consider it wrong to drink alcohol. If you believe in what your religion teaches, then *for you* drinking alcohol is wrong, but what about people who do not practice your religion? Is the drinking of alcohol actually wrong, or is it a personal preference depending on your own personal beliefs? Obviously, it is a personal belief; it is subjective.

But there are things that are universally right and universally wrong. Take murder for instance. Murdering someone is wrong, period. You may be thinking, "Yeah, but certain cultures do not value life as much as ours. To them, it may not be wrong." That does not make it right. Some things are absolutely right or wrong, and the fact that some culture or religion believes it is okay, does not make it okay.

There are things in our world that are absolute and things which are subjective, right or wrong according to someone's belief about them. So which does your conscience abide by? The answer is – it depends.

Of course, your conscience will always convict you when you have done something which is absolutely wrong, such as murdering someone, raping someone, or stealing something which belongs to someone else. That goes without saying. But it will also convict you if you go against your personal belief system or code of ethics.

When I say that your conscience will convict you if you do not do what's right, "what's right" encompasses the things which are universally right or wrong, and your personal beliefs concerning your code of ethics, what you have decided is right or wrong for you. If you believe something is wrong, and you do it anyway, then your conscience will convict your spirit until you make it right.

To continue with my example of alcohol, if you firmly adhere to your religious beliefs that alcohol is wrong, but you go out for a drink anyway, your conscience would convict you because you have implanted the belief in your subconscious that drinking is not right. But if you have no such belief about alcohol being wrong, going out for a drink would not bother your conscience in the least.

In addition to those things which we all know are wrong, you must decide what is right or wrong for you *personally* and adhere strictly to your beliefs or code of ethics. Once those beliefs have been implanted into your subconscious mind, then your conscience uses those beliefs to help keep your words and actions in line with your beliefs.

For this reason, it is important that you know what you believe and why. It would be helpful for you to take some time and develop a code of ethics or honor code by which you live your life. Most people never stop and take the time to actually think about what things are truly important to them and how they want to live their life, but this is something that everyone should do.

An honor code or personal code of ethics helps you understand your deeply held beliefs and makes it easier for you to make those difficult decisions when they do come up. Once you have your personal belief system organized, making decisions about what you will and won't do is easy. Then all you have to do is discipline yourself to live by the standards which you profess to believe are right or wrong.

I strongly urge you to take some time and make a list of the things which you consider wrong for you. Do you consider smoking marijuana wrong? What about drinking? Cursing? Eating meat? Brainstorm your beliefs and come up with your own personal code of ethics. Then live by the standards which you set for yourself.

Keep a close watch over your thoughts, words, and actions to make sure they are in line with your code of ethics. Don't lower your standards for anyone or anything once you know what is right and what is wrong for you personally.

Also, note that not everything has to be right or wrong. Most things will simply be a matter of choice. Maybe you think it is okay to drink alcohol, but you simply don't like alcohol or consider it unhealthy, so you don't drink it. That does not mean that drinking alcohol is wrong; it simply means that you have decided that it is not for you, and that is perfectly fine.

Your code of ethics should be for things that you consider absolutely wrong and won't do, and standards that you want to integrate into your life because you consider them right for you according to your beliefs. Your list may have 20-30 things on it, but it does not need to list every single thing you can think of. Focus on standards which direct your overall actions.

Also keep in mind that you can go back and change your code of ethics, or add to them, if your core beliefs about something change or need to be adjusted. This is *your* personal code of ethics and has nothing to do with anyone else. Make it work for you, not the beliefs of everyone else.

Keep your code of ethics as specific as possible. Really think about your true beliefs. For example, don't say, "It is always wrong to lie." I can guarantee you that this will put your conscience in a tight corner.

An example would be if you were living in Nazi Germany and you were hiding a Jewish girl in your home, which would be an honorable act. If Nazi soldiers came to your door and asked if you were hiding any Jews, would it be wrong to lie to them in order to save the girl's life or wrong to turn the girl over to the Nazis? In this case, wouldn't lying be the honorable action to take? Be careful about being overly rigid when it comes to certain beliefs.

Making your code of ethics is not something you should do quickly or half-heartedly. Take your time and really think about what you believe, then live by the standards which you have set for yourself. Many things will not be black and white. That is why you must take some time and really think about what you believe and be clear about what is right for you.

Once you are satisfied with your personal code, then you have to hold yourself to the standards you have set. You have to discipline yourself to uphold your standards during your everyday life. There will always be temptations to lower your standards, but lowering them will cause a conflict in your conscience, which will, in turn, disrupt your inner peace.

To maintain a clear conscience, you must develop discipline and self-control. As Henry Ward Beecher stated, "Hold yourself responsible for a higher standard than anybody else expects of you. Never excuse yourself. Never pity yourself. Be a hard master to yourself and be lenient to everybody else." If you will do this, your conscience will not only be at peace but will constantly make you feel good about yourself and your decisions.

On the other hand, be careful not to be too hard on yourself when you fall short. You are human, and humans do make mistakes and will falter at times. Don't beat yourself up when you fail to live up to the standards which you have set for yourself. Forgive yourself as quickly as you would forgive someone else. Beating yourself up because you made a mistake, or were weak when you should have stood strong, will not do you any good. Remember what I said about your subconscious hearing everything you say? Never talk bad about yourself!

When you fall short, (I say "when" instead of "if" because everyone makes mistakes or falls short of their goals at some time during their life), forgive yourself, set things straight, and get back on track. Once you have done this, your conscience is satisfied and will not continue to nag you about your failure to live up to your code. The important thing is to keep pushing forward; never allow a mistake or moment of weakness to cause you to give up on living the kind of life that you want to live.

Always do your best to do what's right according to your code of ethics, and your conscience will allow you to live in peace with yourself. Without a clear conscience, inner peace is impossible. Keeping your conscience clear is another cornerstone of maintaining consistent inner peace and tranquility.

Never do anything against conscience
even if the state demands it.
Albert Einstein

Thoughts to Ponder

If the heart is right the deeds will be right.
Japanese Proverb

If you compromise with your own conscience,
you will weaken your conscience.
Napoleon Hill

I expect to pass through this world but once;
any good thing, therefore, that I can do, or any kindness
that I can show to any fellow creature, let me do it now.
Stephen Grellet

Whatever the outcome may be, the important thing
is to step forward on the path that you believe is right.
Daisaku Ikeda

It is no easy thing for a principle to become a man's own
unless each day he maintains it and works it out in his life.
Epictetus

If we are ever in doubt what to do, it is a good rule to ask
ourselves what we shall wish on the morrow that we had done.
Sir John Lubbock

In whatever position you find yourself,
determine first your objective.
Marshall Ferdinand Foch

Behavior is the perpetual revealing of us.
What a man does, tells us what he is.
F. D. Huntington

Don't hold onto negative feelings by justifying
why you are right and someone else is wrong.
Deepak Chopra

Never explain – your friends do not need it
and your enemies will not believe you anyway.
Elbert Hubbard

Thoughts to Ponder

It's the action, not the fruit of the action, that's important.
You have to do the right thing. It may not be in your power,
may not be in your time, that there'll be any fruit.
But that doesn't mean you stop doing the right thing.
You may never know what results come from your action.
But if you do nothing, there will be no result.
Mahatma Gandhi

Set goals not for the outcome itself,
but for who you get to become in the process.
Jim Rohn

Only the just man enjoys peace of mind.
Epicurus

In my life, nothing goes wrong. When things seem to not
meet my expectation, I let go of how I think things should be.
It's a matter of not having any attachment to any fixed outcome.
Deepak Chopra

If you are not concerned about the outcome of a circumstance,
you will experience no fear. Whatever the outcome will be,
will be, whether you fear it or not.
Chin-Ning Chu

There is no such thing as a failed experiment,
only experiments with unexpected outcomes.
R. Buckminster Fuller

From a spiritual perspective, freedom from attachment to a
particular outcome is the ultimate expression of liberation.
We can choose the actions we take, but we cannot
control the consequences of our choices.
David Simon

There is nothing scary about life if you are not attached to results.
Neale Donald Walsch

The greatest portion of peace of mind is doing nothing wrong.
Seneca

Chapter 6
Your Words are Powerful

Speak little;
protect your own peace.
Swami Muktananda

One of the reasons that a calm, tranquil mind is so important is because a tranquil mind leads to peaceful, well-thought-out words. Your words will indicate your mental state. When your mind is agitated, stressed, or angry, your words will give evidence of that fact.

If your mind is filled with angry thoughts, your words will have an angry tone and will be words of anger or resentment. If your mind is focused on peaceful, loving thoughts, then your words will be more peaceful and loving. Everything you say originates with the thoughts you think, and sooner or later, those thoughts will produce corresponding words.

Our words are much more powerful than we have been taught. In fact, most people have never even considered that their words may contain energy or have an effect on their lives. But words, just like our thoughts, contain energy. We can use our words to calm an irate person, just as we can use our words to anger someone who was previously calm and serene. There is only one reason for that – our words have power and energy and should be used with care.

Most people never give their words much thought. In fact, I would say the majority of people speak without consciously thinking about what they are going to say a lot of the time. In our culture, people are simply uncomfortable with silence, so they continue to talk about anything and everything, never once considering the power contained in their words.

Careless words spoken in haste have destroyed friendships, marriages, caused hate-filled feuds, made life-long enemies, caused fights, cost many lives, and have even led to wars. Keep this in mind the next time you doubt how powerful your words are. And those are just some of the issues careless words can cause; your words greatly affect your own life as well.

The law of attraction states that whatever can be imagined and held in the mind's eye is achievable if you take action on a plan to get where you want to be. Part of the law of attraction has to do with the words that you speak. Your words send images to your brain. As I discussed in an earlier chapter, your brain does not see letters or words, but images. Words form those images; therefore, the words you speak create the images that your mind focuses on and which are amplified in the mind's eye.

According to the Bible, God created the entire world and everything in it through His words. Words have great power, but the vast majority of people either do not know this or do not believe this, and therefore use words carelessly as if they do not matter at all.

If you will remember, in an earlier chapter on cleansing your subconscious mind, I stated that we use words in the form of affirmations to change the thoughts and beliefs of our subconscious mind. Affirmations work because our words have the power to transform our minds. This alone makes your words something which you should take more seriously.

John Wayne said, "Talk low, talk slow, and don't say too much." This was John Wayne's advice on acting, but it is also great advice for maintaining your inner peace. The tone of your voice matters because different frequencies affect humans in different ways. Having a nice, pleasing tone is important and something that you can work towards changing, but for our discussion here, I want to focus more on talking slow and not saying too much.

If you are talking fast, you don't really have time to think about your words; you are simply saying whatever pops into your mind. This can cause you many problems because people who do not think before speaking, many times say things they regret. You should always think before you speak! Slow down, think about what you are going to say, why you are going to say it, and whether or not you actually should say it.

Also, don't talk too much. In our modern culture, people seem to dislike silence or any pause in the conversation, so they speak just to keep the conversation going, even if what they are saying is meaningless or should not be said. When you talk too much, you are always in danger of saying things that are better left unsaid or revealing too much personal information. It is not wise to expose too much personal information to people.

Freely exposing personal or private information to others is something I see people doing all the time. People post all kinds of private and personal information about themselves on social media. And they freely share secrets and private information in casual conversations. Many even post where they are, where they are going, and when they will be away from home or out of town.

Not only is this not wise, but it can be very dangerous. If you are posting on your social media accounts that you are having a great time in Florida on vacation, that is a giant, neon sign to any thief that your home is empty and a possible easy target.

Saying too much in casual conversations can be just as dangerous, as you are giving people who may not have your best interest at heart information that they could use against you. I don't mean to be negative, but this is just a fact. There are people out there who will take information from your conversations, file it away, and later use it against you.

It is best to avoid talking too much. Be discreet and careful with your words; this is hard to do when you talk too much. The more you talk, the more careless you get; that is just human nature. This is even truer if you are having drinks and relaxing with a group of people.

Don't talk too much! You don't have to share your opinion on everything. You don't need to try to impress everyone in the conversation with your vast array of knowledge on every subject. Remember that you learn much more by listening than you do by talking. When you are talking, you are telling people what you already know; when you are listening, you are increasing your own knowledge.

Furthermore, talking too much can increase your stress and disrupt your inner peace. You may start worrying about something you said or wondering if the information you let slip is going to cause you problems later on. And that alone can disrupt your inner peace. You don't have these issues if you are selective and careful with your speech. There is an old Okinawan proverb which states, "Spend words as efficiently as money." That is good advice!

Keep your speech uplifting and positive. Stay away from negative talk and gossip. Remember that affirmations work both ways – they can implant positive, uplifting thoughts into your mind, or they can implant negative, defeating thoughts. If you are speaking and listening to negative, low-energy words and conversations, then you are allowing negative energy to infiltrate your mind, which is the exact opposite of what you want. Be selective when it comes to what you say and what you listen to.

There is always a tactful way to exit the conversation when it disintegrates into negativity or gossip. Learn the lost art of tact and excuse yourself politely. Isaac Newton said, "Tact is the art of making a point without making an enemy." You can leave a conversation without offending people or appearing rude, and you should do so when the conversation begins to turn negative. You don't need that negativity in your life as it will hinder your goal of maintaining your inner peace.

Also, be especially careful about what you say when you are angry. We tend to be careless when we are angry and say things that we may not mean or things that will come back to cause us problems at a later date. It is never wise to allow your anger to dictate your words; always think rationally and speak with purpose.

Moreover, don't be afraid of silence. It is okay if there are periods of silence during a conversation. For some, silence can feel somewhat uncomfortable. We don't know what to do with ourselves when the conversation stops, and no one is speaking. But there is nothing wrong with silence.

Don't feel that you have to say something simply because no one else is speaking. Focus on your drink, enjoy the atmosphere, and digest what has been said. Remember the old saying – wise men speak because they have something to say; fools speak because they have to say something. Learn to speak when you have something of value to add to the conversation, not to break the silence. If there is nothing more to say and the conversation has come to a close, excuse yourself and go do something more constructive.

And refuse to take part in silly, useless arguments or debates. Many times these innocent discussions end up causing hard feelings. You may not even know that your words have offended someone until much later. Stay away from toxic arguments as much as possible, and it is always possible. I will discuss this subject in detail in a later chapter.

Everyone has the right to believe whatever he or she wants to believe, even if it is ridiculous. It is not your job to prove that someone is wrong or prove that you are right. Think about it. Is your objective to prove that you are right or to maintain your inner peace? Many times you can't do both, so choose to maintain your inner peace and let others believe whatever they choose to believe.

So far, I have discussed some wisdom concerning speaking, what to say, and how to conduct your speech around others. But there is a whole other side to your words and speech that I need to discuss, something I touched on just a bit at the beginning – your words have power and energy.

You should use your words wisely, not just in conversation with other people, but in order to develop and maintain your inner peace. You should use positive affirmations, as we have already discussed, but you should also be aware of the power and meaning of the words that you use.

Your words don't just have power when you are purposely reciting your affirmations. They *always* contain power, even when you are not mentally focused on them. You must be careful about what kind of self-talk you are using throughout the day. Miyamoto Musashi, known as Japan's greatest swordsman, stated this perfectly saying, "Do not speak badly of yourself. For the warrior within hears your

74

words and is lessened by them." This was great insight for the 17th century and still holds true today.

You must be aware of the words, thoughts, and beliefs that you are constantly feeding your subconscious mind. It does no good to spend 10 minutes on positive affirmations and then spend the rest of the day carelessly speaking negatively about yourself and putting yourself down. Ten minutes of positive affirmations will not cancel out an entire day of negative, self-defeating speech!

Monitor your thoughts and speech throughout the day. When you catch yourself saying negative things about yourself, stop yourself and replace those thoughts or words with positive, uplifting words which support you and increase your self-confidence and self-worth.

You must always be aware of your words and thoughts, as many of us are in the habit of speaking or thinking negatively about ourselves. We make a simple mistake and say, "That was stupid! I am so stupid. I always do that! I am so dumb." Your subconscious mind hears those words and thoughts and believes them to be true, as I have already discussed. Then it looks for ways to reinforce those beliefs in your life. Not good!

Your choice of words matters. Instead of saying something like, "I will retain my inner peace no matter what," say, "I am in a constant state of inner peace. When you say "I will" do something, that always refers to the future. When you say, "I am," you are making a powerful declaration of what you are right now, in this present moment. And that is where the power resides.

For many people, this will mean changing a large portion of their vocabulary. If you have been in the habit of talking badly about yourself or using words filled with negativity, it is time to delete those words and phrases from your life and replace them with words that support you and bring positive energy into your life. Instead of speaking badly about yourself, start speaking powerfully and purposely about yourself.

Make sure that your self-talk is positive and in line with your goal to cleanse your subconscious mind, replace your negative thoughts with positive thoughts, and maintain your inner peace. Remember, I told you that maintaining your inner peace would be work; well, this is part of that work. Don't let your guard down when it comes to your thoughts and words throughout the day!

Richard Brinsley Sheridan stated it perfectly when he said, "Never say more than is necessary." If you keep your words factual, peaceful, and uplifting and say only what is necessary, you will never have to be concerned with what you have said. Be honest, truthful, and sincere with your speech.

Be Honest with Others and Yourself

Speak with honesty, think with sincerity, and act with integrity.
Roy T. Bennett

Many people find it hard to be honest, either with others or themselves, but honesty is absolutely necessary for your inner peace. Studies show that people lie between 10-200 times a day. That is absolutely amazing! A study done at the University of Massachusetts in 2002 showed that 60% of people lied at least once during a 10-minute conversation and actually told an average of two to three lies during that time. In addition, it discovered that most people tell a substantial number of lies in the course of everyday conversations.

So why does this matter? Studies have been done on the effects that lying has on the body and mind, and they show some interesting results. Lying adds stress and anxiety to your mind. People know that if they are caught lying, it can do permanent damage to their reputation. Therefore, when they lie, they activate the limbic system in the brain, which initiates the fight or flight response that is triggered by stress.

The fight or flight response is a protective response which readies your body for emergency situations. Your body and mind are not designed to experience this response constantly. When your mind activates the fight or flight response frequently, it causes chronic, low-level stress.

In addition, the continual epinephrine surges can cause damage to arteries and blood vessels, which increases your risk of a heart attack or stroke. It also causes an increase in your cortisol levels creating physiological changes. Essentially, your body's energy is depleted each time you activate your stress response. The cortisol increases your appetite in order to replenish your body's energy, which also causes a build-up of fat tissue, leading to weight gain.

Since this is not a scientific book, I am not going to get into all the science behind what actually happens in the body. I will merely simplify the consequences of this process. The result of frequently activating the limbic system is constant stress! It can lead to all the same health problems that are associated with chronic stress from any other source in your life.

So to summarize, lying can cause you to be at a higher risk for heart attacks and strokes, drains your energy, can lead to weight gain, and adds stress and anxiety to your life. All of that alone should be motivation enough to start being honest with yourself and those around you. Additionally, it will lead to your conscience hounding you because you are not living up to your code of ethics, which should include being honest.

When you lie, your conscience will continually remind you of your dishonesty and that what you did was not right. People lie because they are afraid to tell the truth for one reason or another, and fear is a negative, low-level energy. Part of living a life of inner peace is working to remove fear from your life, not enabling it or allowing it to influence what you say.

Lying increases your fear, stress, and anxiety, all of which are negative, low-energy thoughts that disrupt your inner peace. Also, studies have proven that the more you lie, the more you weaken your conscience. It is like your conscience becomes desensitized to your lies. The more you lie, the more your conscience starts to give up on keeping you in line.

Let me give you an analogy. When the movie *Braveheart* first came out, my wife and I went to see it at the theater. The amount of graphic violence and all the bloody scenes actually caused my wife to get up and temporarily leave the movie. She felt sick to her stomach. But in spite of this, we did enjoy the story and the movie. So much so that I decided I would like to see it again.

A few weeks later, we went to see *Braveheart* again. This time, the brutality did not have the same effect on my wife. She was desensitized to the blood and graphic violence after seeing the movie only one time. It does not take much exposure to something to desensitize you to it! This is something that you should keep in mind when it comes to the music you listen to and the movies you watch.

The same principle applies to your conscience. Your conscience will try to keep you in line when you do not live up to your standards, but if you continually ignore your conscience and lower your standards, sooner or later, your conscience will become desensitized to your actions and give up on you living as you should. This is not a good situation to be in, especially if you want to live a life of inner peace and tranquility.

This is one reason that you should be mindful every moment of your life. Each time you do not live up to your standards, you weaken your resolve and your spirit. Don't allow yourself to be dishonest in your daily life. Being honest removes the stress and anxiety which accompany lying. And by removing this unnecessary stress and anxiety, you are becoming more tranquil and at peace with yourself.

Be honest with others and be honest with yourself. Live each moment of your life honestly and in accordance with your standards. In so doing, you are able to maintain your inner peace. It is never advantageous to lie to yourself.

If you have mastered disallowing the opinions of others to affect you (which I will discuss in another chapter), then you have no reason to lie. You lie when you are concerned or fearful about what others will think if you tell the truth. You lie when you are trying to control and manipulate other people. You lie when you don't have the courage to live your life your way.

These are all negative issues that will rob you of your inner peace. If you find that you have issues when it comes to being truthful, spend some time in meditation and discover where the cause of your dishonesty comes from. Then remove that cause from your subconscious mind and develop the courage to be honest. Being honest throughout your life will be easy once you root out the cause behind your perceived need to lie.

Always keep in mind that your words are extremely important. Refuse to speak badly about yourself, even if you are only joking. Refuse to allow yourself to lie and be dishonest, as it weakens you in the same way that speaking badly about yourself does. Your spirit and your subconscious mind hear and are mindful of your words; keep your words positive, truthful, and peaceful. To do this, it is vital that you develop the habits which foster being truthful and honest.

Throughout human history, our greatest leaders and thinkers
have used the power of words to transform our emotions, to
enlist us in their causes, and to shape the course of destiny.
Words cannot only create emotions; they create actions.
And from our actions flow the results of our lives.
Tony Robbins

Thoughts to Ponder

Better than a thousand hollow words
is one word that brings peace.
Buddha

You will always win by not saying the things you don't need to say.
Chinese Proverb

Of what does not concern you, say nothing good or bad.
Italian Proverb

Speak little, and keep your words truthful and sweet.
Say only what benefits others.
Swami Muktananda

Never trust your tongue when your heart is bitter.
Samuel J. Hurwitt

In silence man can most readily preserve his integrity.
Meister Eckhart

Silence is a means of avoiding misfortune.
Sakya Pandit

Where the river is deepest, it makes the least noise.
Italian Proverb

The Indian believes profoundly in silence –
the sign of perfect equilibrium.
Silence is the absolute poise or balance of body, mind and spirit.
What are the fruits of silence?
They are self-control, true courage or endurance,
patience, dignity, and reverence.
Silence is the cornerstone of character.
Ohiyesa

Lower your voice and strengthen your argument.
Lebanon Proverb

Honesty is the first chapter in the book of wisdom.
Thomas Jefferson

Thoughts to Ponder

Your friend has a friend, and your friend's
friend has a friend; be discreet.
The Talmud

Each time you are honest and conduct yourself with honesty,
a success force will drive you toward greater success.
Each time you lie, even with a little white lie,
there are strong forces pushing you toward failure.
Joseph Sugarman

No legacy is so rich as honesty.
William Shakespeare

Language creates reality. Words have power.
Speak always to create joy.
Deepak Chopra

When two men quarrel,
he who is first silent is the better man.
The Talmud

Tell the truth. If you tell the truth all the time you don't
have to worry three months down the line about what
you said three months earlier. Truth is always the truth.
You won't have to complicate your life by trying to cover up.
Benjamin Carson

Lay down for yourself, at the outset, a certain stamp and
type of character for yourself, which you are to maintain
whether you are by yourself or are meeting with people.
And be silent for the most part, or else make only the
most necessary remarks, and express these in few words.
Epictetus

Words can inspire. And words can destroy. Choose yours well.
Robin Sharma

Words are containers for power,
you choose what kind of power they carry.
Joyce Meyer

Chapter 7
Develop Good Habits and Stay Calm

We are what we repeatedly do.
Aristotle

Ultimately, after you have done the initial work to get yourself on the right track, maintaining your inner peace will come down to forging good habits. Developing bad habits comes easily; developing good habits takes perseverance and self-discipline. But once you have successfully created the habits which foster inner peace and tranquility, they will become second nature for you.

The first step to developing habits that support your inner peace is breaking your bad habits. Many people have developed the mentality that they will never allow anyone to treat them rudely or get the best of them. Therefore, as a protective measure, they almost always react in kind when someone is rude to them.

This is very common throughout the world. If someone shoves someone, that person shoves them back. It is an eye for an eye type mentality. The problem with this type of mentality is that it is never-ending and never leads to the inner peace that you are seeking. This mindset will many times lead to ongoing hassles, stress, strife, hatred, feuds, and unforeseen problems. What happens after you shove the other guy back? Does he apologize, smile, and walk away, or does he come back at you even harder?

It is much better to do everything in your power to maintain peace with people. If someone is rude to you walking out of the grocery store, instead of being rude back, smile and say, "I hope your day gets better," and leave it at that. Don't stew about it all day long. If you bump into someone in a pub and spill his drink, and he starts yelling at you, de-escalate the situation. Say something like, "Oh, man, I am so sorry. Here let me buy you a fresh drink."

De-escalating negative situations is always the route to inner peace; whereas, fighting fire with fire ensures that the fire continues to burn inside you, as well as the other person. You have to change the way that you look at things, especially if you have allowed negative people, situations, and events in your life to jade you.

For our purposes here, a bad habit is anything that interferes with developing and maintaining your inner peace. If you get rude or obnoxious when you drink too much, stop drinking. If you sleep in every morning and then get stressed because you don't have time to do what you need to do, stop sleeping so late. If you are in the habit

81

of allowing worry or fear to control your life, then it is time to get rid of those habits. The list of bad habits could fill this book; you know what yours are and what you need to change.

The key to changing your bad habits over the long run is to not only get rid of the bad habit but to actually replace that habit with one that nurtures your inner peace. The Universe abhors a void and will always seek to fill any void in your life with something else. It is crucial that you make sure to fill that void with something beneficial that helps you on your journey to inner peace.

If you are in the habit of responding with a witty, snide comment when someone is rude to you, then replace that habit with soothing, peaceful comments. This may be hard to do at first, especially when every cell of your body wants to put that obnoxious guy in his place. The reason that you may find this hard to do is because for years you have programmed your subconscious mind to react that way. You must break that habit and reprogram your mind to respond in a different way.

When you respond differently, it will start to change how others react to you. Be kind, even if it takes all of your restraint and self-control to do so at first. Start taking pleasure in the knowledge that you may help someone change his or her spirit and even have a better day. Instead of reinforcing his negative beliefs about people, take him by surprise and respond with kindness.

I can speak from experience. I never allowed anyone to get away with being rude to me or even those around me. If I saw someone being rude, I would go out of my way to put him in his place, even if he was not rude to me personally. I was quick with a sarcastic comeback or an underhanded remark, but this didn't foster inner peace in my life.

Now, I look for ways to defuse those situations. I look for opportunities to make people feel good about themselves. I hand out compliments to strangers and feel good about the smile I put on their faces. I changed my confrontational nature to one of soft-spoken peace and tranquility. I actually find more peace and pleasure in being kind to people than I do from putting them in their place.

Whatever habits you have which are obstructing your goal of maintaining inner peace need to be removed from your life and replaced with higher energy habits – ones that foster inner peace in your life. Cultivate good habits that promote inner peace, not only in your life, but in the lives of those around you. You choose your habits; they don't choose you. Choose wisely!

Although you choose your habits, your actions have a deceptive way of becoming habits before you know it. Raging rivers never start as such; they originate from many small streams which continually feed the river until they become one substantial, uncontrollable river. You must constantly monitor your actions and thoughts, especially the negative ones, to ensure they do not become unwanted habits that negatively affect your life.

Nobody ever sets out to become an alcoholic or a drug addict. They try something and find that they like it. Then they try it again and again, and before they know it, they are addicted to the substance. The same principle applies to your bad habits. You must not become complacent about your life; continually monitor your progress and make changes as needed. Don't allow bad habits to develop and distract you from your overall goal of inner peace.

Once you have changed your bad habits and replaced them with habits that help you maintain your inner peace, you will find that maintaining inner peace will become much easier for you. It will become a natural part of your life. Stress, worry, strife, anger, jealousy, and other unwanted emotions will appear less and less often.

Humans are creatures of habit. Make sure you develop the right kind of habits in your life, as your habits become your life. If you want to live a life of inner peace and tranquility, choose to develop practices that foster inner peace and tranquility. The tools and activities I discussed earlier will be a great help to you in developing these habits, but only if you apply them to your life.

Stay calm and controlled, and manage your life like your actions and habits matter because they do. One of the habits you should foster in your life is to always stay calm, no matter what is happening. A flustered, panicked mind will never lead to inner peace.

Always Remain Calm

Only those who are not affected by
external circumstances will always be calm.
Lieh Tzu

No matter what the external circumstances around you may be, you can always choose to remain calm on the inside. Remaining calm is a choice you make. Nothing and nobody can take away your calm mind unless you choose to allow it to happen. If you are at peace internally, then your mind will be calm, as being mentally calm and living with a high level of inner peace go hand in hand.

Your ability to remain calm in any situation comes from the inside, from your mind. If you have cleansed your subconscious mind and learned to control your thoughts, then you will have total control over your ability to remain calm. You simply have to learn to take control and refuse to allow anything to put your mind into panic mode.

The ability to remain calm in the midst of the storm is vital to your inner peace. If you allow your mind to panic because of something that is happening externally, then your inner peace will follow your mental state. It is virtually impossible to maintain your inner peace while your mind is in panic mode. No matter what the situation may be, it is never wise to lose control. Panicking always makes things worse in every situation.

It takes a strong, self-confident mind to remain calm amid chaos, especially when those around you are panicking. This is an excellent opportunity to determine how well you have developed your inner peace. Panic, like anger, is contagious. When people see others losing control because of fear or anger, as we have seen with angry mobs, they tend to follow suit instead of remaining calm and rational.

Staying calm in times like these is not only a sign that you have developed your inner peace to a higher level, but that you have set yourself apart from the average person with your ability to remain calm and rational, instead of panicking, shutting down your rational mind, and losing control. Doing so makes you unique, as most people tend to panic and not think clearly when stress affects their minds.

Dr. Wayne Dyer taught, "Calmness is the peace of God within you." Think about that. If you have the peace of God within you, you are not going to panic or allow external circumstances to put fear into your heart. If you truly trust in God and know that God is omnipotent and omnipresent, you will not panic. The man or woman who truly believes this will be able to maintain his or her inner calm no matter what is going on around them.

I began this section with a quote from Taoist text, *Lieh Tzu*, which states that only those who are *not* affected by external circumstances will always be calm. It takes a while to get to the point that you are not influenced by external circumstances. It takes self-confidence, trust in a Higher Power, and a strong commitment to maintaining your inner peace, but it can be done.

A calm mind is a strong, rational mind. When those around you are panicking and falling apart, remind yourself that a panicked mind is not a rational mind, and an irate, livid mind is a mind which has lost control. There is no inner peace in either a panicked mind or an enraged mind. When you allow fear and anger to take control of your mind, inner peace and tranquility take a back seat; your emotions are in control.

Not only does this disrupt your inner peace, but it causes mental confusion and the inability to think rationally. Many times those who are panicked, or who have allowed their anger or fear to totally take control, do things that not only make the situation much worse but that also have long-lasting, negative consequences for their lives. Both the prisons and the cemeteries are full of people who allowed panic or anger to dictate their actions instead of remaining calm and thinking rationally.

Panic never makes things better; whereas, maintaining a calm and rational mind usually results in a much better outcome, no matter what the situation may be. A calm mind is the best weapon against whatever challenge you may be facing. Thomas Jefferson stated, "Nothing gives one person so much advantage over another as to remain always cool and unruffled under all circumstances."

Of course, you are not in competition with other people when it comes to maintaining your inner peace and tranquility, but remaining calm under all circumstances will give you an advantage over every situation in which you may find yourself.

Confucius even took calmness one step further, stating "Lose your stillness, and you will fail in everything you do." Think about it. If you lose your temper in a heated situation, it strengthens the other person's point and makes you look weak, out-of-control, and foolish. Even if you lose your temper when you are working alone, it has consequences. It disrupts your inner peace and adds to your frustration and stress.

On the other hand, maintaining a calm attitude will strengthen your point, with the added benefit of making people see you as a rational, controlled person, especially when those around you are losing their cool. That calmness also increases the respect which others have for you. Remaining calm will have a positive effect on those around you and will even help them regain their composure. Your calm demeanor gives them confidence that things will be all right.

It also allows you a clearer perception of what is happening around you. Panic and anger cloud the mind; calmness and inner peace strengthen your perception. In every situation, it is to your advantage to remain calm and maintain your inner peace.

When you are tempted to panic or allow anger to take over your mind, focus your attention on your objective. Focus on compassion, tolerance, forgiveness, and self-discipline. Remind yourself that you will only be able to think rationally if you maintain a calm mind.

There is an example that is widely used by Asian sages to demonstrate the importance of maintaining a calm mind. Think about how the moon is reflected in water. If there are waves on the water, the moon is distorted; it is not reflected accurately. The moon is only reflected accurately in calm, still water.

The same principle applies to your mind. Your thoughts cannot be rational and wise if your mind is troubled and agitated. Your mind must be calm and still in order for your thoughts to be clear and rational.

Furthermore, when your mind is troubled, and you can't think clearly, allow your thoughts to settle, and you will regain your calmness. Don't try to force your mind to settle down; allow it to calm down on its own. Use some of the breathing techniques I gave you in chapter three. Calming your mind during those times is not a quick fix; it takes a little time for it to calm down. Just relax, breathe, and allow the confusion and negativity to disperse, and your mind will regain its peaceful state.

Think of the water in a clear lake in which the mud on the bottom has been disturbed, and the water has become muddy. You cannot force the water to become clear; you must simply wait and allow the sediment to settle, and the water will clear by itself. If you go in and try to force the water to clear up, you will only be making it muddier by trying to rush a process that must follow its natural course.

It will take time for your mind to clear, just like the water in the lake. Don't struggle to calm your mind; simply focus on something else until you regain your calm mind and inner peace. Your mind will become clear on its own if you place your focus elsewhere. And the breathing techniques in chapter three, along with meditation are great ways to change your focus and allow your mind to become clear and calm again.

The more you practice staying calm, the more maintaining a calm mind will become a habit. Just refuse to allow anything or anyone to disturb your mind. Once you become proficient at maintaining a calm mind and controlling your thoughts, controlling your fear, anger, and worry will be much easier. And once you have controlled your fear and anger, which I will discuss in the next chapter, you will no longer have to deal with panic.

All of these pieces fit together like a jigsaw puzzle to create and maintain your inner peace. The more pieces that you incorporate into your life, the clearer your path to inner peace becomes.

To be calm is the highest achievement of the self.
Zen proverb

Thoughts to Ponder

Men acquire a particular quality by
constantly acting in a particular way.
Aristotle

The soul, like the body, accepts by practice
whatever habit one wishes it to contract.
Socrates

Habit becomes one's nature.
Japanese Proverb

Habit is a cable; we weave a thread of it each day,
and at last we cannot break it.
Horace Mann

Cultivate only the habits that you
are willing should master you.
Elbert Hubbard

Character is simply habit long continued.
Plutarch

The fire that seems extinguished often slumbers beneath the ashes.
Pierre Corneille

The chains of habit are too weak to be felt
until they are too strong to be broken.
Samuel Johnson

Peace of mind comes from knowing that this too shall pass
and good progress comes from good habits.
Brendon Burchard

The only proper way to eliminate bad habits
is to replace them with good ones.
Jerome Hines

Good habits, once established are just
as hard to break as are bad habits.
Robert Puller

Thoughts to Ponder

Never be in a hurry, do everything quietly and in a calm spirit.
Do not lose your inner peace for anything whatsoever,
even if your whole world seems upset.
Saint Francis de Sales

In the midst of movement and chaos, keep stillness inside of you.
Deepak Chopra

The nearer a man comes to a calm mind, the closer he is to strength.
Marcus Aurelius

If you wear shoes to protect your feet, the pebbles in the
road cannot affect you. Likewise, if you remain calm under all
conditions, the pebbles in the road of life cannot cause you pain.
Narada

Remember to preserve a calm soul amid difficulties.
Horace

To bear trials with a calm mind robs
misfortune of its strength and burden.
Seneca

The master remains serene in the midst of sorrow;
evil cannot enter his heart.
Lao Tzu

The measure of wisdom is how calm you
are when facing any given situation.
Naval Ravikant

The pursuit, even of the best things, ought to be calm and tranquil.
Cicero

The greater the level of calmness of our mind, the greater our peace
of mind, the greater our ability to enjoy a happy and joyful life.
Dalai Lama

Recognize that if it's humanly possible, you can do it too.
Marcus Aurelius

Chapter 8
Ban Fear and Worry from Your Life

You cannot live in fear and maintain
your inner peace at the same time.
Bohdi Sanders

Fear is a reaction to a person, place, thing, or situation, and fear is the source of all worry. Besides the fear of falling from high places and being startled by loud noises, all other fears have been learned or conditioned in us over the years. No one is born with a fear of being assaulted, of offending the boss, or of snakes. Those are all learned from different experiences. Many people have spent so much of their lives worrying about one thing or another or allowing phobias to control them that fear has become a normal part of life for them.

Courage, on the other hand, is a decision. No matter what you are facing in your life, you can always decide to be courageous instead of fearful. Fear is a reaction; courage is a response. When you react, you are rarely in control. But when you respond, you have made a conscious decision about what you will do next. Reacting is your mind on autopilot; responding is being fully aware, thoughtful, and rational.

Some people believe that fear is a good thing and that only irrational people say they have no fear. They will use things such as venomous snakes as an example. They make comments such as, "If you are not afraid of venomous snakes, they will kill you." But that is not exactly true. You don't have to fear venomous snakes in order to have the knowledge of what they can do and the wisdom to stay away from them.

Knowledge and rational thinking control fear. Fear comes from the mind, so you must control your thoughts in order to control and eliminate your fear. And you absolutely must control your fear if you want to live a life of inner peace. You cannot live in fear and maintain your inner peace at the same time. Fearful thoughts will always disrupt your tranquility.

There is a big difference between irrational fears and having a healthy respect for things that could cause you harm. Let's go back to my example of the fear of snakes. Most people understand that venomous snakes can be very dangerous and even deadly. But having an irrational fear of all snakes is not wise. If you are hiking or living in an area known to be inhabited by venomous snakes, you should approach your safety rationally.

Learn how to identify snakes that can be dangerous. Learn their habits, what type of habitat they prefer, how they react, where you are likely to find them, etc. This is having a rational respect for these reptiles and what they can do. Being afraid to go hiking or fishing because there may be a venomous snake on the trail or around the water is allowing your fear of snakes to control you. That is completely irrational!

Fear is based on erroneous thinking and ignorance. I have seen people literally start shaking and run screaming at the sight of a tiny, harmless garter snake, which could not bite them even if it wanted to. They know that the garter snake is not venomous and is not dangerous in any way, but fear controls their mind. I have even picked the garter snake up and shown them that it is harmless, but they cannot get past their irrational fear.

The fear of snakes is just one example of a multitude of fears which can take control of someone's mind. I have seen people so fearful of heights that they cannot take a drive in the mountains and people so afraid of sharks that they are afraid to be in a boat in the Gulf of Mexico. These are all examples of allowing your fear to control your mind.

Instead of fearing things that other people fear, use your knowledge of those things to determine what you should do and what you shouldn't do; then respond accordingly, without fear. Knowledge tells you what you need to know in every situation; fear clouds your mind and causes irrational thinking; courage allows you to act on your knowledge in spite of your fear.

The fear of public speaking is the most commonly held fear of people in today's culture. That fear holds many people back from doing things which they would like to do, but that fear is not rational. After all, what would happen if you stood up to give a speech and totally dropped the ball? Would you be embarrassed? Would people laugh at you? So what!

Stop being fearful and worrying about what other people do or think. Being embarrassed or being laughed at is not the end of the world, but in some people's minds, the fear of being embarrassed or laughed at can be paralyzing. Fear comes from the mind and thus, can be eliminated by taking control of your mind.

Your fear is only as deep as your mind allows it to be. It is your thoughts that make your fears seem much bigger and much more important than they truly are. Once you actually confront your fear, you will discover that it is nothing like what your mind made it out to be. As Emerson stated, "Do the thing you fear and the death of fear is certain."

As a child, I was terrified of deep water. I loved to go to the lake and play in the water, but only as long as I could touch the bottom of the lake without the water being over my head. I could swim and had no problem playing under the water, but I had a fear of the deeper water.

I remember my dad would take me and throw me high up into the air, and I would splash down into the water. I loved doing that, but only as long as the water was not too deep. I knew my dad would not let anything happen to me, but if he tried to throw me up in the air into water that was over my head, I would go into a panic.

Like most fears, that was completely irrational. The deep water was only a few steps away from where I played all the time, but it scared me. I could swim as well in that water as I did in the water six feet closer to the bank, but that did not matter. My mind allowed the fear of the deep water to totally control me.

How did I get over that fear? My dad would not allow it; he continued to throw me up into the deeper water until I finally realized there was nothing to be afraid of. After doing it a few times, I no longer minded it at all. Remember, doing the thing you fear will change the way you *think* about that fear.

You must confront your fear, or it will always control you. Once you face your fear, you destroy your fear. Your mind has a way of making things worse than they actually are, if you allow it to. The cure for that is, once again, to take control of your mind and think rationally.

Even though it may be uncomfortable, you must overcome your fears. If you don't overcome your fears, they will disrupt your inner peace, not to mention, interfere with many of the things you enjoy. Don't allow anything or anybody to control your life. If fear is controlling you in any way, be determined to defeat it and remove it from your mind. The less fear you have, the more inner peace you will experience.

Determine that no fear will influence your actions. If you have a fear that interferes with your life in some way, force yourself to face it and conquer it. If you have a fear of public speaking, force yourself to speak in public, even if it is to a very small group. If you have a fear of snakes, go to a pet store and ask them to allow you to touch and hold one of their snakes. Never allow any fear to conquer you! See your fears as a challenge and rise up to meet each of them.

The biggest fear that people have, besides the fear of public speaking, is the fear of death. How crazy is it that most people fear public speaking more than dying! After all, public speaking is not a matter of life or death. That is how irrational our fears can be if we allow them to take over our minds. The fear of public speaking comes from your ego and being overly concerned with what other people think about you.

The old Jedi Master, Yoda, stated, "Train yourself to let go of the things you fear the most." This means that you should let go of your fear; stop holding on to it as if it is a vital part of you. Fear is not a part of you. Stop owning it by calling it, "My fear of snakes" or "My fear of public speaking." Get rid of all fear; this includes the fear of death.

Be at Peace with Your Death

Peace of mind is that mental condition
in which you have accepted the worst.
Lin Yutang

The fear of death is the second most widely held fear in the world. Being afraid of death is more about being afraid of the unknown. Although we have some ancient teachings and many modern accounts of near-death experiences where people have died for a short period of time and come back to life, what happens when you die is still a mystery for most people.

I want to discuss being at peace with the fact that you, me, and everyone else on this planet will leave our physical body at some time during our life on earth. This is what we call death. From the minute that you are born, you are on a journey towards the physical death of your body. This is just a fact. The question is not whether or not your body will die, but rather how long you will live in the body you have been given.

One point I want to make before I go on is that when I speak of death, I am speaking about the death of our physical body. Almost all sages and religions have taught that although our physical body dies, our spirit or soul lives on. The teachings vary concerning what happens to our spirit once our body dies, but the vast majority of teachings agree that we do not actually cease to exist. We do not die; we simply go back to that from which we came.

Don Miguel Ruiz, the author of *The Four Agreements*, had a great analogy for death in his book. He explains that our body is like a computer. If you buy a new computer, it does not work unless there is a power source to make it work. That power source is electricity. When it is plugged into the power source, it works. It is that source that gives the computer life. But when the computer no longer works, that does not affect the power source which gave the computer life

92

and made it useful. The source of the computer's power is still there, even though the computer has died.

The computer is your body. Your body is the most complicated, most powerful machine ever made. It is simply amazing, but without the energy source which brings it to life, it is nothing more than hydrogen, oxygen, carbon, and nitrogen. That energy source is your spirit, your true essence, who you truly are. And when your body dies, that power source, the real you, lives on. Your body is simply separated from its power source.

Death is a natural part of life and nothing to be feared. Every person who has ever lived from the beginning of time, with the exception of those still alive today, has taken this journey. Since we all have different beliefs about death depending on how we were raised and what teachings we adhere to, I will not go into my beliefs about what happens after we leave our physical bodies. But I do want to help you get past the fear of death.

The fear of death is actually much worse than death itself. Death is inevitable. There is no way to cheat death. There is no magic potion that will make you live forever in your physical body. Our body is like an amazing machine run by an extremely complicated computer system and fueled by what we feed it. Like all machines, sooner or later, it will wear out, no matter how well you maintain it. All machines with working parts wear out sooner or later.

So how do you get past fearing your own inevitable death? First, you must come to terms with the fact that you are going to die and there is nothing that you or anyone else can do about it. If you find that this fact is distressing you, then it is time to do some research on the different teachings concerning death.

When you start to research the different philosophies and teachings concerning death, you will notice a clear pattern developing from the ancient Christian teachings, the ancient Egyptian teachings, the Greeks, the Roman Stoics, the ancient Asian teachings, to the teachings of the Native Americans.

One thing all of these teachings have in common is that when we leave our physical body, we do not die. These beliefs vary on the specific details concerning what happens to your spirit after death, but they all agree that you do not actually die. This should be comforting to you if you are dealing with a fear of death. Study the different teachings from around the world and delve deeper into the ones that resonate with you.

The majority of these teachings agree that, to one degree or another, how you live your life while you are in your physical body plays a big part in how you will live after you leave this earth.

Therefore, you have the power to determine what kind of experience you will have in your life after death; you are in charge. Most religious teachings state that those who have lived a good life here on earth, meaning those who have done their best to be good to other people, loving, kind, giving, helpful, and who have tried to live the best life they could, will be rewarded for doing so.

Some religions get more detailed and state that you have to take this step or that step in order to go to Heaven, but even those religions teach that part of the process is living a good life, loving your neighbor, and helping others. Find the teaching or religion which resonates with you as the truth and do your best to follow it. Those who have a firm faith in what happens after death are more at peace with the fact that they will leave their physical body one day.

This brings us to a point that I covered earlier. You must live your life by a code of honor or a code of ethics. Determine what it means to live a good, upright life, and then do your best to live accordingly. When you fall short, ask God's forgiveness, forgive yourself, correct your shortcomings, and get back on track. Seek to become a better person each and every day.

Being a better person does not mean that you seek to become better than others, but that you become a better person than you were the day before. Live your life by the Japanese concept of Kaizen – continual, never-ending improvement. Never give up on living a life of character, honor, and integrity, and all that those concepts encompass.

Since our lives are so hectic and busy with work, family, chores, and everything in between, it is easy to forget about continually trying to improve ourselves. One way to combat this is to consider a technique that the samurai used to overcome their fear of death.

The samurai lived by a strict code and served ruthless leaders. Those leaders could command a samurai to commit suicide at any time. Consequently, the samurai never knew from one day to another when they would be commanded to commit suicide or be called into battle and killed during warfare.

For the ordinary person, this would cause a lot of mental stress. To combat that stress, the samurai kept his own death fresh on his mind. In a sense, the samurai died before he died. He knew his death was inevitable; therefore, he remained ready for death at all times. He kept his finances in order, his family life in order, his spiritual life in order, and maintained his character and honor.

You should live your life in the same way. Of course, nobody is going to demand that you take your own life, but that does not mean that your life is anymore guaranteed to you than the samurai's life was to him. Accidents happen every day. You are not guaranteed to be alive tomorrow. No one knows the exact time of his own death; therefore, you should get your affairs in order and be ready for the inevitable. Being prepared and having all your affairs in order removes a great deal of the stress associated with dying.

Die before you die. Meditate on your death and be prepared. Live your life to the best of your ability and leave nothing unsaid or undone. Make sure you have your affairs in order. Live each day of your life as if it is the last because in reality, one day, it will be. This is not a negative, dark, depressing exercise, but simply one of preparing yourself mentally, physically, and spiritually for what you know is inevitable.

Look at it this way; if you live on the Florida coast and you get a category five hurricane warning, you start preparing for it to make landfall. You make sure you have plenty of food and water, board up your windows, make sure your generator is ready to go, etc. You prepare in every way you possibly can for what you know is coming your way. You don't sit around in fear; you prepare the best you can and go on living your life. You get yourself and your family mentally prepared for what's coming.

Consider this, when you are packed and ready for a trip, you have double-checked everything around your home, made sure you have everything you need, your agenda is set, and you know exactly where you are going, you don't have much stress about your journey. But if you forget to prepare and it is time to leave, it is very stressful trying to get everything in order in a hurry, wondering what you have forgotten, who you need to call, etc. It is always better to be prepared ahead of time. It does away with a lot of the anxiety.

Your time on this earth is short; use it wisely. Don't allow the fear of death to interfere with the joy of living. Remind yourself what the great Scotsman, William Wallace stated, "Every man dies, but not every man really lives," and start living your life to the fullest each and every day. Don't seize the day; seize every minute of every day and bring each minute in line with how you want to live your life. Don't fear death; live your life to the fullest while you are alive!

Make it a habit to remind yourself that you will not live forever and that you do not know how much time you have left on this planet. When you do that, you will appreciate the people and things in your life more. You will love your family more deeply, you will enjoy the things you have been blessed with more fully, and you will not forget to live your life to the fullest each and every day.

There is an online countdown clock which you may find very helpful in this process. You can use it for many things, but I find it helpful to use as a reminder of how short life truly is. When you understand that life is short, it becomes more precious to you. You can use this countdown clock by programming it to count the days until you are a certain age, say 80-years-old. It then starts the countdown and shows how many days you have left, down to the second, until you turn 80, or whatever age you program it for.

I keep my countdown clock on my favorites list on my computer and check it often. It reminds me that I do not have time to waste and helps keep me focused on living my life to the fullest. Here is the link to this site if you would like to use it to help motivate you to actually live every day of your life to the fullest.

https://www.timeanddate.com/counters/

When you consider that death is the worst thing that can happen to you in any given situation, and you have overcome your fear of death by using the techniques in this chapter combined with your personal beliefs concerning death, all of your other fears start to appear unimportant. And if you remind yourself of this often, you will find that worrying becomes a thing of the past.

Refuse to Worry about Anything

Positively nothing is worth losing your peace of mind over.
Emmet Fox

Worrying about people or situations in our lives is something the majority of people today appear to have issues dealing with in their lives. It seems that people are constantly worried about everything from their job to the weather, and they openly voice their worries as if stating them will somehow make everything better. I hardly go through one day without hearing someone say they are worried about one thing or another. Worry seems to be a pandemic in our modern culture.

I have news for you – worrying has never made anything better and never will. It is a total waste of your time and mental energy. It changes nothing, except for adding to your stress, sleeplessness, and health problems. Yes, worrying does negatively affect your health.

Medical research has shown that as much as 90% of all illnesses and diseases are stress-related, including high blood pressure, heart disease, and cardiovascular disease. Even if worrying accomplished some good things or actually helped in some way, just the fact that 90% of all diseases and health problems are stress-related, and worry

96

is a major cause of stress, should be enough to make you refuse to worry about anything.

But, to add insult to injury, worry does not accomplish anything positive in your life. It causes many problems for you, while at the same time doing nothing to help you in any way whatsoever! And yet, people all over the world appear to be addicted to worrying about one thing or another.

I will lay it on the line for you. Worrying is ridiculous. Either take action to resolve the issue or be okay with the way things are. Those are the only two rational choices you have. Worrying is an irrational choice. It makes no sense to worry about anything for any reason.

When it comes right down to it, there are only two types of situations in your life – situations you have control over and situations that you have no control over. If you can do something about whatever it is that you have been worrying about, then stop worrying and take action.

If you can't do anything about the situation, no matter how badly you may want to, then why are you worrying about it? Everything will work out as it will, period. What good will your worrying do? The only thing that worrying about the situation will do is cost you sleep, stress, and possibly make you sick while you wait to see how things play out.

If you can do something about the situation, get up and do it; if there is nothing you can do about the situation one way or the other, then forget about it and move on to something else. Those are the only reasonable and wise choices you have.

There are some things you have control over and some things you don't. Here is a basic list of things that you can control:

1) Your Thoughts
2) Your Beliefs
3) Your Attitude
4) Your Words
5) Your Perspective (how you choose to see the world)
6) Your Honor and Character
7) Your Behavior
8) Your Gratitude
9) Your Habits
10) Your Response in any given situation
11) Who you associate with

You may be thinking that there are other things in life that you can also control. For example, if your son is being bullied by his baseball

97

coach, there are things you can do to take care of that situation. This is something that you have some control over, but it also falls under "your response in any given situation." You will find that everything you have some control over falls under one of the categories on this list.

Thomas Merton correctly stated that anxiety is the mark of spiritual insecurity. I find it strange when people who proclaim to believe in God go around worrying about everything and everybody. If you really do believe in God and believe that He is all-knowing and all-powerful, and that He blesses those who love Him and are devoted to Him, then isn't worrying contrary to your belief?

If you truly believe what you profess to believe, you would never worry about anything because your faith in God would be all you need. Worry is a sign that your faith in God is weak. After all, if you truly believe that God loves you, is watching over you, and looking out for you, you would not be worrying about anything.

I want to point out that there is a difference between worry and concern. Worry is focusing on problems that may or may not occur; it is a type of "what if" thinking where you are focused on all the negative things which may or may not happen.

Remember that you attract into your life what you continually focus on. When you are worrying about something, you are actually sending more energy to whatever it is that you are worried about happening, and in a sense, enabling it to come to pass.

In contrast, concern is a more calculated thought. Even though some dictionaries list concern as a synonym for worry, they are two separate things entirely. Concern is the consideration and assessment of the actual situation. It deals with the facts at hand and focuses on how to solve the specific problem if it actually does manifest itself in your life. Worry is fear-based; concern is strategic-based. Worry is a waste of time; concern is preparing for a contingency.

The Book of Proverbs states that "A prudent man sees danger and takes refuge; but the simple go on and suffer for it." It is wise to foresee danger and to prepare a plan to deal with it. That is concern. It is unwise to worry about the possibility of danger, replay it in your mind over and over, but never take any action to prepare for it. Again, if you can do something about the situation, do it, even if it is only to prepare for the worst. If you can't do anything about it, then do something else constructive with your time.

Many people indulge in worry because it takes little to no effort, whereas, taking action, or devising a plan of action, actually involves work. Worry is a lazy person's answer to concern. It is much easier to simply sit and worry about what may happen than to think rationally

98

and see the various options, devise a strategy, and do something to prepare for certain contingencies.

If you want to have inner peace in your life, you absolutely have to stop worrying. Refuse to worry about the small stuff and refuse to worry about the important stuff. Just plain refuse to allow yourself to worry about anything for any reason. Have faith that everything will be all right no matter what happens.

This doesn't mean that you become complacent, throw up your hands and say, "Whatever happens, happens. I have no control over anything in this world." That is not the opposite of worry; it is simply apathy. There are many things in your life which you can control, but you have to actually make the effort to control those things.

Saying that you have no control over your life and just going with whatever happens is akin to taking a sailboat out in the ocean and saying that you have no control over where the boat goes. If you take that sailboat out and just sit there doing nothing because you believe you have no control over where the ocean takes you, it will most likely not take you where you want to go and could very well turn into a dangerous situation.

The sailboat is equipped with sails, a motor, a rudder, and a wheel for a reason. If you refuse to use the tools provided for you, the wind and waves will toss, turn, and blow you wherever they will. They may even send you to the bottom of the ocean. There are many things that you can control, but you have to make the effort to control those things which you can while having the wisdom to know what things are in your control and what things are not.

You have no control over which direction the wind blows or how rough the ocean is, but you can adjust your sails to the wind and use your equipment to foresee rough seas before you get yourself into a bad situation.

Concern would be making sure your equipment is working properly before you leave on your journey, checking the weather forecast before you set sail, and having a strategy in case things go wrong. Worry is allowing your mind to dwell on all the things which could go wrong on your trip but not lifting a finger to prepare for those things.

Worry is fear-based, and we have already seen that fear is a low-energy thought. Low-energy thoughts weaken you, add to your problems, and are both addicting and contagious. The more you allow yourself to worry, the more prevalent your worry becomes. And you will find that your worry actually spreads to those around you. Not only are you causing yourself mental stress and health issues, but you are spreading that negativity to your friends and family.

99

If you have a specific fear that consistently torments you, face that fear rationally. Rational thought always defeats worry. Most of the time, the things you worry about never come to pass. You may have spent days or weeks worrying about a specific problem, only to find that it never was a problem to start with, and you have done nothing but waste your time, add to your stress, lower your immune system, and cause yourself unnecessary problems. The vast majority of the time, your worry does more to injure you than whatever you are worried about in the first place.

If you believe in God, then start trusting God to take care of you and the things in your life. If you believe that everything in the Universe always works out as it should, then start acting on that belief and stop worrying. If you say you believe something, but your actions are contrary to what you say that you believe, do you really believe it? Start living your life according to what you profess to believe!

Refusing to worry is a part of controlling your mind and thoughts. When you worry, you are allowing your thoughts to run wild and uncontrolled. Worry and inner peace cannot occupy your mind at the same time; they are like oil and water, not compatible.

Living a life of inner peace requires that you put an end to worrying, not just about the important things in your life, but about everything in your life. Discipline yourself to refuse to worry about anything for any reason. Do not even allow yourself to use the word "worry" or to say, "I am worried." Remember, your words contain energy and power. You must refuse to allow fear and worry to occupy your mind if you are serious about living a life of inner peace.

Worry is thinking that has turned toxic.
Harold B. Walker

Thoughts to Ponder

Life shrinks or expands in proportion to one's courage.
Anais Nin

The cave you fear to enter holds the treasure you seek.
Joseph Campbell

Do not be frightened, and do not be dismayed,
for the Lord your God is with you wherever you go.
The Bible

Ignorance is the parent of fear.
Herman Melville

Fear defeats more people than any other one thing in the world.
Ralph Waldo Emerson

Old and young, we are all on our last cruise.
Robert Louis Stevenson

To conquer fear is the beginning of wisdom.
Bertrand Russell

The first duty of man is that of subduing fear.
He must get rid of fear, he cannot act until then.
Thomas Carlyle

Of all the liars in the world,
sometimes the worst are our own fears.
Rudyard Kipling

Fear is nothing but a lack of trust in God.
Emmet Fox

People living deeply have no fear of death.
Anais Nin

The price of anything is the amount of life you exchange for it.
Henry David Thoreau

Thoughts to Ponder

When nothing can be done about the way things are,
the wise stop worrying about the situation.
Lao Tzu

Rule number one is, don't sweat the small stuff.
Rule number two is, it's all small stuff.
Robert Eliot

God has thrown open the door and says to you, "Go."
Where? To nothing you need to fear, but back to that
from which you came, to what is friendly and akin to you.
Epictetus

There is nothing that wastes the body like worry,
and one who has any faith in God should be
ashamed to worry about anything whatsoever.
Mahatma Gandhi

Only people who see through the illusions of longevity, fame, social
status, and wealth are not burdened by anxiety and fear.
Lieh Tzu

Those who are perplexed by the difficulties and seeming
inconsistencies of life should remember that at the present
time we get only a partial view of things; and that a partial
view of anything never shows the thing as it really is.
Emmet Fox

Worrying does not take away tomorrow's troubles,
it takes away today's peace.
Leo Buscaglia

Worry is a thin stream of fear trickling through the mind.
If encouraged, it cuts a channel into which
all other thoughts are drained.
Arthur Somers Roche

Do every act of your life as if it were your last.
Marcus Aurelius

Chapter 9
Actively Choose Inner Peace

Because a human being is so malleable,
whatever one cultivates is what one becomes.
Lao Tzu

Everything in your life begins with your thoughts because your thoughts are the source of the choices you make, and those choices determine your actions. If you *choose* to react to everything or to every person who is obnoxious, you will never consistently maintain your inner peace. You must actively *choose* to cultivate inner peace in your life. By not making that choice, you are simply choosing to receive whatever energy comes your way. By electing not to choose, you are actually choosing to leave your life up to other people or external situations.

Without actually choosing inner peace, a life of calm tranquility will always elude you. It won't just magically appear in your life. It is not something that you accidentally stumble upon as you go about your daily life. Likewise, inner peace is not like a mystical pot of gold that you can find if you search long enough. You simply *choose* to live a life of inner peace and then do what must be done to develop it and cultivate it in your life.

When you make a firm decision to choose inner peace, you will be compelled to make choices that will foster more inner peace in your life. Constantly remind yourself that the choice is yours. No one can take away your inner peace unless you make the decision, consciously or unconsciously, to allow them to do so. The choice is yours, so stop allowing other people, external events, and adverse situations to rob you of your inner peace.

You must be all in; there is no halfway if you want to consistently live a life of inner peace. Don't *try* to maintain your inner peace; *be determined* to maintain your inner peace no matter what. Don't give yourself an out. Decide, once and for all, that you will maintain a lifestyle of inner peace, and then refuse to allow anyone or anything to change your mind.

In the ancient world, when a general wanted his men to fight as if their lives depended on it, he would put the men in a position where they had no way to retreat. They had to win or die. Some armies, when invading a country across the sea, would actually burn their ships so there would be no way to retreat. Burn your metaphorical ship and be determined to live a life of inner peace. Decide once and

103

for all what kind of life you want to live, and then live it. Don't leave yourself any alternatives!

You are in charge of your life, nobody else. It is you who must choose whether you want to continue to live on an emotional roller coaster, having a peaceful day once and a while, sandwiched between the turmoil and chaos of life, which randomly robs you of your calm demeanor on other days.

Stop allowing other people and external events to pull you into the storms of life. If allowed, they will arbitrarily pull us into their storms, while we complacently ride each storm out and brace ourselves for the next one. It is time to stop allowing other people and events to steer your ship. You do have other options; you don't have to live your life like the majority of people in this world. Why let anyone pull you into their storm when you have the knowledge and ability to sail around the storm?

Make up your mind that anything, and I do mean anything, that costs you your inner peace is too expensive, and you will not pay that price. Stop allowing other people and situations to choose your mood for you; stop giving other people the key to your sanctuary. Many of us are in the habit of allowing external events and other people to choose our moods for us, but that never leads to consistent inner peace. It is time to take control of your life, emotions, and mood, every day and in every situation.

There is power in your intention. Make your intention to choose inner peace no matter what. Choose inner peace as if your life depends on it because in many ways, it does. Once you get to that point, inner peace will become a habit in your life; you will find that it is almost impossible for anyone or anything to disturb your peace of mind. Others may think you're strange, as you won't react to their enticements, but that won't matter to you; you will be at peace.

I have noticed that once someone really decides to do something, he does it. It doesn't matter what his friends say, what his family thinks about it, or what society believes. Once his mind is firmly made up, he will be motivated to do whatever it takes to achieve his goal. Until that time, his resolve is not forged, and his mind will waver.

He may go back and forth, allowing other people's opinions to cause him to doubt what he feels in his heart. He will allow his mind to come up with dozens of reasons why he is making a mistake and should just continue living as he has been. But those nagging thoughts about how he wants to live will not go away; they keep coming back no matter how many times he justifies not acting on his desires. This cycle will continue until he finally makes up his mind that he is going

104

to change his life once and for all, or until he throws in the towel and gives up on changing his life.

If you have a burning desire to do something, it is probably coming from your spirit and means that you were meant to do it. If you have a burning desire to live a life of inner peace, and to stop allowing stress, worry, anger, fear, envy, resentments, and other low-energy emotions to control your life, then decide once and for all that you are going to change your life. Once you make that decision, everything will fall into place. Be determined to get off that emotional rollercoaster once and for all.

The thing about consistently living a life of inner peace is that you have to make this choice more than once. When you commit to this lifestyle, you start making the necessary changes. But you also have to continue to choose inner peace every time you are tempted to allow your negative emotions to dictate your actions. You have to choose inner peace even when you want to prove your know-it-all colleague is wrong. You have to choose inner peace when you had rather put the rude guy in the restaurant in his place.

It is a continual process, but it gets easier each time you are victorious over your old nature. Each victory increases your self-confidence in maintaining your inner peace. Each time you resist the urge to react instead of respond, you have added another layer to the protective force field that is defending your tranquility.

Each victory begins to weaken the negative, lower energy emotions which have plagued you for years. When you choose a peaceful response instead of anger, your propensity towards anger is weakened. When you choose to have faith in God instead of worrying about a situation, your propensity towards worry and fear declines. You have to break those chains which have been holding you back.

Each peaceful encounter brings you closer to the unwavering inner peace which you are seeking. It all boils down to the choice you make in every situation. Determine that you will choose to respond to every situation in a way that fosters inner peace in your life. Just take it one challenge at a time, and each victory will strengthen your resolve.

You don't have to reach enlightenment to change your world; you simply have to start making better choices. Everything in your life originates with your thoughts and the choices that you make. Change your thoughts and you change your choices; change your choices and you change your life. Peaceful thoughts lead to peaceful choices; peaceful choices lead to peaceful actions. And your thoughts, choices, and actions determine your inner peace.

Practice Being Non-Judgmental

Do not judge, or you too will be judged.
Jesus

In order to choose inner peace, you must also practice being non-judgmental. It seems our society has gotten to the point that almost everyone believes it's their responsibility to judge everything. Things have deteriorated so much in this area that people are now going back 40-50 years in someone's past in an attempt to find something that they can pass judgment on in that person's life. It is really sad and ridiculous!

Almost everything in life is personal and subjective; it depends on your perspective. Everyone has made mistakes along the way. That is simply a part of learning and a part of being human. You have no more authority to judge the mistakes of others than they do to judge you for your mistakes. And you certainly have no right to judge others for how they live their lives, as long as they are not hurting someone else. What others do is between them and God. The fact is, you don't know enough about anyone to judge them.

When you look down on others or judge them based on *your* standards, you are setting yourself above them as if you are God. No one on this planet has a God-given right to judge others because of how they decide to live their life; nor do you have the authority to play "gotcha" by going back through their past in some misguided attempt to dig up dirt on them. Those are the dishonest games that politicians, journalists, and internet trolls play. Keep your distance from such rubbish and from those who deal in such underhanded actions.

Judgment is the constant evaluation of everyone and everything in your life, or the life of others, as right or wrong. While there is a time and a place to judge something as right or wrong, it should not be an ongoing practice concerning other people or things that do not concern you. Constantly judging people and external situations leads to turmoil, strife, anger, and irritation, not inner peace.

Don't spend your time condemning others. You cannot possibly know what is going on in someone else's life, nor can you know what all he has had to deal with in his past or the context of his actions. Always remember that you are not perfect and that you are not the same person you were 10 years ago, five years ago, or even one year ago. What if someone judged you today by every word you spoke or every action you took 10-20 years ago? How would you fare?

Instead of spending your time passing judgment, spend your time improving yourself and focusing on the things which do concern you. In fact, spend so much time improving yourself that you have neither the time nor inclination to judge others. Focus on making yourself better, not thinking that you are better.

As Jesus said to the mob who were about to stone a woman for adultery, "Let him who is without sin among you be the first to throw a stone at her." When you judge others, be prepared for them to judge you. Jesus had a lot to say about judging other people, and you would do well to heed his words on the subject.

Do not judge, or you too will be judged. For in the same way you judge others, you will be judged, and with the measure you use, it will be measured to you. Why do you look at the speck of sawdust in your brother's eye and pay no attention to the plank in your own eye? How can you say to your brother, 'Let me take the speck out of your eye,' when all the time there is a plank in your own eye? You hypocrite, first take the plank out of your own eye, and then you will see clearly to remove the speck from your brother's eye.
Jesus

Those are pretty stern words! And even if you were perfect, how does it increase your inner peace to cast judgment on others? My grandfather was a great man. He used to tell me, "If someone is not what they should be, help them to become better. Help them become what they should be." I promise you, helping others will foster a greater sense of inner peace in your life than judging them.

Instead of being judgmental concerning everything around you, accept people and things for who and what they are. Things are as they are, whether you like it or not. Acceptance fosters inner peace and harmony; being judgmental fosters arrogance, smugness, and conceit. Be kind, be loving, try to help as many people as you can, and let everyone live their life as he or she sees fit.

Being non-judgmental doesn't only apply to other people. You should stop judging yourself so harshly as well. Most of us are our own worst critics. We judge how we look, how we speak, what we should have said or done; this list could go on and on. We are harder on ourselves than anyone else. Like judging other people, judging ourselves too harshly does not lead to inner peace but to aggravation, frustration, low self-esteem, low self-confidence, and discontent. Remember that you are a work in progress.

Nobody on this planet is perfect. Stop trying to be perfect in every way, and just continue to work on improving yourself daily. Be the

107

best YOU that you can be at this very moment. You are unique – a one-of-a-kind. Stop comparing yourself to other people. Stop judging yourself and learn to forgive yourself when you fall short.

Replace any judgmental attitudes that you may have with love and acceptance. Stop being so hard on yourself and others. Stop judging every situation as good or bad, and simply start experiencing life as it comes. Find joy in every situation. If there is no joy to be found in a certain situation, create your own joy.

Instead of being disappointed when the sunset is not as beautiful as you expected, enjoy the peace that the sunset has to offer just as it is. Look for the best in every person, every thing, and every situation that you encounter; that is living with a positive mindset.

Stop judging your looks and your speech so harshly, and just be yourself. Determine to enjoy life instead of evaluating it at every turn. Being judgmental will never bring you inner peace; you will find inner peace in acceptance, love, joy, giving, and helping others. Accept others for who and what they are, and accept yourself for who you are and who you are becoming.

It is easy to be non-judgmental when you do not have preconceived expectations concerning life or other people. Instead of judging the actions of others, or every situation in your life, just be present. You do not have to have an opinion on everyone or everything; just be present in the moment. Stop expecting other people, or life in general, to live up to your expectations.

Get Rid of All Expectations

I'm not in this world to live up to your expectations
and you're not in this world to live up to mine.
Bruce Lee

You must stop expecting people to fit into a certain preconceived mold that you have concerning who and what they should be. Stop expecting the world to meet your expectations, and start excepting life as it is. To do this, you must get rid of all of your expectations. Train yourself to never expect anything from anyone. It is your expectations and sensitivities which cause you to be upset or disappointed, not the situation or other people's actions.

Expect nothing and accept everything. By now you should understand that you do not control everything. In fact, you control very little outside of yourself, as I mentioned earlier. Get rid of your expectations and accept everything as it comes. This doesn't mean that you necessarily approve or agree with the way things are; it simply means that you are accepting things as they are, not as you wish they were. This is accepting the reality of life instead of living in the fantasy world created by your own mind and expectations.

You must love other people as they are and life as it is. Don't let your expectations rob you of your inner peace. Things rarely turn out exactly like you expect them to. Having specific expectations about how things should turn out or how others should behave, only leads to disappointment, upset feelings, anger, and frustration. It is much better to simply live life as it comes and respond to each moment as it is, not as you expected it to be.

Living a life of inner peace is all about being at peace with how things are, not how they should be. When you place expectations on your life or on other people, you are simply setting yourself up for disappointment and frustration, which does not lead to inner peace. Instead of placing your own expectations on the world around you, practice acceptance.

Practice Acceptance

Acceptance looks like a passive state, but in
reality it brings something entirely new into this world.
That peace, a subtle energy vibration, is consciousness.
Eckhart Tolle

You must accept things as they are in order to maintain your inner peace. Remember, you have no control over what other people do, what they say, or how they behave. You could not control them even if you wanted to.

It is not for you to judge them, control them, or to form expectations of them; just accept them and do your best to love them as they are. Accept people and things as they are, then respond accordingly. Acceptance is the first step to dealing with any situation in your life. Not accepting life as it is, is simply living in denial.

Refusing to accept something as it truly is, does not change the reality of the situation. As I mentioned previously, deceiving yourself does not help you, and it can actually cause you problems. You must see the world as it truly is, accept things for what they are, and then respond to them in a way that allows you to maintain your inner peace.

Maintaining your inner peace is a process of training yourself to accept life as it is, not as it should be. You have no power to change anyone in this world other than yourself. While you may do what you

109

can to help other people, you can't force them to change or to accept your help. All you can really do is love them, do what you can to help them, and then let them live their life.

Will it always be an easy path to travel? Absolutely not! Some people make it extremely hard to accept them or their actions. Some people will say and do things that are completely unacceptable; accept them anyway. It is their life to live, not yours.

Accepting them doesn't mean that you agree with everything they say or do; it simply means that you realize that is the way they are, and you accept that.

You may have to accept the fact that the way they are is not compatible with the life you have chosen to live, and you may have to choose to distance yourself from them. This doesn't mean that you do not accept them as they are or that you do not love them, but merely that you are doing what you have to do to maintain your inner peace.

Choose inner peace in every situation, get rid of all expectations, stop judging everything and everyone around you, and start accepting life and the people in your life as they are. You cannot allow other people's words or actions to rob you of your inner peace. Don't give anyone that kind of power over you.

Acceptance does not mean that you allow yourself to become a doormat or that you allow others to treat you any way they want. No one has the right to treat you badly or to dump their garbage in your life. I will discuss this more in the next chapter.

The Serenity Prayer

God grant me the serenity to accept
the things I cannot change;
the courage to change the things I can;
and the wisdom to know the difference.

Thoughts to Ponder

It is in your moments of decision that your destiny is shaped.
Tony Robbins

Let nothing disturb thee;
Let nothing dismay thee.
St Teresa of Avila

Accept – then act. Whatever the present moment contains, accept
it as if you had chosen it. Always work with it, not against it.
Eckhart Tolle

A life that is burdened with expectations is a heavy life.
Its fruit is sorrow and disappointment.
Douglas Adams

Don't hope that events will turn out the way you want, welcome
events in whichever way they happen: this is the path to peace.
Epictetus

Love and peace of mind do protect us.
They allow us to overcome the problems that life hands us.
Bernie Siegel

Life is a matter of choices, and every choice you make makes you.
John C. Maxwell

No matter what the situation, remind yourself, I have a choice.
Deepak Chopra

Happiness can exist only in acceptance.
George Orwell

Acceptance of what has happened is the first step
to overcoming the consequences of any misfortune.
William James

Life is a series of natural and spontaneous changes.
Don't resist them; that only creates sorrow. Let reality be reality.
Let things flow naturally forward in whatever way they like.
Lao Tzu

Thoughts to Ponder

Blessed is he who expects nothing,
for he shall never be disappointed.
Alexander Pope

The day you stop judging yourself, including
your appearance, you'll stop judging others.
Harper Daniels

Be wary of making judgments, because even
the ancient sages were ignorant of many things.
Lieh Tzu

Before we determine character from behavior,
we must consider the context.
Dr. Stephen Lennox

One ought to examine himself for a very long
time before thinking of condemning others.
Moliere

We judge ourselves by our intentions.
And others by their actions.
Stephen Covey

Always respect the differences we all have,
do not pass judgement but try to understand.
Catherine Pulsifer

Never judge by appearances.
English Proverb

We can never judge the lives of others, because each
person knows only their own pain and renunciation.
It's one thing to feel that you are on the right path,
but it's another to think that yours is the only path.
Paulo Coelho

Tolerance and patience should not be read as signs of weakness.
They are signs of strength.
Dalai Lama

Chapter 10
Don't Allow Others to Sidetrack You

Do not let the behavior of others destroy your inner peace.
Dalai Lama

Many times it is the words, opinions, and behavior of others that prompts us to be judgmental and to temporarily lose our inner peace. We allow others to get under our skin in one way or another, become judgmental, angry, or offended, and then our inner peace is disrupted. Don't allow other people to disrupt your inner peace. It doesn't affect them at all, but it has a huge effect on you.

It is very easy to allow the behavior or words of others to disrupt your inner peace. You get sucked into the passion of the moment and before you know it, that person has pushed every button you have, and you are ready to wring his neck. Then you place the blame on that person for *making* you angry, upset, frustrated, or stressed.

You must realize that no one can *make* you angry, upset, or offended. No one can *make* you argue with them or *make* you lose your inner peace. We all have the power to control our thoughts, although most people don't use that power as much as they should. It is you who makes the decision to get angry, upset, or offended. You always have the power to disregard what the other person is doing or saying, and to prevent them upsetting your spirit.

Stop giving your power to other people. When you are easily angered or offended, you are easily manipulated. When you allow yourself to be manipulated by the words or actions of others, you are choosing to allow them to control your emotions and disrupt your inner peace at will. Why do that when you can easily make the choice to maintain control of your emotions and your inner peace?

Refuse to allow anyone or anything to control you or to rob you of your inner peace. Hopefully, you have done the mental work that I discussed at the beginning of the book and are well on your way to controlling your thoughts and emotions. Once you have taken control of your thoughts, you have the power to free yourself from being manipulated by the words and behavior of others.

You cannot allow your inner peace to be contingent on everything going smoothly in your life, and you certainly cannot allow your inner peace to depend on other people's opinions, how they act, or what they say. If you do, you will never consistently enjoy inner peace. You must get past the actions, words, and opinions of other people and be secure in who you are as a unique human being. Don't allow other people's opinions to sway you, to make you doubt yourself or your goals, or to rob you of your inner peace.

Everyone has a right to their own thoughts and opinions, and you have the right to totally ignore them. Their opinions belong to them; there is no reason for you to allow them to influence your emotions. Just because they share their opinions with you doesn't mean you have to be affected by them. They are free to think and believe what they want, and so are you.

Keep your focus on your goal of living a life of inner peace. When you are tempted to allow someone's words or actions to get to you, ask yourself, "Will this bring me inner peace and tranquility, or anger, frustration, stress, and strife?" Just remember, anything that robs you of your inner peace is too expensive. If it is going to disrupt your inner peace, leave it where you found it and move on. Refuse to take the bait!

Nobody can upset you or anger you without your permission. Nobody *makes* you angry; you *decide* to be angry. Nobody *makes* you sad; you *decide* to be sad. Nobody *makes* you upset or offended; you *decide* to be upset or offended. And nobody can take your inner peace away from you; you *make the decision* to put your inner peace aside in order to participate in someone else's negativity or drama.

You may be thinking that this is easy when it comes to strangers; all you have to do is walk away, go about your own business, and never see them again. But what about negative family members or hateful colleagues which you work with every day.

Negative, rude family members and obnoxious colleagues do present a bigger challenge than some stranger, which you will probably never see again. However, that does not change the fact that you should not allow them to disrupt your inner peace. You may have to distance yourself from certain family members in order to maintain your inner peace. They know how to push your buttons better than anyone.

Many times your colleagues have an agenda behind their rude, underhanded behavior. Not only will you have to work hard not to allow them to rob you of your inner peace, but you may need to be aware of the motives behind their behavior. Why are they giving you a hard time?

You must mentally separate the behavior of others from your inner peace. Remember the lesson about controlling those things which you have control over and accepting those things which you can't control. Other people will say and do what they please; you have no control over anyone but yourself. Focus on your own improvement and refuse to act like those who are rude, opinionated, mouthy, or judgmental.

114

Remember what Marcus Aurelius taught, "The best revenge is not being like your enemy."

While 99.9% of the people that you deal with in your life cannot be labeled as your enemy, and you definitely should not be focused on any type of revenge, Marcus Aurelius' wisdom is still great advice. Don't be like those who do not live their life by the principles of inner peace; live your life according to your own standards.

Accepting the things which you cannot control does not mean that you have to allow others to treat you rudely or continually disrupt your life. As I said in the last chapter, living a life of inner peace is not the same thing as being a doormat. By all means, stand up for yourself and do not allow others to treat you poorly. But, at the same time, do it in a way that does not interrupt your inner peace.

You can stand up to a bully without getting angry, irate, or emotional. You can stand up for yourself and tell Aunt Paula how things are without allowing it to upset you or ruin your day. Do the right thing, at the right time, and in the right way. There is a right way and a wrong way to do everything, including dealing with conflicts, rude people, and even a malicious enemy.

The important thing to remember is to never allow the behavior of others to affect you. You can't control what other people say or do, but you can always control how you respond to them, even if that means to simply smile and walk away. Remember, reacting is likely to cost you your inner peace; responding puts you in charge of the situation. You don't have to be offended because someone is being offensive. You have a choice, so choose not to be offended by anyone or anything.

Refuse to be offended

Stop looking for occasions to be offended.
Become a person who refuses to be offended by
any one, any thing, or any set of circumstances.
Wayne Dyer

Like anger, being offended is a choice that you make. You can listen to something someone says or observe what someone does, and actually choose not to be offended, no matter how loathsome their words or actions are. Being offended is never a requirement; it is always a choice. It seems like being offended has become a national pastime in today's culture. People are offended by a simple poster on social media, by how other people choose to vote, by something a politician says, even by something you may have said 40 years ago.

Many people actively look for something to be offended about, even if it has absolutely nothing at all to do with them. Not only do they often choose to be offended, but they seem to enjoy it. Refuse to participate in this ridiculous charade. If you want to be offended, you will have no problem noticing things you find offensive. On the other hand, if you desire to live in inner peace, you can refuse to be offended by anything.

If you are one of those people who are constantly offended by something someone said, or some event that happened somewhere in the world, consider the following questions. How did being offended over that action or incident improve your life? Did it change the other person's behavior? Did it help make the world a better place? Did it add to your peace and tranquility? What exactly did your indignation do for you?

Most of the things that offend you actually have little to no effect on your life. It is not the events, the words, or the actions, but rather how you perceive those things, which cause you to be offended. Again, I will refer you to the last chapter about accepting the things which you cannot change.

If you are going to continually allow the thoughts, words, or actions of others to offend you, you will never find your inner peace. There will always be someone somewhere who does something that you can judge to be offensive. It is better to simply observe what is happening around you than to get emotionally involved in everything you see or hear.

As I said, many people, especially in today's culture, seem to enjoy being offended. Not only do they enjoy it, but they seem to revel in retelling how offensive they found it to be. It is as if they get some kind of rush from being upset. And, if you will notice, those people never seem to be at peace; they are always ranting and raving about one thing or another.

Some people enjoy being offended because it makes them feel good in a strange, roundabout way. Being offended becomes a habit to them, much like habitual anger. They get offended, then angry, and their body releases a specific cocktail of hormones, including adrenaline. Although this continued cycle of getting offended, getting angry, and enjoying the accompanying adrenaline rush may feel good at the time, it is detrimental to their health and can be addictive.

Refuse to participate in such conversations, as this attitude can be contagious. After hearing how upset your friend is about whatever offended her this time, if you are not careful, you will start to feel upset about that situation as well. And even though the event had nothing to do with you, before you know it, your peace and tranquility have been replaced with anger and indignation. It is better to remove yourself from such conversations. Don't let other people dump their garbage in your life!

You must guard your thoughts in order to maintain your inner peace. When you are constantly listening to others complain, gripe, or go on and on about something that offended them, you are allowing them to plant seeds of negativity and strife into your mind. It is hard enough to maintain a calm, tranquil state in today's world without intentionally listening to negativity.

Speak to your friend and tell her that you really do not want that negativity in your life. If she continues to bring up negative issues in the conversation, just excuse yourself tactfully and leave. If you refuse to listen to such talk or simply remove yourself every time the conversation starts to turn negative, you will find that your friend will stop bringing up those topics in your company. Sooner or later, she will catch on that you are not going to take part in her negativity.

Saying you are offended is truly one of the most meaningless statements that someone can make. "I'm offended!" So what? What it actually tells people is that you are so mentally fragile that you can't deal with other people having a different opinion, view of the world, or living a different life than you. When you look at it in those terms, it is not something that you want to go around announcing to other people.

I have seen people who get totally offended because some guy was wearing cut-off blue jean shorts on the golf course instead of nice pants and a polo shirt. I have seen people who get offended because someone was not wearing a tie at a wedding or a funeral. If you are going to allow such minor things as how someone dresses or wears his hair to offend you, then you might as well give up on living a life of inner peace. Remember, you don't control what other people say or do, and you should not be judgmental about their decisions concerning *their* life.

God did not put everyone else on this planet to conform to your taste, your ideals, or to make you happy. Everyone has the right to live their life as they please, as long as they are not harming anyone else. Other people have the right to their opinions and thoughts and to live their life as they see fit, just like you do.

And what's more, their decisions are none of your business. They have the right to live as they please, dress as they please, and think as they please. You have the right to ignore their opinions, not care how they choose to live their lives, and to move on with your life. You

117

don't have the right to demand that they conform to your standards. If you want to maintain your inner peace, you have to stop looking for opportunities to be offended.

John Lubbock stated, "What we see depends mainly on what we look for." If you are looking for things that are offensive to you, you are sure to find them. Instead of searching for things to be offended by, start looking for things to be thankful for. Instead of noticing the negative things in this world, start paying more attention to the beauty in our world, the kindness, and those things which are uplifting to your spirit.

The choice is yours. Do you want to continually be offended, upset, angry, frustrated, and annoyed, or do you want to live a tranquil life full of inner peace? It is not what you see and hear that matters; it is how you *perceive* what you see and hear.

You could see the man in cut-off blue jean shorts playing golf and choose to be offended that he is not adhering to some dress code, or you could choose to feel happy that he is enjoying himself in the beauty of nature. It all boils down to how you choose to look at the world around you. Choose never to be offended, and nothing will offend you.

Ignore Other People's Opinions

What I must do is all that concerns me,
not what the people think.
Ralph Waldo Emerson

If you are continually concerned with other people's opinions about what you do, how you look, how you dress, what you say, or how you live your life, you have made yourself a willing prisoner of other people's opinions. Stop living your life according to other people's opinions and set yourself free.

While everyone is free to express their own opinions, they are just that – their opinions. They should have no bearing on your life at all. The opinions of others are nothing more than their thoughts spoken aloud. Other people's opinions are not facts or weighted in truth; they are simply their thoughts and their point of view. Everyone has their opinions, even those who do not publicly share their thoughts.

The opinions of other people do not carry any more weight in your life than what you allow them to. You will never maintain your inner peace if you are continually concerned with what other people think about how you live your life. When it comes right down to it, their opinions on your life have no meaning unless you give them meaning.

Be willing to be judged by others, and keep in mind that their opinions or judgments do not affect you unless you allow them to. When you truly don't care what anyone thinks of your decisions or how you live your life, you have reached the pinnacle of true freedom. Refuse to be influenced by anyone else unless their influence adds value to your life.

So many people disrupt their inner peace by worrying about what everyone else thinks of them. I have news for you; what someone else thinks about you is none of your business. They are free to think whatever they want about anything they want. You need to figure out why you are so concerned about what others think about you. It may be a sign that your self-esteem needs some improvement.

You must develop your self-respect and self-esteem to such a high level that other people's opinions don't affect you. Have confidence in yourself and in your decisions. When you develop your self-respect and self-esteem to a higher level, you will love and accept yourself just as you are; other people's approval or disapproval will no longer matter to you.

Those who are judgmental will judge you no matter what you do. Those who are envious will be jealous of your success and happy when you fail. Those whose hearts are full of hate will look for reasons to dislike you or even hate you. So what! Those are their issues. Let them keep their negativity and low-energy thoughts; refuse to allow them to affect your life.

Stop trying to please everyone and start pleasing yourself. Don't worry about whether people like you or like how you live. You should be more concerned with upholding your own standards than you are about what other people think of you or your standards.

Once you develop a laser-like focus on how you want to live and who you want to be, the judgment of others won't matter to you at all. Let them judge all they want while you continue to move closer to your goal of inner peace and personal satisfaction.

You must stop allowing other people's judgments or criticisms impact you. Never take criticism from someone who you would not go to for sound advice. If someone is not a trusted friend or family member, their criticism or opinions on your life should not matter to you at all. After all, you have no idea why they are sharing their criticism or opinions with you to start with. Maybe they are actually trying to hinder you in some way or throw you off track. Don't be influenced by random criticism!

This same principle applies to advice. You will find that people love to give free advice; for some reason, it makes them feel wise or important. Some just like to talk, and others are truly trying to help

119

you, but their advice is coming from their own perspective and how they see life. They may not share the same goals or views as you. Quit depending on others and start thinking for yourself.

Unsolicited, free advice is usually worth exactly what you pay for it. It is nothing more than that person's opinion on the subject. Everyone has an opinion, but not everyone's opinion matters. Unless someone knows you and understands your life, his or her opinion is probably not very valuable for you and will not apply to your journey.

You will find that most of the advice you receive over your lifetime is nothing more than thoughtless clichés. Most people do not take the time to really think deeply about an issue before giving advice; they simply repeat some old clichés or quotes which have been repeated to them or that they read somewhere. For advice to truly be valuable, one must take time to give the subject some deep thought, unless the person is an expert on the topic. Advice given off the cuff rarely comes from a place of deep thought or true wisdom.

Start putting more importance on your own opinions and less importance on the opinions of others. Marcus Aurelius put it nicely when he wrote, "It never ceases to amaze me: we all love ourselves more than other people, but care more about their opinion than our own."

You must develop your self-confidence to the point that you value your opinion above other people's opinions. After all, you are living *your* life, not someone else's life. When someone gives you bad advice, and you follow it, it doesn't cost the person who gave you the advice anything; it costs you. You are the one who will have to live with the consequences of your decisions, no one else.

Always take advice with a grain of salt when it is given by someone who encounters no risk if his advice doesn't pan out. It is easy to put a lot of money on one spin of the roulette wheel when you are playing with someone else's money and have nothing to lose. If you win, great; if you lose, it cost you nothing.

The majority of people who give you advice are "playing with your money." They have nothing to lose; all the risk of taking their advice is on you. You are the one who will be dealing with the negative consequences if their advice turns out to be bad. Take advice from people you trust, but always do your homework and reflect on the issue; then *you decide* what is best for you.

Most people do not take the time to think for themselves; they see the world through the eyes of other people. Their deeply held beliefs do not come from deep, meditative thought or intelligent study but are simply beliefs that were passed on to them from someone else. Simply put, they believe what they were told to believe. This is

120

particularly true when it comes to customs, religion, education, and traditions.

You must think for yourself. Going around and asking everyone for their opinions, instead of disciplining yourself to do your own research and thinking for yourself, is a form of laziness. It takes effort to think for yourself. You have to put down your phone, turn off the television, spend time alone, and focus your mind. It is much easier to simply text your friend and ask her what she thinks about the subject, but is that really a wise way to make important decisions?

The majority of people are concerned about other people's opinions because they have a deep desire to be liked by everyone or because they do not have enough self-confidence in their own ability to make good decisions. I can tell you right now that you will never be liked by everyone. Stop being concerned about whether or not people like you.

You cannot live an authentic life if you are constantly gauging what you say, what you do, and how you live by whether or not other people like your decisions. No matter how much you try or what you do, some people are going to like you, and other people are not. It is foolhardy to believe that you will be liked and respected by everyone. It doesn't matter how much you help others or how respected you are; there will always be people who can find one reason or another to not like or respect you. That is just the way it is, and you should be okay with that.

Even Jesus was not liked or respected by everyone. Jesus experienced disrespect and personal attacks during his short time on earth just like everyone else. If Jesus was not immune to the judgments and hatred of other people, why would you think you would be? You won't be! And guess what – it doesn't matter. Your goal is not to be liked by everyone but to live a life of inner peace and tranquility.

When you start wanting to be liked or respected by everyone, you will sabotage your own inner peace. It is very stressful to try to please everyone all the time or to tailor your speech and your actions in such a way that everyone will like you. Walking on eggshells to avoid upsetting the delicate sensibilities of the people around you will only add stress to your life.

The truth is that most people don't think about you that much anyway. While you are so concerned about what people will think about the clothes you wear or how your hair looks, most people barely notice. The average person is too wrapped up in his or her own life to be concerned with you. And even if they were totally focused on your appearance, your speech, or your actions, their opinions on your life are moot points anyway, so stop concerning yourself with their thoughts and opinions.

It is fine to listen to other people's opinions, and even wise to do so at times, but always make your own decisions. Never be swayed to act on any matter simply because of another person's opinion. Value your own opinion more than you value other people's opinions. Take the time to think for yourself and then make your decision.

Take the time to get quiet and think deeply about whatever decision you need to make. Meditate on it and listen to your spirit. If you feel uneasy about the decision, then it is most likely not the wisest decision for you. You will feel at peace with your decision when it is the right one for you. Buddha put it this way:

"Do not believe in anything simply because you have heard it. Do not believe in anything simply because it is spoken and rumored by many. Do not believe in anything simply because it is found written in your religious books. Do not believe in anything merely on the authority of your teachers and elders. Do not believe in traditions because they have been handed down for many generations. But after observation and analysis, when you find that anything agrees with reason and is conducive to the good and benefit of one and all, then accept it and live up to it."

There is one last thing that I want to say about the opinions of others. Many people like to argue or debate in order to prove their opinion is right. You don't have to prove you are right or to prove someone else is wrong – don't argue with them. Arguing never leads to peace and tranquility. As Epictetus taught, "If you want to improve, be content to be thought foolish and stupid."

Refuse to Argue

In quarreling about the shadow, we often lose the substance.
Aesop

Part of ignoring other people's opinions is refusing to argue with them. It is your life to live, not theirs. Get rid of the need to convince other people that you are right; get rid of your need for other people's approval. You do not have to defend your beliefs or the way you live to anyone. Don't get sucked into an argument in order to prove a point.

122

The need to prove that you are right comes from your ego, and if allowed, your ego will disrupt your inner peace more often than not. The ego has a burning desire to be right and doesn't like being questioned. If you allow your ego to control your actions, it will always try to prove it is right through debating and arguing the point until the other person gives in or walks away from the discussion.

Whenever you feel your ego taking control, put it in check and remind yourself that it is better to preserve a tranquil spirit than to prove yourself right. After all, is your goal to prove you are right or to maintain your inner peace? Arguing almost always disrupts your inner peace and tranquility.

You do not have to prove yourself to anyone, nor do you have to justify your beliefs or the way you live your life. Others may want you to justify yourself. They may demand that you prove your point or justify your lifestyle. They may even try to push you into arguing or debating with them. But they cannot *force* you to participate in any argument or debate if you refuse to participate.

You don't have to participate in any argument or discussion if you don't want to. If you refuse to argue, no one will argue with you. You can't argue with someone who is not participating in the argument or who simply will not respond.

You may be thinking that it is rude not to respond or to refuse to discuss a topic that someone is trying to get you to debate, but that is not the case. It is rude for someone to continue to try to force another person to discuss or argue a topic in which he has clearly stated that he does not want to discuss. It is rude to try to cause strife or to push your views on others. It is not rude to guard your inner peace and choose not to participate in an argument or debate.

If your goal is to maintain your inner peace, you should avoid strife and arguments at all cost, as they will always disrupt your inner peace. You must put yourself and your pursuit of peace first. If you are constantly putting everyone else's desires ahead of your own, it will be impossible to consistently live a life of inner peace.

Whenever you are tempted to put someone in his place or to prove him wrong, remember your ultimate goal. It doesn't affect your inner peace if the other person thinks you are completely wrong about a certain topic or gets upset because you won't justify yourself. Remember, you are not living your life according to other people's opinions or beliefs; you are disregarding their opinions unless they add value to your life. And arguing rarely ever adds value to your life.

You don't control what other people believe or think, and arguing with them will not change that fact. Most of the time, arguing simply makes the other person dig in his feet and defend his position even

123

more vigorously. The defense of his beliefs is usually strengthened by his own point of view, which he presents during the argument, and his ego will rarely, if ever, allow him to admit that he is wrong. Very rarely do you change someone's opinion or beliefs during an argument; it is a waste of time and energy.

It is better to maintain your peace and harmony rather than try to prove yourself right. Even if you do manage to prove your case during a heated argument, you will lose your inner peace in the process, at least for a short period of time. It is simply not worth participating in arguments.

As I stated earlier, people who love to argue will debate anything and everything. They will always take the contrarian view of whatever is being discussed. People who enjoy arguing get a rush from the challenge of proving themselves right. If that is how they want to live their life, then that is their business. You don't have to participate; you don't exist to provide entertainment for others.

One way to avoid a debate is to simply say, "That is an interesting point of view. I will have to give that some thought." This makes the other person feel good about himself, feel that his thoughts have some value, and also prevents you from having to cut him off or appear rude. How can anyone continue to argue when you just told him that his point of view is interesting and you will give it more thought?

The less you respond to negative people or participate in their arguments, the more peaceful your life will become. Arguments can end in hurt feelings and have even ended friendships. Some arguments have actually started wars or feuds, which have lasted for years. It is just not worth participating in any dispute. Do what you have to do to end the argument before it begins.

This is especially true if you are speaking with someone whose opinion you do not respect. Why would you ever consider arguing with someone whose views you do not respect to begin with? And, if you are speaking with someone whose views you hold in high regard, there is no reason to argue with him since you value his opinion.

It is obvious that arguing is a waste of your time and energy, but if you do find yourself in a position where you absolutely have to get your point across to someone like a loved one, always do so in a calm and controlled manner. Keep your emotions out of it and just make your point calmly and rationally. State your thoughts and beliefs clearly and firmly. If the other person wants to argue the point, just let him know that you have nothing more to add and leave it at that.

Teenagers love to argue in an attempt to get their way. Your children will absolutely rob you of your inner peace if you engage in arguments with them. The principles in this chapter apply to your immediate family, as well as others in your life. Living in the same house together does not give your family members a license to disrupt your inner peace.

Many disagreements start because one person is trying to exert control in one way or another over someone else. As Rousseau stated, "No man has any natural authority over his fellow men." Other arguments originate with one person trying to help another person. It is easy to see what someone else is doing wrong or how he needs to change his life.

When you watch someone ruining his life, it is only natural to want to help him and give him some wise guidance. But unsolicited advice is rarely taken and many times ends in an argument or hard feelings. Do what you can to help, but do not allow your emotions to get too involved.

It is hard to see someone making obvious mistakes and not want to share your knowledge, but it is almost always best to only give advice when someone asks for it. Don't expect other people to be what you think they should be. Everyone is different and unique. Everyone thinks differently, has a different background, and perceives the world around them in a different way. Allow others to be themselves, and be content being who you are.

Learn to be at peace with how others live and with the consequences of their actions. Help people as much as you can, but don't feel like you need to get involved with everyone else's life. Your responsibility is to improve your life and maintain your inner peace, not to control other people's lives or to try to convince them to live as you think they should.

You have no right to tell others how to live or what they should do, and trying to exert control over someone else's life will almost always lead to resentment, arguments, and strife. You must understand that, even if your intentions are pure and honorable, it is not your intentions others will respond to, but your words and actions.

The Book of Proverbs states, "Whoever corrects a mocker invites an insult; whoever rebukes a wicked man incurs abuse." When you get involved in someone else's life without being asked, you are inviting strife into your life and are putting your inner peace on shaky ground. Even when you are asked to get involved, it can be a risky undertaking.

The feeling that you need to help someone put their life in order is another sign that your ego is trying to run the show. It is based on the attitude that you know more about what the other person needs or should be doing than he does. It is his life to live, his mistakes to make, and his responsibility to learn from his mistakes.

125

Along the same line, it is rarely wise to get involved in anyone else's arguments, especially when two of your friends are arguing. This can really cause complications and possibly a friendship, even if you are just trying to help them resolve the argument. Getting involved in their dispute is not the same thing as trying to smooth things over after the argument is over.

It is one thing to do what you can to save your friends' relationship, and another thing altogether to actively get involved in their argument and take one side or another. Getting involved will only cause you to be put in the middle, add to your stress, and most likely will end up with one or both of your friends upset with you. This is definitely not conducive to your inner peace. It is best to stay far away from that trap!

As you can clearly see, not much good comes from getting involved in an argument, especially if you are trying to maintain your inner peace. Most arguments are over things that really do not matter, and certainly do not foster the peace you seek.

Liberate yourself from the need to prove to others that you are right or to justify the way you live your life. Don't allow yourself to be sucked into someone else's chaos. Maintaining your inner peace is more important than proving you are right or proving someone else is wrong. Spend so much time making improvements in your own life that you have no time for arguments.

Be content knowing that you are living your life according to the standards which you have set for yourself. When you are secure about who you are and how you live, you have no need to justify yourself or prove yourself to anyone. Keep your focus on preserving your inner peace and refuse to argue with anyone for any reason. This is easier to do when you mind your own business, as you will discover in the next chapter.

Harmony in discord.
Horace

Thoughts to Ponder

Inner peace begins the moment you choose not to
allow another person or event to control your emotions.
Pema Chodron

Do not let your peace depend on the hearts of men;
whatever they say about you, good or bad, you are
not because of it another man, for as you are, you are.
Thomas a'Kempis

Even as a solid rock is unshaken by the wind,
so are the wise unshaken by praise or blame.
The Dhammapada

The only way to get the best of an argument is to avoid it.
Dale Carnegie

Whatever anyone does or says, for my part, I am bound to the good.
Marcus Aurelius

Behavior is the mirror in which everyone shows their image.
Johann Wolfgang von Goethe

Perfect behavior is born of complete indifference.
Francois de la Rochefoucauld

Don't let the insecurities of others dull your sparkle.
Shine like the star you are born to be.
Karen Civil

Whatever the world may say or do, my part is
to remain an emerald and to keep my color true.
Marcus Aurelius

The wise live among people, but are
indifferent to their praise or blame.
Chuang Tzu

Try to please all and you end by pleasing none.
Aesop

Thoughts to Ponder

People who wish to be offended will always
find some occasion for taking offense.
John Wesley

If you have enough faith in your own beliefs, you'll find that it's
impossible to be offended by the beliefs and conduct of others.
Wayne Dyer

A man's wisdom gives him patience;
it is to his glory to overlook an offense.
The Book of Proverbs

It is the mark of an educated mind to be able
to entertain a thought without accepting it.
Aristotle

That which offends you only weakens you.
Being offended creates the same destructive energy that offended
you in the first place – so transcend your ego and stay in peace.
Wayne Dyer

Who then is invincible? The one who cannot be
upset by anything outside their reasoned choice.
Epictetus

We have the power to hold no opinion about a thing
and to not let it upset our state of mind – for things
have no natural power to shape our judgments.
Marcus Aurelius

A good person does not argue.
Who does so is not one with the Tao.
Lao Tzu

What weakens us is feeling offended by
the deeds and misdeeds of our fellow men.
Carlos Castaneda

Think for yourselves and let others enjoy the right to do the same.
Voltaire

Chapter 11
Mind Your Own Business

Learn to cultivate your own garden.
Voltaire

One of the most important principles of maintaining your inner peace is learning to mind your own business. With the internet and a multitude of television news stations, you are constantly bombarded with information about things that you have no control over and which, when you get right down to it, are none of your business. As Voltaire taught, learn to cultivate your own garden.

While it is good to stay informed regarding what is happening in the world around you, you don't need to clutter your mind with endless information which doesn't concern you. You must learn to cultivate your own garden and stop worrying about what everyone else is doing. Weed your own garden, and let everyone else take care of their garden.

Minding other people's business gets you involved in problems, dramas, and issues that will disrupt your inner peace. Being nosey is akin to gossiping. If you are truly working hard to improve your own life, providing for your family, fostering your friendships, meditating, doing your inner work, and enjoying your life, you won't have enough time to focus on someone else's personal affairs. Keep your focus on your own life and your own improvement.

Unless it clearly concerns you, don't trouble yourself with what other people do or don't do. Remember, not only do you not control what others think, say, or do, but it is truly none of your business. Too many people get a rush by hearing gossip about their neighbors, celebrities, or family members. They get all excited about the latest sordid chatter about who did what.

Let me make one thing completely clear – what your neighbor does is none of your business, period. Unless he is hurting you or someone else, keep your nose out of his business. This is the easiest thing in the world to do, but apparently, it is very difficult for many people.

There are actually several television shows which are purely focused on gossip and news about celebrities' personal lives, and they get high ratings. It is simply mind-boggling to me that people are actually that interested in other people's lives when they appear not to be very interested in doing anything of value with their own life. They live their life vicariously through the lives of others, wasting their own precious time focusing on everyone else's life instead of working to improve their own life.

They watch as their favorite celebrity goes on vacation to exotic places while they sit at home in their living room. They watch as others date different people, and then they get emotionally involved when they break up. Meanwhile, their own relationships are neglected. Many people know more about celebrities than they do about their own family members. It really is a sad way to live.

Start living your own life to the fullest instead of focusing on other people's lives. Once you start minding your own business, you will find that your life is much more interesting and exciting to you than all those people who you don't know and will never even meet.

Moreover, stop getting involved in your friends' and neighbors' dramas. Your goal is to live a life of inner peace, not actively search for as much drama as you can find. Stay so busy maintaining your own inner peace that you have no time for other people's dramas. Refuse to get involved in anyone else's business unless they come to you for help, and you are able to give them sound advice or help them deal with what is going on in their life.

The main problem is that, instead of focusing on their own lives, many people prefer to focus on the lives of others because it takes less effort. It takes effort to improve your life, to control your mind, and to live your life to the fullest. It takes little to no effort to watch other people live their lives, to gossip about your neighbors, or to be entertained by the struggles of others.

Stop being lazy and start cultivating your own garden instead of watching other people cultivate theirs. Refuse to get involved in any drama which does not concern you. If someone comes to you for helpful advice, advise them the best that you can, but do not become emotionally involved in their problems. Becoming emotionally involved in other people's problems and dramas is doing nothing but making it harder for you to maintain your inner peace. Stop it!

It is not selfish to distance yourself from other people's problems and dramas; it is a must if you want to maintain your inner peace and tranquility. You should be very careful about getting involved in other people's personal lives, even if you are asked. Many times, your good intentions to help others only gets you entangled in drama and causes you unnecessary troubles of your own.

As I said previously, be very careful when it comes to getting mixed up in family dramas or quarrels between friends. If ever there was a time to be very selective with your words and your advice, that would be it. Often, when you try to intervene, even if you are asked by one of the parties, it can end up with one person being resentful of you and your participation. It is better to simply not get involved if you can manage it. As the old Danish proverb states, "Keep your nose out of another's mess."

Life provides us all with enough trouble of our own; we don't need to go find more. Deal with your own troubles, and have no interest in things that do not concern you. Be willing to help others, but be prudent about how you do it.

Develop the attitude of Crocodile Dundee and see things yhat don't concern you as none of your business. If someone asked you, "What do you think of your neighbor's big argument in the front yard?" Simply reply, "It is none of my business," and let it go. You do not have to have an opinion on it at all. In fact, when you truly do not have an opinion on what your neighbor is doing, you know that you are taking control of your mind and focusing on the things which you should focus on in your life.

When you stop focusing on what other people are thinking, saying, or doing, you will find that you have more time to focus on the things you need to do. While you are watching your neighbor argue with his wife, weeds are growing in your own garden. Being mentally involved with their spat does nothing to further your goals.

To maintain your inner peace, you must lessen the drama in your life. Find ways to reduce your stress load, not purposely add to it. When you spend time minding other people's business, you are increasing the drama and stress in your life. And this includes participating in gossip.

Refuse to get involved in, or even listen to, gossip that does not concern you. Most gossip is either untrue or only half true. Not only is it none of your business, but most of the time, those who gossip take pleasure in others' pain, problems, and dramas, which tells you volumes about their character. Simply refuse to take part in such behavior.

Gossip is a dirty business. If you think about it, how many times have you heard people gossip about good, positive, uplifting things? Those who gossip about others rarely, if ever, have good intentions or are coming from a place of peace or love. Most gossip is meant to damage someone's reputation, make you see someone in a bad light, or to share someone's private, dirty laundry, which is no one else's business. And the one sharing the gossip is normally not the kind of person that is going to help you better your life in any way.

When it comes to gossip, a good rule to remember is that if someone is willing to spread nasty rumors and make derogatory comments about others, he or she will also do the same when it comes to you. Never trust someone who gossips. They will share negative information, lies, and half-truths about you just as quickly as they share that information about others.

Mind your own business, cultivate your own garden, and have no interest in bringing other people's dirt or drama into your home. Keep your focus on how you want to live your life, on your own affairs, and on your goals, and let others live their lives as they please.

It is always best to stay out of things that do not concern you. The signpost on the path to inner peace reads – "Not my circus, not my monkeys!" For your peace of mind, stay away from both gossip and those who spread gossip.

Selective Associations

Distance yourself from those who bring out the stress in you and move closer to those who bring out the best in you.
Anna Grace Taylor

The people that you associate with matter more than you know, especially when it comes to your inner peace. If you are around someone, for even a short period of time, they will affect your energy either positively or negatively. By being very selective concerning who you associate with, you are keeping your personal energy field free from the contamination of others' negative energy, which can be very infectious.

Just think about how many times you have been in a great mood, with very positive energy, and then you received a phone call from a friend who dumped all of his garbage and negative energy on you. Without a doubt, your mood changed almost immediately. Unhappy, negative people tend to look for others to vent to and unintentionally spread their negative attitude and energy.

Both positive and negative energy is infectious. This is why you should be careful when it comes to those people you spend a lot of time with in your life. You want to spend time with friends and family who lift you up, help you maintain a positive attitude, and foster inner peace in your life, not with those who are constantly negative, complaining, and making it hard for you to maintain your peace and tranquility.

Many times, friends and family will rob you of your inner peace without meaning to. They may be well-intentioned, but their opinions, comments, and overall attitude will bring you down if you allow them to. People can either inspire you or drain you, depending on the energy that they bring to the table with their words and behavior. You have to learn to protect yourself from other people's negative energy!

132

In order to maintain your inner peace and tranquility, it is necessary to surround yourself as much as possible with positive, uplifting people. Even if you are an expert at guarding yourself against negative energy, you will find it difficult to maintain your inner peace if you are constantly bombarded with negativity from people who regularly complain, whine, and gossip.

Distance yourself from anyone who disrupts your inner peace and brings you down. This can be hard to do, especially if it is a family member or a friend. You should have a talk with them about their negativity and how you are really trying to preserve a positive attitude. Many people are very negative without even realizing it, and you may be able to help them change their life, as well as making it easier for you to be around them.

If they are open to examining their behavior and making some changes, help them. Give them books on the subject and maybe discuss how it has been a challenge for you as well. Ask them if they would be willing to help you by not being so negative around you. Ask them to stop gossiping and complaining to you. A lot of times, your friends and family will be willing to make some changes if you bring it to their attention.

Tell them that you know how hard it is to change those habits, as you are in the process of making some of those changes in your life as well. Then you could share with them how much your life has changed for the better since you have been cultivating inner peace. People are always looking for ways to improve their life, so let them see all the positive changes you have made in your life. That said, if they continue to bring negativity into your life, you will want to spend less and less time with them.

Not only do negative people bring negative energy into your life, but they also influence you in other ways as well. You will start to become more like the people you associate with on a regular basis. You will begin to pick up some of their speech patterns and their habits, both good and bad. Whether you realize it or not, those around you are affecting your life.

If you associate with people who are constantly griping, complaining, and who just plain have a negative view of the world, you will find yourself starting to pick up some of those negative traits. If your friends are in the habit of constantly using bad language, you will start to use that same language more and more often.

Whether you believe it or not, the people you surround yourself with will influence your thoughts, your speech, and your behavior. It is vital to your inner peace that you are aware of this and that you choose your friends accordingly. Think about it; you can't spend a lot

133

of time around a mud hole and expect not to get some mud on yourself.

You always get to choose who you will and will not associate with. It is vital to your goals that you associate with people who help lift you to a higher level of inner peace and distance yourself from those who make it harder for you to live the life that you desire. As the Book of Proverbs states, "He who walks with the wise grows wise, but a companion of fools suffers harm."

The people you choose to spend time with will either help you move closer to your goals or make it harder for you to achieve them. This doesn't mean that you have to cut your negative family members or friends off completely, but you will not want to continue spending as much time with them.

The same principle applies to people on your social media accounts. If you have "friends" on your social media who are constantly bombarding you with negative comments, negative posts, and negative energy, you may have to make some changes. Unfollow, unfriend, and disconnect from anyone who robs you of your inner peace!

Removing people from your life doesn't mean that you dislike them or even that they are bad people. It simply means that it is the best thing for you at this time in your life. To maintain your inner peace, you must distance yourself from those who are making it difficult for you to achieve the kind of life that you want to live. You must set boundaries for yourself and for those you allow to be a part of your life. There are all types of people in this world; choose only the best people to be a part of your life on an ongoing basis.

Stay away from a foolish man, for
you will not find knowledge on his lips.
The Book of Proverbs

Thoughts to Ponder

Do not see dirt at others' doors; keep your own porch swept.
Swami Muktananda

Keep your attention focused entirely on what is
truly your own concern, and be clear that what
belongs to others is their business and none of yours.
Epictetus

Like one who seizes a dog by the ears is a
passer-by who meddles in a quarrel not his own.
The Book of Proverbs

Do not give your attention to what others do or fail to do;
give it to what you do or fail to do.
Buddha

No one gossips about other people's secret virtues.
Bertrand Russell

The things most people want to know about
are usually none of their business.
Lewis Carroll

The biggest fool is the one who minds the
business of others rather than minding his very own.
Amit Abraham

Watch out for the joy-stealers: gossip, criticism, complaining,
faultfinding, and a negative, judgmental attitude.
Joyce Meyer

Whoever gossips to you, will gossip about you.
Spanish Proverb

There is so much good in the worst of us, and so much bad in the
best of us, that it hardly becomes any of us to talk about the rest of us.
Edward Wallis Hoch

Who brings a tale takes two away.
Irish Proverb

135

Thoughts to Ponder

If a man's companion is dirty, the person who keeps close
company with him must of necessity get a share of his dirt,
even though he himself happens to be clean.
Epictetus

You become like the five people you spend the most time with.
Choose carefully.
Jim Rohn

The people you surround yourself with influence your behaviors,
so choose friends who have healthy habits.
Dan Buettner

Toxic people make you think you are holding a grudge,
when you are really holding a boundary.
Mel Robbins

Energy is contagious, positive and negative alike. I will forever be
mindful of what and who I am allowing into my space.
Alex Elle

Be careful whom you associate with.
It is human to imitate the habits of those with whom we interact.
We inadvertently adopt their interests, their opinions,
their values, and their habit of interpreting events.
Epictetus

Associate yourself with people who think positively. You cannot
surround yourself with negative people and expect positive outcomes.
Roy T. Bennett

Surround yourself with supportive people.
All the negative people, man you have to push them aside.
Gabriel Iglesias

Make a conscious effort to surround yourself with positive,
nourishing, and uplifting people – people who believe in you,
encourage you to go after your dreams, and applaud your victories.
Jack Canfield

Chapter 12
Overcoming Obstacles and Anger

To bear trials with a calm mind
robs misfortune of its strength and burden.
Seneca

In life, you will have to deal with many obstacles and conflicts throughout your journey. That is simply a part of the human experience. However, you don't have to allow obstacles and conflicts to rob you of your inner peace. Maintaining your inner peace in times of conflict, or while you are overcoming obstacles, is a matter of perspective, how you see the obstacle in front of you.

If you see an obstacle as a terrible thing that is going to totally disrupt your life, then your inner peace is going to be hard to maintain while you are dealing with that obstacle. Whereas, if you simply see the obstacle as a part of your path, it will not upset you or disrupt your inner peace. It is not a roadblock but rather a challenge. Remember what Marcus Aurelius taught:

"Our actions may be impeded, but there can be no
impeding our intentions or dispositions. Because
we can accommodate and adapt. The mind adapts
and converts to its own purposes the obstacle to our
acting. The impediment to action advances action.
What stands in the way becomes the way."

Think about this wisdom from the great Roman Emperor. There can be no impeding your intentions or your disposition. Events and people in life can try to obstruct your goals, but neither have any power to control your attitude or intentions. You have total control over what you intend to do and how you choose to see the obstacle or conflict standing in your way.

You have the ability to adapt and use the obstacle to your advantage. It is up to you. You can use the obstacle to your advantage, or you can allow it to defeat you. If you use the obstacle to your advantage, it becomes a part of your path, and you will be at peace with it. As Marcus Aurelius put it, "What stands in your way *becomes* the way."

Don't focus on the obstacle; focus on your objective and how you can *use the obstacle* to your benefit. Always try to turn every difficulty into a positive in one way or another. Focus on what you

137

want in every situation, and then do what you have to do to make it happen.

See every crisis, obstacle, or conflict as an opportunity or a challenge. See them as a test to see if you are really serious about achieving your goal and maintaining your inner peace. When you look at obstacles in this way, they become part of the chess game of life, instead of something to be upset or distressed over.

Think about it. Chess would be a boring game if there were never any obstacles to overcome or challenges to your strategy. If you sat down and won every game without ever having to think, develop a strategy, or even try to overcome your opponent's moves, you would soon lose interest in playing the game. There would be no challenge to it.

Look at life's obstacles as a challenge, something for you to overcome in order to win the game. See them as nothing more than a part of the game that adds interest and challenges your skills and your mental ability to overcome and become victorious. When you look at obstacles in this way, they become less serious, less stressful, and more interesting.

Learn to flow around obstacles peacefully instead of allowing the obstacle to cause you stress and disrupt your inner peace. One of Bruce Lee's most famous teachings is to be like water. Lee taught:

> "Be water, my friend. Empty your mind. Be formless,
> shapeless, like water. You put water into a cup, it
> becomes the cup. You put water into a bottle, it
> becomes the bottle. You put water into a teapot,
> it becomes the teapot. Now water can flow
> or it can crash. Be water, my friend."

What Lee was trying to teach us is to flow around any obstacle put in your way. When you think about it, this makes perfect sense. If you put a giant boulder in the middle of a river, the river doesn't give up flowing to the ocean; it simply finds a way around the obstacle. The water will flow around the boulder or it will flow into it and splash over the top. The water in the river will do whatever is necessary in order to continue its journey downstream. The obstacle does not stop the water from reaching its destination.

The boulder, the obstacle, never gets the best of the river. The river never gives up, never gets frustrated or angry, and never feels defeated because the boulder is in its path. The river simply does what it has to do to achieve its goal. It adjusts its flow and its path accordingly, and continues on its journey.

138

Develop this same attitude in your life. When an obstacle presents itself, instead of getting upset, angry, or discouraged, simply flow around it. Go over it, go through it, go around it, or go under it; do whatever it takes to continue on your journey. Don't let it stop you or frustrate you. Take it in stride, knowing that the obstacle is a part of your journey. Be flexible with your strategy, but never with your objective.

Of course, some obstacles will be bigger and harder to deal with than others. But no matter what kind of obstacle you face, always remain calm and maintain your inner peace while you are riding the storm out. Getting frustrated, upset, and angry about the situation only clouds your mind, adds to your stress, impedes your objective, and disrupts your inner peace.

For many people, those reactions have become an automatic response to obstacles and annoyances. They have reacted the same way for so many years that they automatically react to even small obstacles with frustration and anger. This is a pattern that must be broken in order to maintain your inner peace and successfully overcome the difficulties in your life.

Refuse to allow yourself to get angry or frustrated because of obstacles or the inevitable conflicts which you will encounter on your path. Remind yourself that getting annoyed or frustrated only deprives you of your inner peace and makes it harder for you to reach your goal. Remember Friedrich Nietzsche's famous teaching, "What doesn't kill you makes you stronger."

Be determined to use every obstacle, every challenge, and every conflict to your advantage in one way or another. Learn from it and use it to improve your skills when dealing with the next obstacle. The more you do something, the better you become at it. Obstacles are just like everything else in life – the more you successfully overcome the present one, the better you become at dealing with the next one. Each victory strengthens your mind and your resolve.

One of the obstacles that is common to everyone is learning to deal with anger. Most people would not consider anger to be an obstacle to their goals, but for many, it is one of the biggest obstacles that they have to face. This is especially true if you have developed the propensity towards getting angry over and over again because of minor hassles in your life.

Anger can be very addictive. While anger is a natural response to certain situations, if you are constantly getting angry, it can become a problem. Anger releases a chemical cocktail in your body. You get a surge of adrenaline, noradrenaline, and endorphins which trigger a positive feeling that has been compared to that of morphine.

139

When we get angry, we have an increased heart rate and an increase in blood pressure, and along with the surge of adrenaline, that combination creates an almost euphoric feeling. In addition, many people physically manifest their anger by hitting something, throwing something, or yelling. This causes the body to release dopamine which creates an even greater sense of exhilaration.

The problem is that this good feeling is short-lived and comes with quite a few adverse side effects. When anger becomes habitual, the constant flood of the stress chemicals such as cortisol, and the changes which accompany them, can cause many health problems such as headaches, digestion problems, increased anxiety, insomnia, high blood pressure, skin issues, depression, and even heart attacks and strokes.

You must learn to control your anger. Don't get angry except on purpose. Yes, there is a time and a place for righteous anger, but it is not every day or multiple times a day. It is not each night while you are watching the national news or something else on your television. You should control your anger; it should not control you. Anger should be used as a tool; it should be a response, not a reaction. When anger is controlling you, it is a reaction; when you are controlling your anger, it is a response.

Allowing yourself to get angry repeatedly about minor inconveniences causes anger to become habitual. It is not that you become addicted to the emotion, but to the hormones and the physical feelings that accompany the adrenaline and dopamine rush. There is also an element of stress relief that comes from an angry outburst.

Constant anger is not conducive to inner peace or good health. There is no way you will consistently live a life of inner peace when you allow small, insignificant things in your life to continually provoke you. And the negative health issues will only lead to more stress in your life, which will make it even harder to maintain your inner peace.

Many times, anger comes from the people you encounter in your life. No matter what you do, some people will push your buttons and try to make you angry, or simply do things that will annoy you. They may *try* to make you angry, but they have no power to *make* you angry if you don't allow them to do so.

Don't give anyone the power to *make* you angry. If you are going to allow others to anger you, then you are giving them the power to control and manipulate you. If someone can make you angry, then they can manipulate you at their will. The reality is that no one can *make* you angry. You, and you alone, control when you allow yourself to be angry; you simply use other people's words and actions to justify your anger.

If you are easily angered, you are easily controlled. Furthermore, if you give others the power to anger you, you are giving them the power to rob you of your inner peace as they will. You are putting them in control of your tranquility instead of maintaining that control yourself.

This is why we are told in the Kabbalah that nothing should disturb you. If you allow external events or other people to disturb your inner peace, then you will always find a reason to be upset, angered, and agitated. Remember, inner peace resides in your mind; don't give anything outside yourself the power to control your mind or disrupt your tranquility.

You must remind yourself that when you get angry at someone else, circumstances, or some external event, your anger has no effect on that person or situation. Your anger is only affecting you. And although it may temporarily feel good to vent your frustrations, that good feeling is not worth disrupting your inner peace or dealing with the adverse health effects which accompany your anger.

There is an old Asian story about a monk who was asked, "What is anger?" The monk answered, "Anger is a punishment you give to yourself when someone does you wrong. The person who wronged you does not feel your anger, does not feel your anguish. They are not affected by your self-induced suffering. If you become angry, do not let it set up home in your heart; acknowledge it, and with kindness to yourself, let it disperse. Your own mental well-being is more important. Be kind to yourself. Look after yourself like you are someone you are responsible for." This short parable is good advice for anyone who has challenges with anger.

If you hold on to your anger towards someone, you are not hurting that person, but you are depressing your own energy and robbing yourself of your own serenity. Remember, resentment and unforgiveness are low-energy, negative emotions.

If you do get angry about something, let it go as soon as you possibly can. The longer that you hold on to anger and resentment, the more it will take root in your mind. Moreover, the more you revisit the event or situation mentally, the more your anger concerning that incident will grow.

Think of your temper as a weed in your mental garden. If you remove it from your garden quickly, it doesn't have the opportunity to grow strong roots. But if you allow it to remain there for a period of time, the roots of your anger will grow deeper in the soil of your mind and become much harder to remove. Even after you remove the weed,

141

the roots may remain hidden and continue to grow, causing you to deal with the same weed (anger and resentment) over and over again.

You must remove your anger at the roots and get over it once and for all. If you allow the root of your anger to remain, that weed will pop up over and over again; it will become stronger and stronger until your anger actually turns to hatred. And have no doubts about it, if you hold on into anger towards someone for too long, without removing it and forgiving your transgressor, your anger will grow, and the roots will get stronger.

I quickly summarized some of the health issues associated with anger, but those are not the only dangers that accompany prolonged anger. Uncontrolled anger, especially directed towards another person, can quickly turn into hatred and bitterness.

The Dhammapada teaches, "They insulted me; they hurt me; they defeated me; they cheated me. In those who harbor such thoughts, hate will never cease." Buddha also taught that holding on to anger is like holding on to a hot coal with the intention of throwing it at the person you are angry with. The problem with that is you are the one getting burned, not the other person.

Confucius taught that if you hate a person, then you are defeated by him. But the truth of the matter is that if you allow your anger towards someone to turn to hate, you are not defeated by that person; you are defeated by your own lack of self-control and your refusal to forgive that person for his wrongdoings. It is *you* who is refusing to take control of your emotions; *you* have defeated yourself.

When you hate someone, he is controlling your mind without even trying. That hate will eat you up inside, while the person you hate is enjoying life and not giving you a second thought. You are giving him free rent in your mind and allowing him to continue to hurt you and to get the best of you without even trying. This is unwise anyway you look at it!

Stop hatred before it starts by controlling your anger at the onset. And if you have already reached the point of hatred towards someone, remove that hate by forgiving the other person. (I will discuss this more later.) Trust the Universe to deal with those who have wronged you. Your goal is not to get revenge but to maintain your inner peace. Thoughts of retaliation are not compatible with your peace of mind.

As you continue on your journey, people may push your buttons to try to make you angry. They may disrespect you, treat you badly, disappoint you, and some will even maliciously try to hurt you, but you must refuse to allow them to control your emotions.

A good rule to follow is when you are angry, be silent. A lot of times, we get angry about something, and instead of controlling our

142

words, we allow our anger to control what we say, causing us even more problems after our initial anger has subsided. This is a trap that many people step into when they are enraged.

People will do something to anger you, hoping that you will take the bait and say or do something which they will be able to use against you at a later time. And this shrewd strategy works more times than not, as many people throw self-restraint out the window when they are extremely angry.

Again, don't be easily manipulated or controlled. When you are angry, either stay silent or choose your words very carefully after you have given the situation some thought. See other people's attempts to get under your skin for exactly what they are and refuse to allow them to control you. You have to be aware of the dishonest ploys of those who enjoy causing problems for other people.

In addition, refuse to become angry, antagonistic, or upset when confronted with a negative situation. An angry response will lead to an angry reaction. What you sow, you will reap. If you respond in anger, the other person will react to you in kind. Every action produces a corresponding reaction.

Instead of responding with anger, you can neutralize anger by responding with kindness and love. This always takes the other person off guard. When someone does something to anger you, he or she expects you to react with anger and indignation. It is a good strategy to never give them what they are hoping for or what they expect. Instead, turn the tables on them by responding in a way which they are not prepared for, catching them off guard. Respond calmly and peacefully.

Refuse to be a victim. Refuse to be manipulated or controlled by anyone. Never blame anyone else for your anger, as that is acknowledging that they have power over you. Train yourself to only get angry on purpose, for your own reasons, and when you decide.

If you want to maintain your inner peace and tranquility, then you must come to the realization that you are, in one way or another, responsible for everything in your life, even if you don't understand exactly how at this time. While you are not responsible for the other person's actions or for external events, you are responsible for how you allow them to affect you and for how you respond to them. Taking responsibility prevents you from being a victim.

The more you accept this reality, the more power you will have over your life. While you may be able to identify people who you believe are responsible for your unhappiness or your situation, those are only justifications for what is happening in your life. Nobody is responsible for your happiness but you.

143

You can change the way you see any situation; you can decide to be happy in any situation in which you find yourself. You can choose to see things from a different angle; ultimately, it is up to you to make that choice. Remember, change your thoughts, and you will change your perception; change your perception, and you change your life. This applies to every situation in your life.

I can already hear some of you objecting to this, saying, "But you don't understand what he did to me" or "You don't know what she said about me." Stop "butting" yourself! When you use the word "but" at the end of a statement about getting over something that someone did to you, you are justifying being a victim and holding on to your anger. You can always find some reason for not letting go of your anger or resentments, but those reasons will not help you reach your goal. A victim mentality will never bring you inner peace.

For example, if you say something like, "I would have made a million dollars, but Joe stole my idea and crushed my family." You just turned yourself into a victim. Stop giving your power to other people! Take responsibility for your own life and everything in it. Don't give anyone the power to turn you into a victim, to make you angry, or to make you hate them.

When you take responsibility for everything in your life, you are in charge of your life. No one else is to blame for your failures or your hardships, and no one else is responsible for your victories, success, or inner peace.

Dealing with obstacles, conflicts, and anger is something that everyone has to do; they are not unique to you. It is not the obstacle or anger which robs you of your inner peace, but your perception of the obstacle and your lack of control over your anger. When you are capable of flowing around the obstacles in your path, you will restore a sense of balance to your life. Learn to control and use your anger, and simply let go of it when you need to. Absolutely refuse to allow anger to defeat you!

The value that any experience has for us is the value that we put upon it in our own thoughts…The same unpleasant happening that one man will laugh off and forget, will to another man mean a broken heart followed by death. A big difficulty is what we consider big…Big and little are qualities that lie in our own thoughts…Minimize the problem you are treating. Do not give it importance in your thought.
Emmet Fox

144

Thoughts to Ponder

As quickly as you discover yourself roused,
let intelligence blow the retreat.
Baltasar Gracian

A good person dyes events with his own color
and turns whatever happens to his own benefit.
Seneca

If you are distressed by anything external, the pain
is not due to the thing itself, but to your estimate of it;
and thus you have the power to revoke it at any time.
Marcus Aurelius

When anger speaks, wisdom veils her face.
Chinese Proverb

If you don't wish to be a hot-head, don't feed your habit. Try as a first
step to remain calm and count the days you haven't been angry...
For habit is first weakened and then obliterated.
Epictetus

The first rule is to keep an untroubled spirit. The second is
to look things in the face and know them for what they are.
Marcus Aurelius

Let cold deliberation take the place of sudden outburst.
Fine proof of judgment to keep your
head when the fools have lost theirs.
Baltasar Gracian

No person is important enough to make me angry.
Carlos Castaneda

I permit no man to narrow and degrade
my soul by making me hate him.
Booker T. Washington

A man who never opens his mouth in anger
can close his eyes in peace.
Chinese Proverb

Thoughts to Ponder

My life is in the hands of any fool
who makes me lose my temper.
Dr. John Hunter

Anger breeds confusion.
To be clear-minded you must avoid being angry.
The Bhagavad Gita

Anger is the wind that blows out the lamp of the mind.
Robert G. Ingersoll

How much more harmful are the consequences of anger
and grief than the circumstances that aroused them in us!
Marcus Aurelius

Frequent fits of anger produce in the soul a propensity to be angry.
Plutarch

If you are always getting angry,
you'll turn your nature against the Way.
Bodhidharma

Keep in mind that it isn't the one who has it in for you and
takes a swipe that harms you, but rather the harm comes from
your own belief about the abuse. So when someone arouses your
anger, know that it's really your own opinion fueling it. Instead, make
it your first response not to be carried away by such impressions,
for with time and distance self-mastery is more easily achieved.
Epictetus

Someone despises me. That's their problem.
Mine: not to do or say anything despicable.
Someone hates me. Their problem.
Mine: to be patient and cheerful with everyone.
Marcus Aurelius

If you allow compassion to spring from your heart,
the fire of anger will die right away.
Thick Nhat Hanh

146

Chapter 13
Be Patient and Practice Forgiveness

Infinite patience produces immediate results.
Helen Schucman

Dealing with obstacles, anger, other people, and living a life of inner peace, in general, is much easier when you develop patience. We have become a society that wants everything now. Even waiting a few seconds for a web page to open frustrates some people, and frustration is definitely not conducive to inner peace. If you are going to consistently live a life of inner peace, you have to develop patience.

Time and patience will conquer most things if you allow them to work their magic. The problem is that most people are impatient. They do not want any hassles, challenges, or deviations to their plans or their day. This goes back to the issue of having expectations about everything in your life.

When you expect things in your life to be a certain way, and you are annoyed when they do not go as planned, you get frustrated, angry, and impatient. Those feelings often cause your inner peace to vanish, at least until you compose yourself and get back on track.

To live a life of inner peace, you must get rid of your expectations and embrace going with the flow. A flexible person is able to handle whatever comes his way and not get frustrated or upset every time something does not go as planned. Remember, the willow bends and survives the storm, while the oak tree is inflexible, unbending, and breaks during the inevitable storms of life.

Flexible people adjust their sails when the wind is blowing in the wrong direction. They are not willing to allow external events or situations out of their control to affect their day. They plan their work and work their plan, but when the plan doesn't work out, they simply adjust their sails and continue doing the best that they can do.

If you lack patience, you will find that the people and situations in your life will always find a way to frustrate your inner peace. You cannot allow the things in life which you have no power over to rob you of your inner peace, or you will find it almost impossible to preserve your tranquility. You must be patient, especially with other people.

Everyone is dealing with different issues in their life; always remember, other people's lives do not revolve around you or your plans. When you think about all the different people you deal with each day and all the possible challenges that each one, including yourself, have to deal with, it is amazing that our lives flow as smoothly as they do. Be patient with everyone; each person is dealing with a multitude of difficulties that you are not aware of.

When you develop patience for others, you will find it much easier to deal with your anger and frustrations. A lot of the time, the anger in your life comes from your attitude towards people who have not lived up to your expectations. When you get rid of your expectations, as we have already discussed, and you replace them with acceptance and patience, your life will inevitably become easier.

And don't just develop patience for other people, be patient with yourself as well. You are going to have good days and bad days. You are going to have successful days when it comes to maintaining your inner peace and days that are much more trying.

You may not see the improvements you want as quickly as you hope to, but if you keep working on your inner peace and tranquility, you will make progress, whether you actually see it manifesting in your life or not. If you get impatient and start to believe that the principles in this book are not working for you, you will only slow down your progress.

Think about the people you see every day. When you see someone every day, you don't notice how much they are changing. But if you don't see someone for a few months or a year, you will be shocked at how much they have changed. Most changes are not immediate; they happen gradually over time.

Since I have used gardening as an example throughout this book, let's continue with another gardening analogy. Once you plant seeds in your garden, you must be patient as the plants grow and mature. If you go and dig them up to see if anything is happening, you will only disrupt the growing process. Just because you don't see the seed producing results yet, doesn't mean that the germination process is not working.

Changes are happening even though you don't see the transitions in the life of the seed. But if you go on vacation and have someone else water your garden while you are gone, you will be amazed at how much your garden has grown in your absence.

The same principle applies to the changes in your life. I can promise you that if you are applying the principles in this book, you are making life changes, even if you don't notice as much progress as you would like. You may not perceive how you are changing yet, but be assured, changes are happening deep in your subconscious mind. Once again, I will remind you that changes must take place on the inside before you see the results on the outside.

Give the process time to work. The amount of time it takes to see results in your life will differ with each person, but as long as you don't lose faith and dig up your seeds, they will grow.

Patience allows you to endure whatever comes your way and to maintain your inner peace no matter what else is going on in your life. It enables you to give yourself the time that is required to change your life. And patience allows you to be forgiving of others when they make mistakes or do things that frustrate or anger you. All people make mistakes, be patient with them and forgive them, just as you would want them to do for you.

Practice Forgiveness

Forgiveness equals inner peace –
more peaceful people equals more world peace.
Richard Branson

If you want to maintain your inner peace, you must forgive everyone; refuse to hold on to resentments, no matter how valid you feel they may be. Holding on to past insults, injuries, and negative feelings towards others will always disrupt your inner tranquility. You will never get past those hurt feelings and negative associations until you make a firm decision to forgive. And once you do forgive those who have hurt you or done you wrong, you will immediately feel free and feel a sense of inner peace about that situation which you could not imagine feeling before.

Forgiving someone who has truly hurt you can be very hard. Some people have been hurt so badly that it is all they can do to let go of the anger and resentment that they feel towards the other person. For some people, they have held on to these negative feelings for so long that their sentiments have actually hardened into an unforgiving hatred of the other person.

The problem with not forgiving that person is that you are allowing your thoughts and emotions regarding what he did to continue to hurt you after the fact. He has probably moved on and doesn't think about you at all, but your unforgiveness has allowed his actions to stay fresh in your mind as if it only happened yesterday. By holding on to that anger, frustration, or hatred, you are choosing to allow that person to continue to hurt you and hold you back from your goal of living a life of inner peace.

Consider a venomous snake that bites someone; it is not the bite that causes a problem; it is the venom that is injected into the body and continues to circulate throughout the body. The bite itself is

149

nothing more than the equivalent of being stuck with a needle at the doctor's office. If it were not for the venom circulating throughout the body, it would be no big deal at all.

When someone betrays or hurts you in some way, it is nothing more than a bite. Their actions only injure you to the point that you decide they have injured you. It depends on how you perceive their actions. Once again, the problem resides in your mind. Of course, it is going to be hurtful, disappointing, and upsetting when a trusted friend or family member betrays you or does something to hurt you. But, just like the snake bite, it cannot injure you if there is no venom left in your body, or in this case, your mind.

Unlike the venomous snake bite, when someone hurts you, you get to choose whether or not the poison stays in your body, or for our purposes, in your mind. If you choose not to be affected by his actions, then they have no power over you. You make this choice by choosing to forgive him and move on. This doesn't mean that what he did is okay or that you are okay with his actions; it simply means that you are refusing to allow him to disrupt your life.

It takes a strong person to forgive others and move on with your life. It takes a strong will and, depending on the situation, a lot of discipline and effort. What you must understand is that forgiveness is not for the other person; it is for you. You are not hurting the other person by refusing to forgive him for what he did; you are only hurting yourself.

When your mind starts remembering how someone hurt you, you go through the same emotions that you had when the incident occurred. Basically, you are reliving the whole thing again and again. This disrupts your inner peace and makes you feel angry, hurt, and disappointed all over again.

Meanwhile, the person who hurt you has moved on. He most likely did not care when he hurt you the first time and certainly does not care now. By reliving what he did over and over again, you are only hurting yourself. And have no doubts about it; there are many consequences of unforgiveness.

Holding on to a grudge, for whatever reason, can lead to depression, anxiety, stress, bitterness, anger, resentfulness, and hatred. I have already discussed the negative effects of prolonged anger. Unforgiveness can hinder your spiritual life and cause you to be so caught up in what happened in the past that you do not enjoy the present. Also, dwelling on how someone betrayed you or broke your trust can program your subconscious mind with a deep distrust of people in general, causing you to doubt others' intentions, even when there isn't a reason.

150

Refuse to hold on to resentments. Although you may be able to justify your feelings of resentment towards the other person, you are simply hurting yourself. The benefits of forgiving the other person far outweigh the costs of holding on to your unforgiveness. The costs associated with holding on to a grudge are simply too high. Forgive the other person and move on with your life.

Anger, resentment, jealousy, hatred, and thoughts of revenge are too heavy a burden to carry around with you, but they are only heavy if you continue to carry them. Once you let them go, they weigh nothing and no longer weigh you down.

Forgiving the other person not only removes the toxic thoughts from your mind, but it decreases your stress, anxiety, and feelings of anger or frustration. It improves your immune system, your self-esteem, and your blood pressure. It eliminates all of those negative effects and allows the situation to subside, subsequently increasing your inner peace.

I also want to point out that forgiving the other person does not mean that you have to allow that person back into your life. It simply means that you are refusing to allow what he did to continue to disrupt your inner peace or to negatively affect you in any way.

Many teachers teach that you should forgive and forget, but I disagree with that. Just like everything else in life, you should learn a lesson from your experience and use it to your advantage. That person taught you something about his character and who he is as a person. If you forgive and forget, you are losing that valuable knowledge. Forgive, but don't forget.

This does not mean that you revisit the incident frequently or bring it up anytime that person's name is mentioned. That would not be advantageous to your inner peace. Put it out of your mind completely, but keep that information filed away in case you ever need it to prevent yourself from being hurt or taken advantage of by this person again in the future.

Another reason that you should forgive others is that we all need forgiveness. We are all guilty of saying or doing things that hurt others, even if they are unintentional. If you refuse to forgive others, why should others forgive you? When you are tempted to hold on to a grudge, remind yourself of this fact. Remembering that you are not perfect and that you make mistakes will help you increase your patience with others when they make mistakes.

In addition to forgiving those who have caused you pain in your life, you must learn to forgive yourself for the slip-ups you have made. Refuse to dwell on past mistakes! Forgive yourself and move on, or those past mistakes will continue to hold you back. And let go of all regret. Dwelling on your regrets will almost always disrupt your inner peace.

Forgive yourself but remember the lessons you learned from your shortcomings. This doesn't mean that you continue to remember or dwell on your mistakes, but rather that you learn your lesson from them, so you do not repeat the same mistakes again.

Stop beating yourself up over and over again for a mistake you made once. Deal with it, make amends if you need to, forgive yourself, and be done with it. You need to let it go and start making positive deposits into your karma account.

The Law of Karma states that whatever thoughts, energy, or actions you send out into this world will come back to you. If you give others love, patience, and forgiveness, then more people will be loving, patient, and forgiving towards you. Jesus put it this way, "As you sow, so shall you reap."

If you want people to be patient and forgiving towards you when you fall short, you must be patient and forgiving towards others, even when you don't feel like it. You are working towards your goal of living a life of inner peace. As a part of the process of changing your life, you may have to do some things that you don't necessarily want to do. That is where self-discipline comes into play.

You will have days where your patience has run out, and you may want to snap at someone. Someone may have done something to you that you consider to be so bad that you simply do not want to forgive him. Those are the times when you must remember what it is that you truly want and stay positive in order to manifest inner peace in your life.

Never allow your emotions, especially negative emotions such as anger, hurt, and frustration, to call the shots in your life. Think rationally and stay focused on maintaining your inner peace. Be determined that nothing and nobody is going to disrupt your inner peace, no matter what. Then discipline yourself to maintain your tranquility. This means developing patience and forgiving those who have wronged you in some way.

I will not be distracted by noise, chatter, or setbacks.
Patience, grace, and purpose will guide me.
Louise Hay

Thoughts to Ponder

No great thing is created suddenly, any more than a bunch of grapes or a fig. If you tell me that you desire a fig, I answer that there must be time. Let it first blossom, then bear fruit, then ripen.
Epictetus

Patience and fortitude conquer all things.
Ralph Waldo Emerson

He that can have patience can have what he will.
Benjamin Franklin

Have patience. All things are difficult before they become easy.
Saadi

Patience is the calm acceptance that things can happen
in a different order than the one you have in your mind.
David G. Allen

The stupid neither forgive nor forget;
the naïve forgive and forget;
the wise forgive but do not forget.
Thomas Szasz

He that cannot forgive others breaks the bridge over which
he must pass himself, for every man hath need to be forgiven.
Edward Herbert

How much better to heal than seek revenge from injury.
Vengeance wastes a lot of time and exposes you to many more
injuries than the first that sparked it. Anger always outlasts hurt.
Best to take the opposite course. Would anyone think
it normal to return a kick to a mule or a bite to a dog?
Seneca

Forgiving those who hurt you is the key to personal peace.
G. Weatherly

Patience manifests in confidence, decisiveness, and a feeling
of peaceful satisfaction…attempt to see the larger picture.
Wayne Dyer

153

Thoughts to Ponder

Our patience will achieve more than our force.
Edmund Burke

Patience is the road to wisdom.
Kao Kalia Yang

Trust the process. Your time is coming.
Just do the work and the results will handle themselves.
Tony Gaskins

Perfection is attained by slow degrees; she requires the hand of time.
Voltaire

He who plants a forest in the morning
cannot expect to saw planks the same evening.
Chinese Proverb

Patience is bitter, but its fruit is sweet.
Aristotle

Those who are free of resentful thoughts surely find peace.
Buddha

Inner peace can be reached only when we practice forgiveness.
Forgiveness is letting go of the past, and is therefore
the means for correcting our misperceptions.
Gerald G. Jampolsky

Forgive them, Father, for they know not what they do.
Jesus

Forgive, son; men are men; they needs must err.
Euripides

To lose patience is to lose the battle.
Mahatma Gandhi

Patience, persistence, and perspiration
make an unbeatable combination for success.
Napoleon Hill

154

Chapter 14
Practice Kindness and Compassion

Practice random kindness and senseless acts of beauty.
Anne Herbert

Once you have developed patience and learned to forgive those who have wronged you, it is easier to treat others with kindness and compassion. Treating those around you with kindness and compassion costs you nothing but has great value, both to you and others.

Living a kind, compassionate life leads to happiness all the way around. It makes those who come in contact with you happier, and it makes you feel good about yourself as well. And you don't have to limit your kindness and compassion to people; respect all living things.

When you get to the point that you are treating everyone and everything in your path with love, kindness, and compassion, you know that you have made some major changes to your subconscious mind. Your actions are now coming from a place of inner peace and tranquility, and you are sharing your inner peace with those around you.

For years I would tell people that small children, old people, and animals love me; it is the people in between which I have problems with. I said this so often that it manifest in my life and became my reality. I was programming my subconscious mind with this statement, and my subconscious mind made sure that it manifested in my life.

I would treat young children, elderly people, and animals with kindness and compassion, but other people I looked at with suspicion, distrust, and a defensive mindset. Many of my experiences taught me that people could not be trusted and that I had to protect myself from them. This attitude towards people was further cemented into my mind every time someone cheated me or betrayed me. It was like a continuous, unescapable cycle.

I was continually programming my subconscious mind to believe that people could not be trusted every time someone harmed me in some way. As a result, I was attracting those kind of people into my life. Remember, you get more of whatever you focus on. That had become one of my core beliefs, and it manifested itself in my life over and over again. Each time it happened, it reinforced my belief that people could not be trusted.

When you see people from this angle, it becomes hard to practice kindness and compassion. It is hard to act from a place of love when you see everyone as a potential problem. My walls were always up, and I trusted no one.

On the other hand, I did not look at young children, elderly people, or animals in the same way. I was always kind, compassionate, and patient with them. As a result, they seemed to like me, and I got along well with them. The difference was my attitude and the way I perceived people.

It becomes very hard to practice kindness and compassion with people you do not trust and do not want to be around. I know that there are many people in this world who have had the same experiences and who are thinking, "Yeah, you are right. You can't trust people. They are dishonest and will do you wrong."

Let's look at it from another perspective. Out of all the people you have known, the number who have hurt you or betrayed you is a very small percentage. The problem is that when someone has harmed you, you give that person's actions more weight than you should because it caused you to have very strong negative emotions concerning that incident. As a result, you started to distrust more and more people, and your walls went up.

To practice kindness and compassion, you must change your perspective. That doesn't mean that you blindly trust everyone and live your life naïvely. You should keep your eyes wide open and not be an easy target for those who are determined to mistreat others. As I stated earlier, living a life of inner peace is not the same thing as being a doormat or being blindly naïve.

The fact is that you can be aware of a person's character, or lack of character, sense his intentions, and practice self-defense to keep yourself safe from being taken advantage of, all the while, still practicing kindness and compassion. You can be kind to everyone and still watch your back.

And the more you practice kindness and compassion, the more you will find that others will treat you with kindness and compassion. What you send out in this world always comes back to you in kind. Meet bitterness and resentfulness with kindness. Yes, you should be aware of what others are doing and their motives, but you can still treat them respectfully and be considerate. It takes a strong person to be kind to the unkind or to treat a malicious person with courtesy. It takes someone who walks in inner peace.

Be kind and compassionate, not because someone else deserves it, but because that is the kind of person you want to be. Deserve has nothing to do with it. If you are only focused on being kind to people

156

who absolutely deserve it, you may find yourself like I was and only wanting to be around young kids, elderly people, and animals. I am not exaggerating. I actually had a bumper sticker on my car for many years which read, "The more people I meet, the more I like my dog!"

You treat others with kindness and compassion because you have decided that this is the kind of person you are going to be. If you have had a bad attitude towards other people for years, then this can be a challenge, but it is worth it.

My wife has always been better at this than I am. Some rude guy would flip her the bird for driving too slow or whatever she may have been doing, and she would just smile and wave as if she did not even know what his middle finger meant. I, on the other hand, would roll down the window, and tell him where he could stick his middle finger.

If you are more like my wife, it will be much easier for you to treat others with kindness and compassion. If you are more like I used to be, then you will have some work to do in this area. I have always been kind to everyone, except those who were not kind to me. But that is not good enough; to consistently live a life of inner peace, we must make kindness and compassion our way of life.

We all have our own specific challenges when it comes to living a life of inner peace. Some guy flipping me off and cursing at me going down the road could temporarily rob me of my inner peace, whereas it would not bother my wife at all. And things that would disrupt my wife's inner peace would not phase me.

Certain things trigger certain people depending on their past experiences and how their subconscious mind has been programmed. Practicing compassion for others may come easy for you, but you may have a problem with forgiving someone who has treated you wrong.

As you continue your journey of living a life of inner peace, your weak areas will surface, and those will be the areas which you will have to spend more time perfecting. For some of us, opening our hearts to help others is challenging.

Open your heart to help others

In everything, do unto others as
you would have them do unto you.
Jesus

Part of being kind and compassionate is helping others when you can. Give as much as you can whenever the opportunity presents

157

itself. This doesn't mean you have to give money; there are many ways to help other people. You can find small ways to help other people every day. Even something as small as a smile, a nice compliment, or just being helpful, kind, and considerate can make a big difference in someone's life when they are having a really bad day. The ways you can help other people are virtually unlimited.

For example, I live in Colorado just outside Rocky Mountain National Park. We get a fair amount of snow here, as you might expect. When it snows, my wife and I try to shovel our neighbor's driveway, as he is an elderly man. We also take him meals when my wife prepares a big dinner. I even keep meat scraps to give to his dog. When it comes to helping others, you are only limited by your imagination.

Just this week, I was buying some things from Home Depot, and there was a woman in a car across from me who had bought something in a large box. She was unsuccessfully trying to get it in her hatch back and was obviously struggling. I went over and asked her if I could give her a hand and loaded the box for her. This took very little time or effort, but I am sure it was very appreciated and helpful to this lady who was struggling with it.

If you look for ways to help others, you will find that there is always something you can do. Even if you are very busy, there are hundreds of ways you can lend a hand. It only took 30 seconds for me to go over and load that box for the woman who was struggling with it. If you don't have a few minutes to help someone during your day, you are too busy and need to make some changes in your life.

And the icing on the cake is – when you help other people, it not only makes them happy and helps them have a better day, it brings you happiness as well. I was shopping in the grocery store a few weeks back, and there was an elderly lady who seemed kind of down and out. She was shopping in the same aisle as me and happened to have beautiful, long, gray hair. I smiled at her and said, "Wow, you have gorgeous hair." Her face lit up with a huge smile. And when I saw her later as she was leaving the store, she was still smiling.

Something as small as a nice compliment can completely change someone's day, especially if she rarely hears positive feedback. And when I saw how happy that compliment had made that lady, it made me feel good too. Always remember, you reap what you sow; what you send out into the world always comes back to you in one way or another. No matter how busy you are, you are never too busy to give someone a compliment or a sincere smile.

Always treat others with respect and dignity. This should go without saying, but from what I have seen in our society, it needs to

158

be said much more often. There are many people who rarely experience someone who treats them with respect or even dignifies them as a human being. And I can promise you that the simple act of treating someone with respect can have a huge impact on someone's life.

I was driving on a long trip from Colorado to Louisiana a while back and stopped in a small Texas town in the middle of nowhere. It was late at night, and I was pretty much wiped out, having driven for 12 straight hours. I had just gassed up my car and was going into the store for a snack, and there was a young black couple in their early 20's going into the store at the same time.

I reached the door first, opened it, and held it open for the woman and her boyfriend. At first, they paused and had a strange look on their faces. I smiled, nodded, and motioned them to go ahead, and didn't think anything else about it. I always hold the door open for someone if they are walking in the store at the same time as me, so I didn't think anything about it.

After I had bought my snack, I was outside walking back to my car, and the man started to approach me. It was around 12 o'clock at night, so my warrior radar clicked on, as I thought this was a bit unusual.

I looked at him, wondering what was about to happen here, when he politely said, "Excuse me sir, I just wanted to thank you for holding the door open for my girlfriend and me. No one has ever done that before, and I just wanted you to know that it meant a lot to me."

You never know when the smallest action will mean the world to someone else. Look for ways to make other people feel good, and in the process, you will find that you are increasing your own happiness and inner peace. Open your heart to help others as much as you can, and always act from a place of love.

Always Act from a Place of Love

Always nurture unconditional love for all beings.
This is what it means to be truly human.
Lao Tzu

If you always act from a place of love, then being kind, compassionate, and helping others will come naturally to you. Acting from a place of love starts with loving yourself, and the more inner peace you have, the more you will love yourself and others. It is extremely hard to have the desire to treat others with kindness and compassion when you do not even love yourself.

159

You may think that this is a silly statement because everyone obviously loves themselves. But not everyone does love himself or herself. Some people are in the habit of blaming themselves, speaking badly of themselves, and even hating themselves. If you don't love and respect yourself, it is hard to love and respect anyone else. Being compassionate to others must start with loving yourself. If your compassion doesn't include yourself, it is incomplete; if you can't be compassionate and forgiving to yourself, how can you be compassionate and forgiving to anyone else.

Practice unconditional love for yourself and others. This doesn't mean that you will like everyone or even want to be friends with everyone you meet. It merely means that you have made a firm decision that you will give unconditional love to everyone in your life. This also means that you will forgive those who have hurt you, as I discussed in the last chapter.

When you love yourself, you will love others as well, and when you have love in your heart for others, you will have the desire to be kind, compassionate, and helpful to those around you. Moreover, when you have a deep desire to always act from a place of love, you strengthen your inner peace and tranquility. This, in turn, increases your happiness, your gratitude for the people and things in your life, and helps you maintain a good attitude towards people and life in general.

As you begin to develop your inner peace on a consistent basis, your inner peace will affect every area of your life, including how you treat those around you. As your inner peace increases, so will your desire to act from a place of love, to be patient, forgiving, kind, compassionate, and to help others. And the more you do for others, the happier you will become, and the more you will find that other people start treating you better as well.

Again, what we put out in this world always comes back to us. So if you want to be blessed, happy, content, prosperous, and constantly have a spirit of inner peace, the easiest way to achieve this is to consistently help others achieve these things in their lives. Be determined that you will bless everyone you come in contact with in one way or another. Have a giving spirit. Give of your time, your knowledge, or even a simple blessing. Make regular deposits into your karma account and watch your happiness and inner peace follow.

Remember, there's no such thing as a small act of kindness.
Every act creates a ripple with no logical end.
Scott Adams

160

Thoughts to Ponder

Hold yourself responsible for a higher standard
than anyone else expects of you. Never excuse yourself.
Henry Ward Beecher

Wherever there is a human being,
we have an opportunity for kindness.
Seneca

Love and compassion are necessities, not luxuries.
Without them, humanity cannot survive.
Dalai Lama

Instead of putting others in their place, put yourself in their place.
Amish Proverb

Our task must be to free ourselves
by widening our circle of compassion to embrace
all living creatures and the whole of nature and its beauty.
Albert Einstein

Let us love one another; for love is of God.
The Apostle John

Spread love everywhere you go.
Let no one ever come to you without leaving happier.
Mother Teresa

If you want to be loved, start loving others who need your love.
If you want others to sympathize with you, start showing
sympathy to those around you. If you want to be respected,
you must learn to be respectful to everyone, both young and
old. Whatever you want others to be, first be that yourself;
then you will find others responding in like manner to you.
Paramahansa Yogananda

Those who are happiest are those who do the most for others.
Booker T. Washington

He who serves the most, reaps the most.
Jim Rohn

161

Thoughts to Ponder

Thousands of candles can be lighted from a single candle,
and the life of the candle will not be shortened.
Happiness never decreases by being shared.
Buddha

When we treat man as he is, we make him worse than he is;
when we treat him as if he already were what he
potentially could be, we make him what he should be.
Johann Wolfgang von Goethe

There is no exercise better for the heart
than reaching down and lifting people up.
John Holmes

Only a life lived for others is a life worthwhile.
Albert Einstein

Selfless giving is the art of living.
Frederic Lenz

Until we have seen someone's darkness, we don't
really know who they are. Until we have forgiven
someone's darkness, we don't really know what love is.
Marianne Williamson

We cannot love ourselves unless we love others, and we cannot
love others unless we love ourselves. But a selfish love
of ourselves makes us incapable of loving others.
Thomas Merton

You cannot do kindness too soon, for you
never know how soon it will be too late.
Ralph Waldo Emerson

Focusing on helping others is a fast and
powerful way to make yourself feel better.
Victoria M. Gallagher

A part of kindness consists in loving people more than they deserve.
Joseph Joubert

162

Chapter 15
Determine to be Happy and Grateful

*Happiness is when what you think, what
you say, and what you do are in harmony.*
Gandhi

You have everything you need to be happy right now at this very moment. Like inner peace, happiness is a choice and comes from within. You don't need anything outside yourself in order to be happy; all you need to do is determine that you will be happy no matter what.

Most people are not happy because they are constantly searching for something outside themselves to *make* them happy. Decide once and for all that your happiness will depend as little as possible on anything outside yourself. You don't need to search for anything to make you happy. When you search for something externally to make you happy, your quest will always lead back to where you started – your own mind and attitude.

Nothing can *make* you happy; you make yourself happy by the thoughts you choose to entertain. You can choose to be happy even in the worst possible situation, if you have cleansed your subconscious mind and learned to control your thoughts. Since happiness comes from within, happiness is always within your grasp.

You have everything you need to be happy at all times. This may sound like a ridiculous statement, but it is true nonetheless. All you need is to use what you already have and determine that you will be happy no matter what. We have everything we need at our fingertips, but most of the time, we do not use it.

Look at your kitchen, for example. You have everything you need to cook and prepare good, nutritious food. We have more options for food than at any time in the history of the world, but most people do not choose to buy healthy foods; they decide to put other foods in their bodies.

It does not matter if you have a variety of nutritious foods to choose from if you regularly choose to eat fast food or junk food. You must choose to buy and prepare nourishing, healthy food in order for it to nourish your body. You have the power to heal your body, cleanse your mind, and change your life, but you have to make the effort to use what is available to you.

Happiness is available to everyone, no matter what their circumstances may be, but the vast majority of people do not choose to be happy. They have a wrong idea about happiness; they think that happiness comes from something external. And no matter how much they search for it, they never seem to find it. This is because nothing external can bring you lasting happiness.

It is like the woman who has misplaced her car keys and searches the entire house for hours looking for them, only to find out that she had them in her pocket the whole time. When you search elsewhere for something that only exists within you, you will never find it. You have to come to the realization that happiness is only found within your own mind and spirit.

Your happiness has resided inside you all along, whether you have been happy, sad, or upset. You may have spent years unsuccessfully searching everywhere for happiness. You may have read dozens of books on the philosophy of life, studied several religions, and tried everything that the world has to offer in your quest for happiness. But until you understand that only you hold the key to your happiness, your search will be in vain.

You may be thinking that it is impossible to be happy when you are broke and barely scraping by in life. You can list all the negative things in your life as proof that you really cannot be happy because you are dealing with too many problems. Those thoughts are simply justifying the fact that you have made the decision, most likely unconsciously, that you can't be happy in your current situation.

Wrong thoughts never produce positive outcomes. If you are focused on all the negative things in your life, of course, you are going to be unhappy. Again, you always get more of whatever you focus on. You must change your thinking.

When you start feeling sorry for yourself and thinking about how you hardly have enough money to pay your bills, you dislike your job, your kids are causing you stress, you don't feel well, etc., change your thoughts. Consider the fact that there are millions of people in this world who would absolutely think they had won the lottery if they lived your life. You are abundantly blessed!

There are people who don't have enough money to feed their family, who do not have a decent home, who live on less each week than you spend on your Starbucks coffee, yet they are happy. That's right, they are happy. They do not have even a fraction of the material things which you have, but they are happy. How could this be?

That is because true happiness does not come from money, material things, or anything else outside yourself; happiness only comes from within. It is a decision that you make; it is an attitude toward life. It is being content with the life that you have and not allowing what you don't have to saturate your thoughts. Instead of focusing on all the negative things in your life or the things that you lack, start focusing on the positive things in your life and be content with what you do have.

Learn to be Content with Your Life

Fortify yourself with contentment,
for this is an impregnable fortress.
Epictetus

True happiness comes from being content with your life. Being content with your life doesn't mean that you are not striving to be better or that you should not work to get the things that you want in life. It simply means that you are happy with who you are and the things that you have in your life at this time, while you are working to improve your situation and achieve the things that you want to achieve.

Even if you have very little in your life, you can still be content and happy. There are people all over the world who have much less than you, who are content and happy with what they have in their life. Contentment simply depends on how you see your life and the world around you. Benjamin Franklin's insight still holds true today – "Contentment makes poor men rich; discontent makes rich men poor."

If you are constantly focused on what you don't have or how much other people do have, it will be extremely hard to be content with the blessings that you actually have in your life. That is because you are allowing thoughts of envy, lack, and unhappiness to bring negativity into your current mindset.

You can be just as happy with very little as you can with an abundance of material things. Our society has become very materialistic, so this truism will be hard for many to understand. Happiness and contentment never come to those who are constantly comparing their lives with the lives of others.

When you are focused on people who have much more than you, it causes you to want what they have and to live a life as they live instead of being grateful and content with your own blessings. And as Bilal Zahoor stated, "Happiness will never come to those who fail to appreciate what they already have."

If you are not grateful for what you already have, you will constantly be focusing on what you lack. And when you focus on what you lack instead of your blessings, you manifest more lack in your life. When you are grateful for all the blessings in your life, you manifest more blessings. Being grateful for everything in your life leads to contentment, and contentment leads to happiness.

Be Grateful for Everything in Your Life

When you arise in the morning, give thanks
for the morning light, for your life and strength.
Give thanks for your food and the joy of living.
If you see no reason for giving thanks,
the fault lies in yourself.
Tecumseh

If you find yourself having a hard time being happy because you are struggling with problems, bills, family issues, or things you lack, stop focusing on those things, and start being grateful for all that you do have in your life. When you start being truly grateful for everything in your life, all the other stuff will seem less important to you.

If you are constantly focused on not having enough money, or all the things you lack, then you are going to find that your deficiencies will continue. But if you start sincerely showing gratitude for everything you do have in your life, you will find that the good things in your life will increase until they overshadow the insufficiencies in your life.

Don't take anything for granted. Many people wrongly believe that they don't have much to be grateful for in their life. That is simply because they have the wrong mindset. When you start listing all the things which you have to be grateful for, you will find that you are truly blessed.

The problem comes from focusing on the wrong things. A friend of mine had a son in high school who was very embarrassed by his home. It wasn't that they did not have a nice house. It was a five-bedroom, two bath home with two levels, but it was an older home, and all of his friends had nicer, more modern houses. Their home was a rental house, and the exterior paint was beige with a tinge of pink to it.

He was embarrassed because his friends called his house pink, and it was not as nice as their homes. He had the wrong mindset and was focused on what he didn't have instead of what he did have. He had his own bedroom, which was the master bedroom with a walk-in closet. His room was very large, and he not only had a nice, full-sized bed, but a desk, a couch, an entertainment center with his own television, Play Station, a computer, and a stereo.

He also had a large backyard with a hot tub, a trampoline, a nice garden, apple trees, and plenty of room to play. But he was unhappy and embarrassed by his home. This was purely because his mindset was wrong.

Instead of being grateful for all the things he had, he was focused on what he lacked. He was comparing his life to the lives of other people, instead of appreciating what he had.

If you want to be happy and content, you should never compare your life with anyone who has more than you. Life is not a competition; it is a blessing. Enjoy the blessings you have. You will always be able to find someone who has more things, newer things, more money, or a perceived easier life than you. Stop comparing yourself to others and simply enjoy your life and everything in it!

A good practice that will help you avoid this pitfall is to start off every day with gratitude. Before you even get out of bed in the morning, as Tecumseh said, give thanks for the blessings in your life. Mentally go through all the blessings in your life – your health, your home, your job, food, water, clothes, your car, and the bed you woke up in, whatever you have in your life.

And, as Tecumseh said, if you see no reason to be grateful, the fault lies in yourself. If you feel that you do not have a multitude of things in your life to be grateful for, you need to do some soul searching and wake up to reality.

If you do find that you need to compare your life with someone else's, don't compare it to all your friends or celebrities who have more than you. Compare your life to the lives of the millions of people in this world who do not have a decent home and who are lucky if they have any food to eat when they wake up in the morning. Compare your life to those who do not have access to clean water, food, shoes, or clothing.

Many people have a warped perspective on life. They have a hard time appreciating what they have because they are focused on what they don't have. Instead of being grateful that they have a car, they gripe that their car is a piece of junk. Instead of being grateful that they have a nice dinner, they gripe because they don't have steak. Gratitude is the cure for their shortsightedness.

When you start recognizing and being thankful for all the blessings in your life, both your perspective and attitude will change. Change your perspective and your attitude, and you will change your life. Your heart will go out to those who have less, and you will find that you want to do more to help them. Gratitude will always change your attitude. The truth is you are extremely blessed, so be grateful and adjust your attitude!

167

Always Maintain a Good Attitude

The problem is not the problem.
The problem is your attitude about the problem.
Captain Jack Sparrow

Your attitude actually contains the power to change your life. When you change your attitude, you simultaneously change your life. As Captain Jack Sparrow stated, "The problem is not the problem. The problem is your attitude about the problem." At first, this seems silly. How can the problem not be the problem?

The answer lies in how you perceive the so-called problem. If you see it more like a challenge, then your attitude towards it will change. When someone says to you, "We have a major problem," if you haven't taken control of your thoughts, your mind automatically starts thinking thoughts of failure, hassles, stress, fear, and even panic.

On the other hand, if instead of calling it a "problem," you say, "We have a major challenge," your thoughts are more focused on getting ready to meet the challenge, finding solutions, fortitude, and refusing to accept defeat. Remember, words matter, and so does your attitude.

No matter what you are facing, maintaining the right attitude will make it better. Always strive to have a good outlook. No matter what is happening around you, accept reality with a positive mindset. The right mindset will change your perspective, and changing your perspective will change your reality.

When asked about his failures, Thomas Edison stated, "I have not failed, not once. I've discovered ten thousand ways that don't work." Now that's a positive attitude! No matter how many times Edison's experiments failed to produce his desired outcome, he never considered any of them to be a failure. Remember, the problem is not the problem. The problem is your attitude about the problem.

Develop this mindset about your happiness and your inner peace. Refuse to allow any challenge, any situation, or any person to rob you of your happiness or your inner peace. If a situation is not what you want it to be, change your perspective. When you change your perspective, your attitude will change as well. And your attitude towards what is happening around you is what determines your happiness.

If you think something is *making* you unhappy, change your perspective, which will change your attitude towards it, and by changing your negative attitude, you positively affect your happiness.

Stop taking everything in your life so seriously; lighten up and determine that you are going to enjoy your life, period. Don't allow anything to stop you from being happy. You have that power; all you have to do is change your perspective on your life.

Imagine that you are in a sailboat, and in front of you are two islands. One island is called Happiness, and the other is called Discontent. Your attitude is the wheel of the sailboat that allows you to guide your boat (your mind) to the island of Happiness. Even if the wind (the trials of life) is trying to blow you to the island of Discontent, you can always use the wheel to guide your boat exactly where you want it to go, in spite of the wind or weather.

You control your sailboat, not the wind. The wind will vary, but a skilled sailor knows how to use the wind to his advantage, no matter which direction it is blowing. If the wind is blowing in the wrong direction, he simply adjusts his sails to get to where he wants to go. He is in charge of where his boat goes, not the wind.

This same principle applies to your attitude. If you live in the present moment, you can always control your attitude at any given time. It is simply a matter of choice and developing the right mindset. One way to control your attitude when you are dealing with a trying situation is to simply find the humor in it – laugh in the face of your challenges. It is virtually impossible to have a bad attitude and laugh at the same time. Laughter will change your attitude almost immediately and has many health benefits as well.

When you laugh, you are actually changing the chemistry of your body. Science has proven that laughter produces endorphins which produce feelings of euphoria, well-being, and happiness. These endorphins are a natural way to relieve pain and have the ability to relieve stress, relax muscles, and increase the power of your immune system.

As Jimmy Buffett wrote in one of his songs, "If you want to be happy, be a comedian." Stop taking life so seriously and be grateful for all of your blessings. Be thankful for them each and every day. Stay focused on the positive things in your life. If you have had a negative attitude, change it. Focus on all the good things in your life, and stop concentrating on the negative side of things. Start seeing your life from a new perspective. Lighten up and start truly enjoying your life!

You must understand that inner peace and the contentment which comes from inner peace are the real sources of happiness. The flowers of inner peace and happiness grow in the same garden – your mind. You are in complete control of what you grow in your garden. If you want happiness and inner peace, then plant seeds of happiness and inner peace, water them, keep them weeded, and cultivate them in your life. The choice is yours.

Remember, change your perspective to change your attitude; change your attitude to change your life. Determine that you are going to be happy no matter what. Stop comparing yourself to those who have more than you. If you simply must compare your life to others, compare it to those who have much less than you. Be grateful, be happy, be content, and start living your life your way.

There is no happiness so great as peace of mind.
Cicero

Thoughts to Ponder

To live happily is an inward power of the soul.
Marcus Aurelius

Happiness depends upon ourselves.
Aristotle

Happiness has nothing to do with wealth
and prestige, but is a result of harmony.
Lao Tzu

To be happy, we must not be too concerned with others.
Albert Camus

We don't see things as they are, we see them as we are.
Anais Nin

A joyful outlook helps peace to unfold.
Sri Satya Sai Baba

When you drink of the spring, be thankful for the source.
Chinese Proverb

Saying thank you is more than good manners. It is good spirituality.
Alfred Painter

He is a wise man who does not grieve for the things
which he has not, but rejoices for those which he has.
Epictetus

There is a calmness to a life lived in gratitude, a quiet joy.
Ralph H. Blum

It is our attitude at the beginning of a difficult task which,
more than anything else, will affect its successful outcome.
William James

When you are distressed by an external thing, it's not the
thing itself that troubles you, but only your judgment of it.
And you can wipe this out at a moment's notice.
Marcus Aurelius

Thoughts to Ponder

There is only one way to happiness, and that is to cease
worrying about things which are beyond the power of our will.
Epictetus

I have learned, in whatsoever state I am, therewith to be content.
The Apostle Paul

Contentment consist not in adding more fuel,
but in taking away some fire.
Thomas Fuller

Reject your sense of injury and the injury itself disappears.
Marcus Aurelius

The man who makes everything that leads to happiness
depend upon himself, and not upon other men,
has adopted the very best plan for living happily.
Plato

The essence of philosophy is that a man should so live that his
happiness shall depend as little as possible on external things.
Epictetus

Very little is needed to make a happy life.
It is all in your way of thinking.
Marcus Aurelius

The sage is happy everywhere, the whole earth is his.
Nowhere and in no situation is the sage
dissatisfied with his condition.
Confucius

Happiness is not a station you arrive at, but a manner of traveling.
Margaret Lee Runbeck

The greatest happiness is tranquility of mind.
Sakya Pandit

Gratitude is the sign of noble souls.
Aesop

Chapter 16
Live Your Life Your Way

There is only one success –
to be able to spend your life in your own way.
Christopher Morley

If you are going to live a life filled with inner peace and tranquility, you are going to be walking a different path than the vast majority of people in our society. Many will not understand why you excuse yourself when the conversation turns negative or starts focusing on gossip. Some may think that you are too timid to stand up for yourself when you walk away from some rude guy instead of reacting to his ill-mannered words or behavior.

Living differently than the majority of people in your life takes great strength and determination. If you want to live life your way, you must develop a strong sense of self-confidence and self-esteem. You must truly be dedicated to living a life of inner peace in order to stand up to those who will do everything to get you to continue to live the same life you have been living.

You must decide who you want to be and how you want to live your life, and then have enough confidence in yourself to not care what anyone else thinks or says about it. Become comfortable being unique, responding differently, and thinking differently from most people. Decide who and what you want to be, then work backward to figure out what you must do to achieve that objective. In this case, most of that work is laid out for you in this book.

Be courageous enough to be yourself in a world which will try to persuade you to be like everyone else. Don't be concerned with what others think about how you live your life; don't be concerned with societal norms or how the vast majority of people live. Remind yourself that most people do not live a life filled with inner peace and tranquility. If you want to have something in your life that most people don't have, then you are going to have to choose to do things that most people prefer not to do.

Living your life your way means being self-reliant – physically, spiritually, and mentally. You must understand that you are living your life your way because you are working towards a unique goal – inner peace and tranquility. Live your life by your own personal code of ethics, not other people's rules or norms. Refuse to do anything simply because everyone else is doing it. Always stay true to yourself, your personal ethics, and maintain your inner peace.

You are unique, and nobody can live your life better than you. Likewise, nobody is in a position to tell you what is best for you and how you should live your life. If you allow others to persuade you to be anyone besides your true, authentic self, it will cause you regrets and disrupt your journey to inner peace. You will live with an internal conflict between yourself and your true life objectives.

Be mentally faithful to yourself and your goal of living a life of inner peace. Don't allow other people to get inside your head or make you doubt the decisions which you have made concerning how you will live your life. In the long run, being mentally faithful to yourself and living the life that you choose will bring peace to both your mind and your spirit.

If you allow other people to pressure you into lowering your standards or living a life other than your own, both your mind and spirit will feel as if something is just not right. Until you get back on your path, you will feel like something is off, even if you can't figure out exactly what it is. Conforming to others' desires will eat away at your soul until you no longer feel like yourself and are confused about who you really are.

Don't try to imitate others; be a first-rate version of yourself. Be kind, compassionate, and giving, but don't live to please everyone else. Find your own purpose in life; find your own path and follow it to the end. This is your journey, your adventure, don't allow others to dictate which path you must take.

While you should help others, be kind, compassionate, understanding, and forgiving, that doesn't mean that you have to lose yourself in the process. All of those aspects are a part of living the kind of life which you have chosen, but you also need boundaries. When it comes down to a choice between making others happy by conforming to their wishes or staying on your path, you have to put yourself first.

You will find that when people are unhappy with their own life, they like to have others around them who are just as blasé as they are. Their life is not going to change until they make a personal decision to change it, just like you have. Lowering your standards and disrupting your inner peace to make them happy is not truly helping them or you. If you want to help someone who is struggling in life, let them see your inner peace and happiness, and then show them how to improve their own life instead of joining them on their level.

Instead of lowering your standards, help them raise their standards, but you should not try to force your lifestyle on them any more than they should try to force theirs on you. When they see how happy and content you are, they will want the inner peace that you have. When they come to you and ask, "How are you always so happy, tranquil, and content? Nothing ever seems to bother you." That is when it is time for you to share how you live and how you have found inner peace and serenity.

Unsolicited advice rarely makes a difference in anyone's life. When they are ready for your help they will ask for it. If you are living a life that they admire, sooner or later, they will ask you for your secret. That is when they are ready for help, and possibly ready to change their life.

Many times, other people truly believe that they are helping you when they suggest that you should change the way you are living. But they do not know who you truly are, what is in your heart, or what your ultimate objective is. Be yourself, not who the world wants you to be. As I stated earlier, don't let the opinions of others dictate your actions or how you live your life. Remember what Shakespeare wrote, "This above all, to thine own self be true."

Live your life your way! You are a unique individual. Do not lose your individuality by living a life that is not authentically your own or in some misguided attempt to be like someone else. While it is completely acceptable to admire certain qualities in another person, you should not try to imitate that person. If someone has specific qualities that you admire, integrate them into your own life and make them uniquely your own.

The Japanese people are known for taking different things from other countries and then making them uniquely their own. They don't try to copy another country and be exactly like it, but rather, they take what they like, integrate it into their culture, and make it distinctively Japanese. You should do the same thing whenever you see a quality that you really admire in someone else. This is very helpful on your journey to inner peace.

The principles and ideas in this book are not set in stone. You must customize them to work for you and your personality. Introverts and extroverts may handle the same type of trying situations in a totally different way. When you see someone handling a bad situation in a way that you admire, learn from it, take what you liked about their response, and make it uniquely your own. Develop your own personal strategies, responses, and approaches to dealing with negative situations or difficult people.

For example, if you like the way that John Wayne's characters speak and handle themselves in his movies, integrate his slow, thoughtful tone and his self-confidence into your own personality. But do not try to be John Wayne. When you try to be or act like someone else, you appear awkward and unauthentic. On the other hand, when you take a trait or quality from someone you admire, and make it your own, it becomes a part of you.

Think of your favorite soup. It probably has many different ingredients, such as thyme, rosemary, salt, pepper, and other herbs. Each ingredient has a unique smell, texture, flavor, and purpose. But when you take that ingredient and add it to your soup, a transformation occurs. You can no longer separate all the herbs, the salt, or the pepper; they have simply become the soup. They are no longer separate ingredients but have combined to form something totally unique.

The same principle applies when you take a quality that you admire from someone else and make it your own. It becomes a part of who you are. And that is what you should do. Take the qualities that you admire in others, from wisdom literature, or wherever you find them, integrate them into your life, and make them a part of you. All of those qualities, along with those which are already exclusively yours, make you who you truly are. The combination makes you uniquely you.

You may be thinking that in doing so, you are trying to be someone that you are not, but that is not the case. If you are trying to change your true nature to be more like someone else, that is trying to be someone you aren't. You are not trying to change your true nature; you are improving who you are and becoming someone completely unique – you are becoming the true you!

What you are doing by integrating the good qualities and character traits you see in others, and positive character traits from the teachings of the sages, is becoming the person you are meant to be. You are purposely creating yourself. You are not losing yourself; you are becoming who you are meant to be. If those traits weren't meant to be a part of who you are, you would not be so attracted to them; they would not excite your spirit, and you would have no desire to integrate them into your life.

Understand that it is okay to live a life that others do not understand. You were not put on this earth to impress other people or to be liked by everyone; you were put on this earth for a specific, unique purpose that only you can fulfill. Don't sell yourself short! Self-improvement is not the same thing as trying to be something that you are not; it is taking who and what you are and making yourself the best that you can be.

Don't let others or your past define you; *you define who you truly are*. If you see a quality or trait that you admire, and it stirs your heart, then don't hesitate to integrate it into your life. Decide who you want to be, develop the qualities that you want to assimilate into your life, and then live your life your way. Then you are ready to figure out your purpose in life.

Dharma – Your Purpose in Life

Your purpose in life is to find your purpose
and give your whole heart and soul to it.
Buddha

Dharma is a Sanskrit word that refers to one's duty in life. According to the theory of dharma, it is believed that everyone has a specific duty in life that they were born to perform or achieve. Once you know your purpose and you decide to live for that purpose, you will feel at peace. Basically, this means that you should discover what it is that you were meant to do in life and do it.

Everyone has talents which are soley his or her own, something that they do better or different than anyone else. Finding what that talent or purpose is will lead you to deeper inner peace.

It is harder to maintain your inner peace when you are working at a job that you completely dislike. If you come home every day drained from your work, your head pounding from being in a stressful environment all day long, and feeling like there has to be something more to life, you are not living your dharma; you are simply trading your time for money.

Robert Byrne wrote, "The purpose of life is a life of purpose." Just working to make money, dreaming about the weekend so you can get away from that job for a couple of days, and dreading every Monday, is not living a life of purpose. When you are living a life of purpose, you are excited to get up and start a new day. Fridays and Mondays are not a big deal because you enjoy every day of your life to the fullest.

When you get to that point in your life, you know that you are on the right track and doing what you are meant to do. Those who simply go through their week to get to the weekend have little meaning in their life. Victor Frankl stated, "When a person can't find a deep sense of meaning, they distract themselves with pleasure." This perfectly describes people who spend their lives working jobs they dislike. That is no way to live life and is not conducive to living a life of inner peace and tranquility.

Find out what it is that comes naturally to you, what you love and enjoy. Then develop those talents and find a way to make a living doing what you love. You may have to supplement your income while you are working towards making a living at what you love, but

177

in doing so, you will be working for a totally different reason. Your attitude will be very different. You will not feel trapped in a job you dislike, but you will feel excited that you are moving towards your goal, your purpose in life.

Discover the path that captures your heart and follow it to the end. That is what you are on this earth to do. Find what excites your spirit and feels right to you. And once you discover it, don't allow anyone to talk you out of living it. Likewise, don't allow temporary defeats or hardships to sidetrack you or cause you to doubt yourself.

Defeat and Failure are just an Opinion

Defeat is a state of mind; no one is ever defeated
until defeat has been accepted as a reality.
Bruce Lee

Never allow temporary defeats, thoughts of failure, or hardships to cause you to turn away from your purpose in life. Defeat and failure are nothing more than opinions. The truth is that you are never defeated until you give up and declare defeat. Failures are nothing more than the dues you have to pay to get where you want to be in life. They can only stop you when you decide to give them the power to do so. If you don't quit, you can never be defeated!

How can you be defeated if the game is not over yet? Until you throw in the towel and declare defeat, the game is still being played. Consider a football game. It is played in four quarters. I have seen teams that have played awful during the first half of the game and were behind by more than five touchdowns by halftime, but that did not mean they were defeated because the game was not over. I have also seen a lot of those teams come back and win the game in the fourth quarter because they refused to give up and declare defeat.

This same principle applies to your goal of living a life of purpose and inner peace. You may have had some rough times, and you may have even felt defeated along the way, but the game is not over yet. As long as you are still working toward living your purpose in life, there is still time on the clock. The game is not over until you decide it is over, and you are not defeated, no matter what has happened in the past until you declare defeat. So don't quit! Just keep playing the game and doing your best each and every day.

Your duty is to do your best, not to worry about the outcome. Don't focus on being the best; focus on being the best that you can be. When you live according to your purpose in life, the outcome will be that you are at peace with your life. That peace will not be affected by whether or not you are achieving a specific outcome, as you know you are doing what you are meant to do.

Anytime you start to have thoughts of defeat or failure, go back to the chapters on your thoughts and subconscious mind and change those thoughts. When you learn from your temporary defeats, you turn them into knowledge and then can use them to your advantage. Refuse to declare defeat when you know you are doing what you are meant to do! Let your mantra be, "I never lose; I either win, or I learn." As Jeffrey Fry put it, "Failure, loss, and defeat are just mile markers on the road to success."

If you are doing what you know in your heart that you are meant to do, and you are living your life your way, the only way you can possibly fail is if you quit and walk away. That would be the ultimate failure in life.

Giving up living life on your own terms, and conforming to what the world tells you that you have to be, is giving up on yourself. It will be extremely hard for you to find your inner peace when you know in your spirit that you have thrown in the towel and allowed the trials of life to defeat you.

Never let yourself get to that point. If you discover that you were wrong about your purpose in life, or if your purpose changes, as it might for one reason or another, that is one thing. But giving up on living the kind of life that you want to live will never bring you inner peace and tranquility. You will always have a nagging feeling that you sold out and gave up on yourself.

This sometimes happens when you are struggling to be successful at your passion, and you see others living in nicer houses, driving nicer cars, going to nice, expensive restaurants, etc. You can start to doubt if living your passion is really worth it. Those thoughts come from comparing your life to other people's lives. Control your mind and don't allow yourself to compare your life with anyone else's.

Don't Compare or Compete

Egotism causes a lack of inner peace.
Sri Satya Sai Baba

Most of the people that you are comparing yourself to are not what they seem to be. People tend to compare themselves on their worst days to other people on their best days. This is especially true if you are comparing yourself to some celebrity. The celebrities that you are comparing yourself to have spent hours having their make-up done, their hair perfectly styled, their clothes custom-fitted just for them. That is not real life. Their photos have been airbrushed and doctored. Their speech has been scripted and rehearsed. What you see is a carefully constructed illusion to impress you. It is silly to compare yourself to a fantasy! Just practice self-acceptance and be content with being real; be the unique, special person that you are meant to be.

And don't compare yourself to your neighbors or family who may be making more money and appear to have nicer things. Your goal is to live a life of inner peace and live your life your way, not to keep up with the Joneses.

Comparing yourself with how others look, their lifestyle, their income, or the things they have, is a form of envy when you get right down to it. Remember, jealousy is one of the negative, low-energy thoughts which you are trying to remove from your life. Comparing yourself with others or trying to compete with them in order to look good opens the door to negative thoughts and will absolutely disrupt your inner peace.

When you compare your life with someone's life, it ultimately leads to thoughts of jealousy, envy, frustration, resentment, and doubts about how you live your life. It never leads to thoughts of love, compassion, happiness, or contentment.

When you are competing with others or scheming about how to be better than someone else, your ego is in charge. And when your ego is in charge of your life, it will overshadow your inner peace. No matter how successful you become or how good-looking you may be, you can always find someone who has more money, a bigger house, more toys, is better looking, etc. Comparing yourself to others only leads to negative thinking and unhappiness.

Live your life your way and be content with the outcome. Don't allow other people's opinions or lifestyles to cause you to doubt your purpose in life. Remember, a unique, one-of-a-kind item is always worth more than some cheap imitation or mass-produced replica.

Instead of using other people as a template to evaluate yourself or your accomplishments, judge yourself by your own happiness and inner peace. Comparing yourself to others disavows your own uniqueness that makes you special. Love and accept yourself just as you are. Live your life your way and follow your passion.

Inner peace doesn't come from getting what we want,
but from remembering who we are.
Marianne Williamson

Thoughts to Ponder

Do not wish to be anything but what you are,
and try to be that perfectly.
Saint Francis De Sales

In our short time here, we should listen to our own voices and
follow our own hearts. Why not be free and live your own life?
Why follow other people's rules and live to please others?
Why not let your life be guided by your own heart?
Lieh Tzu

The wise are not bound by the norms of society.
Those who are caught up in cultural customs are inevitably
constrained physically and drained mentally. This is the
price of allowing themselves to be directed from the outside.
Lao Tzu

It is necessary to the happiness of man
that he be mentally faithful to himself.
Thomas Paine

There is just one life for each of us: our own.
Euripides

The minute you start caring about what other people think,
is the minute you stop being yourself.
Meryl Streep

The person without a purpose is like a ship without a rudder.
Thomas Carlyle

Failure is an attitude, not an outcome.
Harvey Mackay

Nothing will kill what you've been called to do
more than comparing yourself to someone else.
Beth Moore

Follow your bliss and the universe will
open doors where there were only walls.
Joseph Campbell

Thoughts to Ponder

Don't ask yourself what the world needs;
ask yourself what makes you come alive.
And then go and do that. Because what the
world needs is people who have come alive.
Howard Thurman

The wise are not bound by the norms of society.
Confucius

As long as we make the best effort we are capable of,
we cannot feel discouraged by our failures.
Mother Teresa

Don't live to please others. Don't think everyone else
knows what's right or true. Listen to yourself, and
be true to yourself. That way, no matter what else
happens in life, you will always have your self-respect.
Jane Porter

Listen to yourself, not the noise of the world.
Only you know what is right for you.
Leon Brown

It is better to fail in originality than to succeed in imitation.
Herman Melville

Always be a first-rate version of yourself,
instead of a second-rate version of somebody else.
Judy Garland

Can you remember who you were, before
the world told you who you should be?
Charles Bukowski

First keep the peace within yourself,
then you can also bring peace to others.
Thomas a'Kempis

Make the most out of what you have now.
Victoria M. Gallagher

Chapter 17
Live in the NOW

You must concentrate upon and consecrate yourself wholly
to each day, as though a fire were raging in your hair.
Deshimaru

I want to encourage you not to procrastinate in your journey to finding inner peace. As humans, we have a habit of wanting to wait until the perfect time to start a new project, work out, or make changes in our lives. That is why so many people make New Year's resolutions. They could just as easily decide to change their habits immediately instead of waiting for January 1, but they put things off until the New Year as if that is a magical day that will make them more motivated. It isn't. That is just a form of procrastination. It shows a lack of motivation to actually make changes in their life now.

Life is much shorter than you realize. Even what we consider to be a long life goes by so fast that you will hardly believe it. And the older you get, the faster time seems to fly by. You do not have any time to waste, NONE, not one minute! You have no idea how much time you have left on this earth. The time to start living a life of inner peace is NOW!

The only time you have to make changes in your life is NOW, in this present moment. The past is gone, and the future only exists in your mind; NOW is the time to live your life and to make all the changes that you know you need to make. You only have this present moment, or what I like to call the NOW.

Refuse to waste one more minute of your life regretting things that happened in the past or fantasizing about the future. Focus your attention on the NOW. Worrying about tomorrow or regretting the past causes mental stress, sadness, anger, regret, worry, fear, and other negative, low-energy thoughts.

Most people don't fully enjoy the NOW because their mind is somewhere else. They are rarely fully present. To get the most out of your life, you must be fully aware and present in the NOW. Being fully present in the NOW means that you are continually mindful of your thoughts, words, actions, and responses. You must treasure the present moment because the present moment is all you truly have.

Commit yourself to live each moment of your life fully in the way that you want to live, being mindful to foster and maintain your inner peace. Weigh every choice on whether or not it is consistent with your goal of living in inner peace and tranquility.

183

Live every minute of your life to the fullest. Don't allow yourself to get bogged down with the challenges of life; don't allow yourself to get stressed out by overthinking your options. Use what is right and what nurtures your inner peace as a gauge in making each decision of your life.

We all have visions of what we are going to do and how we are going to live "someday," but for most people, "someday" never arrives. If you have something you want to change in your life, change it NOW. If you have something you really want to do in life, do it NOW. NOW is the time to be who you want to be and live the life that you want to live. Live in the NOW is the mantra for the wise!

Make the choices that you have been putting off your main priority. No more putting things out of your mind until another day; today is the time to put your life in order. We all put things out of our minds from time to time because we simply do not want to deal with those decisions, choices, or actions right now.

Things that we don't want to do tend to build up in our life because we never get to the point that we actually want to deal with them. In fact, most people never address those things until life finds a way to force them to do so. As these things build up, they stay in the back of your mind and can rob you of your inner peace. Stop procrastinating and get your life in order NOW. It has been proven that a cluttered desk or lifestyle adds stress to your life; just think how much stress a cluttered mind will add to your spirit. Free your mind and spirit, and stop procrastinating!

Many people have no purpose, meaning, or direction for their life. Living this way requires little thought or effort, which is why so many choose to live life without a purpose or direction. But living your life in that manner can also be very dull, depressing and will stifle your motivation, creativity, and inner peace. Deep inside, you know something is missing, and you know that there has to be something more to life.

When you start living life your way, you begin to find purpose and meaning in your life; you have a direction that you want your life to go. And when you live your life your way with inner peace and tranquility, you will love life and look forward to each new day with gratitude, excitement, and wonder.

Be who you want to be and do what you want to do, as long as it is in line with your standards and it moves you closer to the inner peace you are seeking. Keep your thoughts in the present moment and focused on your goals. Your life is created by how you live each NOW. Your thoughts in each instant lead to your choices, and your choices move you closer or further away from your destiny.

184

Live your life NOW. Don't get so focused on your goal and what you are becoming that you forget to enjoy where you are at this very moment. Appreciate and be thankful for every minute of your life, as that minute will be gone in sixty seconds. Every minute you waste is one that can never be recovered; it is lost forever. Remember that count-down clock that I mentioned earlier; it is a great reminder of this fact.

Once you have made a firm decision to live your life your way, with purpose and inner peace, reject anything which is inconsistent with who you have decided to be and how you have decided to live your life. Don't seize the day – seize the present moment! Everything you do is a choice, and each choice either moves you closer or further away from inner peace.

You don't *have to* do anything; you choose your behavior. Make every choice in your life consciously and bring it in line with who and what you have decided to be. The average person lives unaware. He allows most moments to pass unappreciated and unrecognized as if he is going through life on auto-pilot. Living life in this way is living life as if it doesn't really matter. It is simply allowing it to happen instead of using your thoughts and actions to create the kind of life that you want to live.

Don't focus on what has happened or what may happen; focus on what *is* happening at this very moment. Live each NOW as if it truly matters because, in the grand scheme of things, it does. Each moment is special, unique, and fleeting; treasure it because it will never come around again. Live each moment with purpose, enthusiasm, conviction, and direction.

To some, this may sound exhausting. After all, how can someone live every single second of his life in this way? This is wrong thinking. Once you develop your inner peace, you will find that you are grateful for your blessings in each and every moment. Living your life with awareness and purpose is the opposite of exhausting; it is energizing and invigorating. You will be happy, and you will have the desire to accept everything in your life with peace and tranquility.

Living a life of inner peace is an art, hence the title of this book. And, as with every art, it will take time to master it. It will take time to change your habits and start to appreciate every moment of your life. Most of us are accustomed to going through our lives with the same habitual thoughts, attitudes, and behaviors that we have always had.

We go through each moment without giving it much thought. And before you know it, another year has gone by in much the same way as the previous year and the year before that. In what seems like a

185

blink of an eye, decades have passed by, and you sit and wonder where your life went and how it could have possibly gone by so fast. Don't let this happen to you!

Take the time to examine your life and bring it in line with your desires, goals, and dreams. If you are not living the kind of life that you want to live, it is because of the choices you are making. Change your choices, and you will change your life. And the great thing about this is that you can start changing your choices right now, this very moment. Refuse to be ordinary; be extraordinary!

Examine your life and make whatever changes are necessary to put yourself on your ultimate path. The time to take control of your mind, your life, and your inner peace is NOW. If you want more out of life, make the choices that give you more. If you want more inner peace in your life, start making the necessary choices that will move you towards more inner peace.

Be fully awake and alive. Take control over your thoughts and be mindful of every minute of your life. Live each moment in a manner that is consistent with maintaining your inner peace, tranquility, and the life you have decided to live. Be honest with yourself and others about what you truly want and start living your life your way.

Develop Self-Discipline

The man of principle does not forget
who he is because of what others are.
Baltasar Gracian

Self-discipline provides you with the determination to continue on the right path and to live in the NOW. If you don't have the self-discipline to put the principles in this book into action, they will do you no good at all. Every single thing I have discussed requires self-discipline on your part; without it, you are merely spinning your wheels and going nowhere.

It takes self-discipline to bring your thoughts under control, to be careful with your speech, and to remain calm when others are panicking. It takes self-discipline to train your mind to constantly live in the NOW. Self-discipline is vital to your inner peace and to living life your way.

You may believe everything I have written in this book, but unless you have the self-discipline to put it all into action, it will not change your life. If you are struggling to integrate these principles into your life, ask yourself if you really believe in them, or are you simply agreeing with them because you can see their value?

186

There is a saying that you are what you do, not what you believe. While it is good to believe in the power of your thoughts and words and in living by a personal code of ethics, your belief in these things will not change your life until you transform those beliefs into the necessary actions to bring about changes in your life. Being mindful and living in the NOW keep you focused on the life you want.

You may love martial arts. You may love going to the tournaments, watching martial arts on television, reading about martial arts, thinking about martial arts, but you are not a martial artist if you are not actually *practicing* martial arts. Learning about gardening, knowing everything about the different plants, soils, nutrients, and weeding is great, but until you get out in the dirt and actually garden, you are not a gardener.

Inner peace requires action, not simply agreeing with the principles, reading about the principles, or desiring to live a calm, peaceful life. As I said before, it takes work; it is not easy or automatic. It is easy to read the principles and agree with the information, but it takes a lot more effort to actually live them. And that is where self-discipline comes into play.

Even after you have done the work on your subconscious mind and your life is going the way that you want, there will always be temptations to lower your standards, to allow anger to cloud your mind, or to entertain low-energy thoughts, all of which will disrupt your inner peace.

The vast majority of the time, it will be other people who will offer you the opportunity to trade your inner peace for temporary turmoil. Others may be rude or confrontational, but that doesn't mean you have to take the bait. Always keep Baltasar Gracian's teaching fresh in your mind, "The man of principle does not forget who he is because of what others are."

Developing self-discipline allows you to respond instead of reacting to the world around you. Reacting is natural, and it is the path that most people take. Your objective is not to be like most people but to maintain your inner peace in spite of what everyone else does.

Many people say that they want to change their life, but few actually do. That is because, even though people say they want to change, they don't really mean it. What they mean is that they want to continue to live as they are living, but they want the same results as people who live a disciplined life. It doesn't work that way. If they really wanted to change their life, they would buckle down and do it. But that takes self-discipline, and they prefer to take the easy road instead.

The best things in life come from disciplining yourself to live the kind of life that you choose. It takes very little effort to form bad habits, but a strong self-discipline and determination to break those habits and replace them with habits that will better serve you. Once you develop self-discipline, you can cultivate good habits which allow you to consistently live in the NOW and to live a life of inner peace.

I want to add one final thought on living in the NOW. You are going to live in the NOW one way or the other; you have no choice about that. NOW is the only time that anyone can live in. The present moment is the only time that truly exists. The only question is whether you are going to be fully mindful in this present moment or simply continue to go through the motions as if you are on autopilot, only to later wonder where the time went. Choose wisely!

The secret of health for both mind and body is to
live in the present moment wisely and earnestly.
Buddha

Thoughts to Ponder

One of the illusions of life is that the present hour is not the critical
decisive hour. Write it on your heart that every day is the best day
of the year. He only is right who owns the day, and no one owns
the day who allows it to be invaded by worry, fret and anxiety.
Finish every day, and be done with it. You have done what you could.
Ralph Waldo Emerson

Do not dwell in the past,
do not dream of the future,
concentrate the mind on the present moment.
Buddha

The Tao is not far away from where you are.
Those who go looking for it elsewhere always return to here and now.
Lao Tzu

This is not a dress rehearsal. This is it.
Tom Cunningham

Now is the watchword of the wise.
Charles H. Spurgeon

Every moment of life is the last.
Basho

Each of us lives only now, this brief instant.
Marcus Aurelius

Live now, believe me, wait not till tomorrow;
gather the roses of life today.
Pierre de Ronsard

No man is free who is not master of himself.
Epictetus

Delay not to seize the hour.
Aeschylus

Those who lack self-control live disoriented and disturbed lives.
Seneca

Thoughts to Ponder

The superior man is watchful
over himself even when alone.
Chung Yung

Self-control brings calm to the mind,
without it the seed of all the virtues perishes.
Fo-shu-hing-tsan-king

The superior man does not give up good conduct
because the inferior man rails against him.
Hsun-Tzu

A really self-restrained person grows every day from strength
to strength and from peace to more peace. The very first
step in self-restraint is the restraint of thoughts.
Gandhi

If you are depressed you are living in the past,
if you are anxious you are living in the future,
if you are at peace, you are living in the present.
Lao Tzu

Our attention is apt to be so fixed upon tomorrow or next week
that we forget to relish this day. People are always going to
be happy a little later on when they have done something
else first…enjoy each hour of the day as it passes.
Emmet Fox

While walking, examine the walking; while sitting, the sitting.
Zen Proverb

Many people are constantly subjecting their minds
to totally unnecessary wear and tear. They rehearse
past troubles mentally, and often they even rehearse
trouble that they think is likely to happen tomorrow.
Emmet Fox

Be happy in the moment, that's enough.
Each moment is all we need, not more.
Mother Teresa

Chapter 18
The 12 Laws of Karma and Inner Peace

The principles outlined in the *12 Laws of Karma* are very helpful in tying everything together to help you live a life of inner peace. These ancient principles have been used for thousands of years and are harmonious with teachings ranging from common-sense philosophy to New Age philosophy and everything in between. These laws pre-date all religions with the possible exception of Hinduism and are compatible with all religious teachings.

I have integrated the *12 Laws of Karma* with the principles of inner peace to help you better understand how the principles work and to drive home why you need to apply these principles in your life. These principles not only apply to developing and maintaining your inner peace but to all aspects of your life. I promise you, if you apply these principles to your life and integrate them with the principles of inner peace, you will see results.

Law #1
The Great Law

This is the law of cause and effect. The law of cause and effect simply means that everything you think, say, or do has an effect or consequence. As I discussed in the first chapters of this book, your thoughts and beliefs have been programming your subconscious mind since your birth. The thoughts and beliefs which have been deeply embedded in your subconscious mind continually guide your thoughts, words, and actions.

Every thought, word, and action has an effect on your subconscious mind, as well as consequences in other parts of your life. The effects that they have on your life depend on their content. Good, loving, positive, peaceful thoughts and words have positive effects on your life and your inner peace; whereas negative, low-energy thoughts and words will have a negative effect on your inner peace and life in general.

Remember, like attracts like. In order to achieve the inner peace which you desire, you must ensure that your thoughts, words, and actions are in line with living a life of inner peace and harmony. Whatever thoughts or energy you send out into the world come back into your life in one way or another. If you want to consistently live a life of inner peace, you have to embody that inner peace.

Jesus put it simply when he said, "You reap what you sow." That is the Great Law. Jesus used the example of growing seeds. If you plant a lot of seeds in your garden, you will get a much larger harvest than if you only plant a few seeds. If you want an abundant harvest in your life, then be very generous with the seeds that you plant.

The key to inner peace is planting the right kind of seeds to get the harvest that you want. If you want an abundance of inner peace and tranquility, then you must plant an abundance of those seeds in your life and the lives of those around you. Don't just develop inner peace in your life and keep it to yourself; share your inner peace and tranquility everywhere you go. Be generous in planting the seeds of inner peace and tranquility in the lives of everyone you meet.

The more you think and focus on thoughts of peace, tranquility, and a sense of inner calm, the more those qualities will appear in your life. You attract the things you focus on into your life, so start focusing your thoughts on peace and tranquility. Start speaking words of peace. Use your calm demeanor to bring a sense of peacefulness to those around you.

Every action carries with it a consequence of one kind or another. Everything that happens in your life is the consequence of some action. The Great Law teaches us that nothing in our world happens on its own – something causes it to happen. This is true even when you cannot figure out what caused it. Just know that somewhere down the line, something caused what you now have in your life.

Constantly remind yourself that whatever you send out into the universe has consequences and will affect your life in one way or another. Start becoming more mindful about everything you say, do, or think – everything matters; even the smallest actions. Sow seeds of peace, and you will harvest more peace in your life. Make the Great Law of the Universe work in your favor instead of against you!

Law #2
The Law of Creation

The Law of Creation basically means that you must actually take action to get what you want in life. Sitting around and wishing that you could live a life of inner peace will get you nothing. If you really want inner peace in your life, you have to take action to develop and maintain it.

Your environment and everything in it is influenced by your actions or your lack of action. Nobody is going to magically appear in your life, fix everything that is wrong, and grant you inner peace; you have to do that for yourself. If something is not right in your life, you

192

need to take action to change it. Don't look for a savior, a guru, or some self-help expert to change your life for you. Be your own liberator and take charge of your own life.

If something in your life needs to be changed, take action, and change it. The events in your life don't just randomly happen; you make them happen through your thoughts, words, and actions. If you have an abundance of chaos, stress, and challenges in your life, that is a sign that you need to make some internal changes to create the kind of life that you want for yourself.

I have given you many principles which can change your life, but they are worthless to you unless you actually take action and use those principles and exercises to make positive changes in your life. As the Dhammapada teaches, "It is you who must make the effort; the sages can only teach."

If you want inner peace in your life, then make it happen. Besides this book, there are many great teachings that can help you live a life of inner peace, but you must use what you read and learn and put it into action in order for it to truly matter. You have the power to create the life that you want, but you must actually develop that power before it will benefit you.

Law #3
The Law of Humility

This law has to do with your ego. You must accept that you have made mistakes in the past that are affecting your life today. Don't think so highly of yourself that you disregard your weaknesses or refuse to own your mistakes. We all have our strong points and our weak points, and we all make blunders in life. Be humble enough to recognize your mistakes.

If you refuse to acknowledge your mistakes or deny that they have affected your life, you will not be able to correct those mistakes and change the impact that they have had on you. If you deny that you have negative thoughts and beliefs implanted in your subconscious mind, then why would you ever want to do the work to cleanse your subconscious mind and replace those limiting beliefs that are holding you back?

You must be humble and accept the fact that your current environment and the things which you are now experiencing are the results of your past thoughts, beliefs, words, and actions. In order to change anything in your life, you must first acknowledge it, and then do what needs to be done to change it. If you refuse to acknowledge that your garden has weeds, why would you take action to remove

193

them? Recognizing the need to make changes in your life is the first step towards making those changes.

If you want to live a life of inner peace, you must first acknowledge that there are some things that are negatively affecting your life. Then use the principles in this book to negate the effects of those mistakes or limiting beliefs, and replace them with thoughts and beliefs which will develop your inner peace.

Many people allow pride to stop them from making life changes. If you are too proud to acknowledge your mistakes, limiting beliefs, or negative programming, you will never take action to change those things. And you will continue to get the same results that you have been getting. Humble yourself, admit that you need to make some changes in your life, and then take action to develop your inner peace.

Law #4
The Law of Growth

This law concerns personal growth, which is necessary to develop inner peace. Every change in your life begins with you. When you start making changes within yourself, then the things around you change as well. Remember, there are things that you can control and things that you can't control. There are things you can change, and there are things that you must accept.

You only have control over yourself – your thoughts, your words, and your actions. The way you handle the things in life which you can control, as well as the way you respond to the things in life that you can't control, determine your inner peace.

Personal growth always starts from within. Start by cleansing your subconscious mind and controlling your thoughts. Once you have made those changes, then it becomes easier to control your words and actions. Be consistent in controlling the things which you can control, and you will see changes in your life and a lot of personal growth.

Accepting the things which you have no control over is a must. Focus only on those things which you can control. If you try to control other people or events which you have no control over, it will only frustrate you and disrupt your inner peace. Focus your energy on your own personal growth and the things that you can control.

If you want to grow spiritually and develop your inner peace, you must place your focus where your spirituality and inner peace reside. When you make the correct adjustments on the inside, all of the changes that you want to see on the outside will soon follow. Your external environment will respond to your internal changes. Things must get right on the inside before they get right on the outside!

Law #5
The Law of Responsibility

Everything in your life is your responsibility. You must accept and take responsibility for the life that you have created. Don't blame your situation or your lack of inner peace on anyone or anything outside yourself. Don't allow yourself to develop a victim mentality. Take ownership of everything in your life; only then will you make the positive changes you want.

You choose your environment. You are the one who decides who you will associate with, what you allow in your life, and what thoughts you allow to take root in your mind. You have no one to blame for anything in your life except yourself.

At the same time, it is not constructive to live in regret or dwell on thoughts that place blame on yourself. Acknowledge that you are responsible for everything in your life, and then take action to change the things that you want to change.

Always own everything in your life. Many people are in the habit of blaming themselves for everything bad that happens to them and giving credit to others, or to luck, for the good things in their lives. You are responsible for both. Take your power back, and don't shortchange yourself!

Remind yourself that we all make mistakes. Many of the things in your life came from incorrect information or beliefs, which led you to make decisions that did not manifest the kind of life that you wanted. The good news is that you can change those beliefs and change your life.

Everything in your life begins with your thoughts. You have a thought, you choose to act on that thought, and then your actions produce a result. Every result in your life is a manifestation of the choices you have made. If you do not like the results you have been getting in your life, then start making better choices. With better choices, you produce better results.

When you take responsibility for everything in your life, even the things which you cannot mentally understand how you could have possibly created, you take your power back. If you blame anyone or anything else for the challenges in your life or give others credit for your successes, you are giving your power away.

Even though you cannot mentally connect the dots and see how you are responsible for everything in your life, accept that belief on faith. Just take responsibility for everything in your life, and then get to work creating the kind of life that you want to live – a life filled with inner peace and tranquility.

195

Law #6
The Law of Connection

This law is closely related to the Law of Responsibility. The Law of Connection states that everything in your life is connected. Everything in your life comes from some action; it is all connected in one way or another. Everything you do is important and carries some consequence, even if you are not aware of what that consequence may be or if you never understand how the consequences of your actions are connected. Sometimes the consequences of your actions do not manifest in your life until much later.

The past, present, and future are all intertwined. The things you think, say, and do today have their roots in the thoughts, beliefs, and experiences from your past. And your thoughts, beliefs, and actions today will have an effect on your experiences in the future. It is all connected. Every action sets in motion a ripple effect that causes repercussions that you may never be aware of. Even if you can't see how something in your past is connected to your life today, there is a connection somewhere down the line.

If you had the ability to see the origins of everything in your life, you would be able to trace everything back to a specific choice that you made or action you took. Consider the movie *Wild Things*. The interesting thing about this movie is the way it was written and directed.

As you watch the movie, you think you know what is happening with the plot, but there are many actions and repercussions that you have no way of understanding because you cannot see the hidden connections. Just like in life, there are many aspects that you are not privy to. It is not until the end of the movie when they go back and fill in the blanks, that it all makes sense to you.

At the end of the movie, the director goes back in time and shows you how decisions were made that changed the lives of each of the characters. Then you can plainly see how the fate of each character was determined by the choices that they each made. Their life was determined by choices in their past which carried consequences that they could have never imagined.

Many of the things in your life are like this movie. You can see the results, but you cannot consciously piece together how you had anything to do with those results, much less how you are responsible for them. But, if you were able to sit down and have a conversation with God and asked Him to explain how you were responsible for specific things in your life, God could connect the dots, and it would all make sense to you.

196

Every action produces either good or bad karma, which is to say that every action you take produces a consequence of one kind or another. When you do negative things, you create negative karma; when you do positive things, you create positive karma. Karma is essentially the law of cause and effect. Whatever you put out into the universe will come back to you in one way or another.

In order to have a positive future and gain control over your life, you must offset your negative karma and replace it with an abundance of good karma. Think of this as a bank account. If you spend more than you have in your account, you will have a negative balance, and it will have negative effects on your life.

What you want to do is continually make positive deposits into your karma account, which will help negate the effects of your negative actions. You will still have to deal with the consequences of your past actions, but you can start creating a positive future by making more and more positive deposits into your account.

You have a karma account and everything you think, say, or do makes either a positive or a negative deposit into your account. Positive thoughts, words, and actions, based on high-energy thoughts and actions such as love, peace, patience, helping others, etc., build up your positive karma. Negative thoughts, words, and actions based on negative, low-energy thoughts and actions, such as anger, hatred, jealousy, envy, resentments, etc. add to your negative karma.

Your thoughts, words, and actions of today determine what you will have in your life tomorrow. Which is to say, the karma you create today determines the life you will live tomorrow. Make sure you are making abundant positive deposits into your karma account every day!

Law #7
The Law of Focus

What you focus on and how you focus on it matters. This law is concerned with directing your attention fully to the task at hand. You cannot hold two thoughts in your mind at the same time. When you are trying to accomplish several things at once, your attention is dispersed and divided, which weakens your focus.

In order to make the necessary changes to your subconscious mind, you need a laser-like focus on your goal. You will experience much better and faster results if you completely focus on one thing at a time. Meditation is an important practice that will help you focus your attention.

197

Be mindful concerning how your attention flows. Being unfocused, or only focusing on your goal occasionally, will not bring about the changes that you want to see. Concentrate fully on one thing at a time. Keep the old Zen proverb in mind – "When walking, walk. When eating, eat." Whatever you are doing at the time, give it your full attention.

Not only should you focus your attention completely on your task at hand, but be mindful about what you are focusing on as well. If you keep your focus on your goal of inner peace, it will be much harder for your thoughts to wander to negative, low-energy thoughts of anger, resentment, jealousy, greed, envy, or hatred. Maintain control of your mind!

Law #8
The Law of Giving and Hospitality

If you have trust and faith in the principles that you believe in, it should show in your actions. In other words, your behavior should follow your beliefs. If you believe that living a life of inner peace is how you should live, then your life should exhibit the qualities of inner peace and tranquility. A part of this is sharing those qualities with others through your interactions.

You should not only talk the talk, but you should also walk the walk. Your inner peace and tranquility should be evident to those around you. There has to be a connection between what you profess to believe and how you live your life. If you want to live a life of inner peace, make it a part of your life to share that inner peace with others. Help them to cultivate inner peace in their lives.

We all know someone who professes to be Christian, Buddhist, or a practitioner of some other religion, but whose actions go against much of what is taught in their chosen religion. Not only does this reflect badly on that person, but it also raises doubts about his religion if that is the kind of person his religion produces. Don't live your life in that way!

If you want to cultivate inner peace in your life and help others do the same, make sure that you are living according to the principles you profess to live by. You shouldn't tell others how great inner peace is and then lose your temper or get stressed out over minor things in your life. That is talking the talk but not walking the walk, and it is hypocritical.

If you are thinking negative, low-energy thoughts and trying to act as if you are living a life of inner peace, sooner or later, the truth will show. Remember, inner peace resides within your mind; it will not

198

consistently exhibit itself in your behavior until it is firmly rooted in your thoughts and your subconscious mind.

You can't give something to someone else if you don't have it to give. If you want to spread inner peace and tranquility in the world, you first have to cultivate inner peace within yourself. Then your inner peace has to demonstrate itself through the way you live your life. Only then will you be able to be truly hospitable and help others enjoy inner peace and tranquility in their lives.

Help others as much as you can on your journey. Share your knowledge and inner peace with them and help them on their path. When you are filled with inner peace, it will show in how you treat those around you. Hospitality and consideration of others will come naturally to you.

Law # 9
The Law of Here and Now

This law encourages us to live in the present moment – the NOW. I have already covered living in the Now in a previous chapter, so I will only touch on it here. Living in the NOW has a lot to do with your focus. You can't live in the NOW if you are constantly thinking of the past or planning for the future. Focus your attention on the present moment.

In order to have inner peace, you have to live in the present. When your thoughts start to drift to the past, often they are focused on things that do not foster inner peace. You begin to think about all the things that you regret, sad thoughts about the people you miss, or how you should have done one thing or another differently. All of these thoughts are unproductive and impede your inner peace.

When your mind starts to focus too much on the future, you are wasting time in the present. While it is good to make plans for the future, don't spend too much time dwelling on them. Make your plans and then get focused on the present so you can manifest the kind of future you want. Thinking about what you want to do will not get it done; you must take action.

Too many people dream of what they will do someday, but someday never comes. The only time that you truly have is in the here and now. As Robert Balzer stated, "Life is what happens to you while you're making other plans."

Inner peace always resides in the NOW. It is never found in the past or the future. You live in the NOW; the past is only memories, and the future does not exist yet. The NOW is the only time you have to experience inner peace, tranquility, and life itself.

Law #10
The Law of Change

The law of change states that the past will repeat itself until you have learned your lesson from it and made the appropriate changes in your life. The one thing you can count on in life is that everything changes, but there are some negative things that seem to appear in your life over and over again. And to make matters worse, we tend to reinforce those events by getting upset and confirming them in our life by stating something like, "Every time I start feeling good about things, this happens again!"

Not only are you experiencing the same frustration time after time, but you are programming your subconscious mind to continue to find ways to manifest that frustration in your life by affirming it through your emotion-filled words.

It is said that the definition of madness is doing the same thing over and over again and expecting different results. If you find that you are experiencing the same problem or annoyance over and over again, that is a signal that you need to make some changes. When you want a different result, you must take different actions. If the same thing is disrupting your inner peace repeatedly over time, it is most likely a sign that you need to change either your thoughts, words, or actions.

If a certain action seems to trigger you over and over again, it is time to deal with it directly. Figure out why it triggers you, and change your thought process concerning it. Take steps to remove yourself from that cycle of being triggered, temporarily losing your inner peace, and having to spend time getting rebalanced again.

Use the techniques in this book to change your subconscious mind. Remove the trigger and replace it with a higher energy thought. And then the next time that situation appears, stop yourself before you allow it to rob you of your inner peace. Change whatever needs to be changed to maintain your inner peace.

Law #11
The Law of Patience and Reward

The law of patience and reward states that you must take action and be patient in order to receive the reward which you are working towards. Living a life of inner peace requires patience, not just with other people and the situations of life, but with yourself while you work towards your goal. As I stated in the chapter on patience, everything in nature takes time to grow. You don't plant your garden

200

one day and then harvest your vegetables the next day; you have to be patient, do the work, and cultivate your garden.

The same principle applies when it comes to developing your inner peace. You can't cleanse your subconscious mind of a lifetime of negative thoughts, limiting beliefs, and bad habits overnight. You have to be consistent in doing the mental work necessary to change your mind and replace negative thoughts and beliefs with ones that foster inner peace. You have to be patient with yourself and the process.

Long-term rewards require that you put in the work and not lose your patience with the process. Losing patience will result in giving up and going back to your old ways of thinking and reacting to the people and events in your life.

I discussed your karma account earlier. Think of the work that you are doing to change your subconscious mind, thoughts, and behavior as your savings account for the future. You are saving now by doing the work that needs to be done so that you can comfortably live a life of inner peace in the future. The more you make those changes in your life, the more your inner peace savings account grows.

You will have good days and bad days, but as long as you don't give up, you will keep moving closer and closer to the inner peace that you long for. Consistently bring your thoughts and actions under control, and refuse to give up on your goal.

Law #12
The Law of Significance and Inspiration

This law can be interpreted as you get what you deserve in life. Every thought, every word, and every action is significant in your life, and either brings you closer to inner peace or moves you further away. Nothing in life comes for free; if you want something worth having, you have to work for it.

Everything you do affects your environment in one way or another. When you allow someone to push your buttons and you react badly, you are reinforcing bad behavior, not just in yourself and in your subconscious mind, but in the world as a whole by your bad example.

When a rude driver cuts someone off in traffic, and the other person reacts by flipping him off, hitting the horn, yelling, etc., it does nothing to bring peace or compassion to the situation. It most likely results in the rude driver reacting in the same manner and escalating the situation. Remember, like attracts like. These actions are the seeds of road rage and can quickly deteriorate into a very ugly situation.

201

Whereas, if the driver who was cut off in traffic had just chalked it up to the other guy having a bad day and not allowed it to disrupt his inner peace, there would have been no further reaction from the careless driver.

Your attitude and actions matter, not just to your life, but to the lives of those around you. When you respond kindly and compassionately to someone who maybe doesn't deserve it, you are making the situation better for everyone. You have changed the energy of that situation and maintained your inner peace.

Everything you do affects the world in some way. You never know when your kind, compassionate, patient, and peaceful response may truly make a lasting impact on someone's life. There are no insignificant actions. Instead of reacting without thinking, choose a calculated response meant to maintain your inner peace and set an example for those around you.

~~~~~~~~

This chapter was a quick overview of how the 12 Laws of Karma connect to the art of inner peace. Use the wisdom in the 12 Laws of Karma to help you maintain your goal of inner peace as you go through your daily life. Be mindful of your thoughts, your words, and your actions, and work to bring them in line with the kind of life that you want to live. Remember that every thought, word, and action matters, and live your life mindfully.

Freely share your inner peace and tranquility with others. Deposit into your karma account daily until you have an abundance of good karma that will provide you with an increasingly blessed future. Use your actions and words to inspire those around you. Be a good example of what it is like to live a life of inner peace and share your peace with everyone you come into contact with each day.

Individuals create karma;
karma does not create individuals.
Bodhidharma

Thoughts to Ponder

We gather the consequences of our own deeds.
Garuda Purana

We choose our joys and sorrows long before we experience them.
Kahlil Gibran

Events, circumstances, etc. have their origin in ourselves.
They spring from seeds which we have sown.
Henry David Thoreau

Everything in nature is a cause from which there flows some effect.
Baruch Spinoza

Now, though I do no wrong, I am punished by my past.
Neither gods nor men can foresee when an evil deed will
bear its fruit...When you meet with adversity don't be upset,
because it makes sense...If we should be blessed by some
great reward, it is the fruit of a seed planted by us in the past.
Bodhidharma

Your goodwill towards others returns to yourself in the end.
Japanese Proverb

The good deeds you do now are the treasure of the future.
Philippine Proverb

Kindness gives birth to kindness.
Sophocles

There is no act, however trivial, but has its train of consequences.
Samuel Smiles

What is man's chief enemy? Each man is his own.
Anacharsis

Sow much, reap much; sow little, reap little.
Chinese Proverb

Take away the cause and the effect must cease.
English Proverb

203

Thoughts to Ponder

Chance is a word void of sense; nothing can exist without a cause.
Voltaire

Every man is the son of his own works.
Cervantes

Hidden things always come to light. Do not sow bad seeds.
Be sure, they will come up...We can't know where our pain is from.
We don't know all that we have done. If you cause injury to someone;
you draw that same injury toward yourself.
Rumi

I stumbled over the roots of a tree I had myself planted.
Goethe

How people treat you is their karma; how you react is yours.
Wayne Dyer

As she has planted, so does she harvest; such is the field of karma.
Sri Guru Granth Sahib

When you truly understand karma, then you realize
you are responsible for everything in your life.
Keanu Reeves

Learn to see. Realize that everything connects to everything else.
Leonardo da Vinci

The law is simple. Every experience is repeated or suffered
till you experience it properly and fully the first time.
Ben Okri

Do evil thoughts of retaliation injure oneself or one's enemy?
Nagarjuna

Do not judge, and you will not be judged.
Do not condemn, and you will not be condemned.
Forgive, and you will be forgiven. Give, and it will be given to you...
For with the measure you use, it will be measured to you.
Jesus

Chapter 19
Your Inner Peace Roadmap

He who conquers others is strong;
he who conquers himself is mighty.
Lao Tzu

The principles and wisdom that I have shared with you in this book will change your life if you consistently apply them in your pursuit of inner peace. I have given you a lot to think about in *The Art of Inner Peace*. In this chapter, I am going to summarize all of the principles I have shared to make it easier for you to refer back to and keep yourself on track. Let's get started.

~~~~~~~~

Inner Peace Comes from Within

Inner peace comes from within and resides in your mind. Therefore, you have the ability to completely control your inner peace and tranquility at all times. No one can disrupt your inner peace or take it from you since you are the only person who is in charge of the inner workings of your mind.

Whenever you are feeling stressed or out of sorts, take the time to go within and rebalance yourself. Things must get right on the inside before they can be right on the outside. If you want to develop inner peace in your life, you must go within.

Your Thoughts Create Your Reality

Everything in your life originates with your thoughts, including every word you speak and every action you take. Therefore, your thoughts create your reality. If your life is not what you want it to be, the issue is to be found in your mind. Change your thoughts, and your external life will change.

Everything you have ever thought, believed, said, or done resides somewhere in your subconscious mind. Your subconscious mind controls around 95% of the beliefs in your life. It is thought that the subconscious mind is close to a million times more powerful than your conscious mind.

Your subconscious mind has been programmed over many years to believe the thoughts, beliefs, and words you have conditioned it to believe over the years. And since it accepts those core beliefs that you have fed it as absolutes, the subconscious mind works to manifest them in your life. True change starts with cleansing and reprogramming your subconscious mind.

Cleansing Your Subconscious Mind

In order to take control of your mind and your life, you must cleanse your subconscious mind of the negative thoughts and limiting beliefs which it has accepted as truth over the years. It is important not to simply remove those negative thoughts and limiting beliefs; you also have to replace them with thoughts and beliefs that foster inner peace and tranquility.

The Universe abhors a void. If you do not replace the negative thoughts and limiting beliefs in your subconscious mind with positive, self-affirming thoughts and beliefs, it will simply revert back to its old ways, and you will be no better off. You must be consistent! There are many techniques and practices which help you cleanse and change your subconscious mind. Below are the exercises included for you:

1) Meditation
2) Positive Affirmations
3) Visualization
4) Your Vision Board
5) Spending Time in Nature
6) Breath Work
7) Stop Complaining
8) Reduce Your Time Watching the News
9) Scratching the DVD

Your Mind Versus Your Emotions

Once you have cleansed and reprogrammed your subconscious mind, you must reinforce that work by disciplining and controlling your thoughts. You must make your choices according to your own standards and how you want to live your life. To do this, you must spend some time in meditation and deep thought in order to understand what your standards or code of ethics entail.

Do not allow your emotions to dictate your actions. Doing so will disrupt your inner peace more often than not. Your emotions originate in your mind. Control your mind and get your thoughts in line with your goal of inner peace.

206

There are two categories of thoughts/emotions which will determine what you manifest in your life:

1) Positive, Higher Energy Thoughts – Empower You
   (love, gratitude, patience, forgiveness, kindness, etc.)
2) Negative, Low-Energy Thoughts – Disempower You
   (Anger, hatred, jealousy, fear, worry, resentfulness, etc.)

You must work to rid yourself of the negative, low-energy thoughts and emotions and increase your positive, higher-level thoughts and emotions. Negative thoughts and emotions will disrupt your inner peace if you do not control them and remove them from your life.

Correct Actions Lead to Inner Peace

Since your thoughts give birth to your actions, positive, higher-energy thoughts lead to actions that maintain your inner peace. Never act before you think. Think about things rationally, keeping in mind your goal is to maintain your inner peace.

Instead of reacting to circumstances or other people, respond. When you react, you are allowing other people or events to control you; when you respond, you are in control. Always strive to do what's right, regardless of the consequences. Don't be attached to the outcome of your actions but to the action itself.

Correct actions based on higher-level, positive thoughts and inner peace lead to a clear conscience, which is a must in order to maintain your inner peace. Never go against your conscience, as it is there to help you maintain your code of ethics. Ignoring your conscience will disrupt your inner peace.

Your Words Are Important

Your words are more powerful than you think. That is why practicing personal, positive affirmations is such a powerful tool. Words affect your spirit, your subconscious, and your life. They can heal, or they can destroy, depending on how you use them. Your words can bring peace to your life, or they can totally disrupt your inner peace.

Being dishonest and lying will disturb your inner peace. Lying causes your conscience to convict you, increases your stress and anxiety, and can actually lead to health problems. Discipline yourself to be honest with both yourself and others. Self-deception never leads

207

to positive outcomes. Be honest, be mindful, and choose your words carefully.

Develop Good Habits and Stay Calm

Ultimately, your habits become your life. You must rid yourself of your bad habits, which are not in line with living a life of inner peace. In addition to removing your bad habits, you must replace them with good, life-affirming habits. Human beings are creatures of habit. In order to consistently live a life of inner peace, you must develop good habits which help you maintain inner peace in your daily life.

One of those habits is to always remain calm, no matter what is happening around you. Not only does remaining calm help you maintain your inner peace, but the ability to stay calm is actually a sign that you are succeeding in your quest to live a life of inner peace. Panicking and losing control are never conducive to your inner peace and tranquility.

Ban Fear and Worry from Your Life

Fear is a reaction to a person, place, thing, or situation, and is the source of all worry. Worry is nothing more than a lack of faith in God. It is always focused on things that you cannot control and causes your mind to concentrate on the future instead of the NOW. Both fear and worry are negative, low-energy thoughts that will absolutely rob you of your inner peace. You cannot allow fear and worry to reside in your mind and live a life of inner peace at the same time; the two are not compatible.

Take control of the things that you actually can control, and stop focusing on the things that are out of your control. The only things you truly control are your thoughts, words, and actions. If you can do something about a specific situation, do it; if you can't, move on. Refuse to worry about anything.

One of the biggest fears is the fear of dying. In order to live a life of inner peace, you must be at peace with the fact that you are going to leave your physical body one day. Come to grips with this fact, and you will want to live every moment of your life to the fullest.

Actively Choose Inner Peace

Since inner peace resides within your mind, you have the ability to choose to be at peace at any time and in any situation. It is a choice that you make. Decide once and for all that you are going to live a life of inner peace and then stand by your decision. Don't allow anything to disrupt your tranquility.

Part of that process is removing expectations from your life. Expectations can lead to sadness, frustration, and disappointment. Remember, you are not in this world to live up to the expectations of others, and other people are not here to live up to your expectations of them.

Instead of placing expectations on other people and situations, practice acceptance. Accept people as they are and life as it is. Stop judging everything in your life. Practice being non-judgmental. Getting rid of expectations and being non-judgmental will foster inner peace.

Don't Allow Others to Sidetrack You

Don't allow the opinions, words, or actions of others to sidetrack you. It is okay to ignore other people's opinions. You are not responsible for the thoughts, words, or actions of others, only for your own. Refuse to be offended. Nobody can offend you if you refuse to be offended. Don't allow yourself to be offended by anyone or anything.

Stop allowing other people to pull you into their drama. You do not have to justify your opinions or your life to anyone. It is your life to live, nobody else's. Others are entitled to their opinions, and you are entitled to your opinion. Arguing gives birth to strife, resentments, and hard feelings; refuse to take part in arguments. No one can argue with you if you refuse to participate.

In the same way, refuse to take part in or listen to gossip. Gossip is almost never uplifting and positive, and does not lead to inner peace. Excuse yourself when a conversation turns negative or when someone starts gossiping.

Mind Your Own Business

If you want to live a life of inner peace, you must focus on *your* life, not that of others. Too many people focus on what everyone else is doing and neglect to get their own life in order. Don't get involved in other people's business or dramas. Focus on cultivating your own garden instead of watching others cultivate theirs, and then judging them for how they do it. Remember, the signpost on the path to inner peace reads – "Not My Circus, Not My Monkeys!"

The people that you associate with matter. They will either help you move closer to your goals or make it harder for you to achieve

209

them. Be selective when it comes to your associations. You tend to acquire some of the traits of the people you spend time with, so make sure you are spending time with people whose lives or character you admire. Allowing the wrong people into your life will always disrupt your inner peace sooner or later.

Overcome Obstacles and Conflicts

No matter how much you try to live a peaceful and tranquil life, you will have to overcome conflicts and obstacles from time to time. Remember to be like water and flow around the obstacles in your path with a calm and tranquil spirit. Others may try to trigger your anger, but you do not have to take the bait. Instead of getting angry, see obstacles and conflicts as challenges and respond instead of reacting to them.

Nobody can *make* you angry; you choose to be angry. Getting angry and frustrated only robs you of your inner peace. Long-term anger can lead to hatred, and hatred will completely throw you off track. Don't try to control the actions of others; just observe, accept, and respond when needed.

When you allow someone else to *make* you angry, you are allowing that person to manipulate and control you; you are making yourself a victim. Refuse to be a victim! Take responsibility for everything in your life.

Develop Patience and Forgiveness

It is easier to deal with obstacles and conflicts if you develop patience and forgiveness in your life. Instead of getting angry about what someone else says or does, practice patience and forgiveness. We all make mistakes. Don't always assume that their actions are malicious or even have anything to do with you. You have no idea what is really going on in other people's lives.

Forgive others when they mess up, even if they are maliciously trying to hurt you. Forgiveness is for you, not for the other person. Holding on to anger and resentment will not only disrupt your inner peace but can cause long-term stress and health issues. Forgive everyone all the time. Forgive, but don't forget. When someone shows you his or her character flaws, make a note of them in case you ever have to deal with that person again. This is not holding a grudge but simply protecting yourself.

Also, be patient and forgiving with yourself. You are only human, and you will make mistakes; you are not perfect. Understand that

210

mistakes are opportunities to develop inner peace in your life. Quit holding on to past regrets, forgive yourself, and move on. Regrets will rob you of your inner peace.

Practice Kindness and Compassion

Instead of being impatient and unforgiving, practice kindness, compassion, and act from a place of love. Be kind and compassionate, not because the other person deserves it, but because that is the kind of person you want to be and because it helps you maintain your inner peace.

Practice unconditional love for yourself and for other people. When you act from a place of love and compassion, you will be kind. It is hard to be compassionate while being angry and resentful at the same time. When you develop your inner peace, the qualities of love, kindness, and compassion will become second nature for you, and you will be happy and grateful for the blessings in your life.

Determine to Be Happy and Grateful

You can choose to be happy no matter what is happening around you. You don't have to be sad, depressed, or unhappy simply because that is what others expect of you. Choose to be happy, even in the worst situations. Happiness is a choice, and like inner peace, it comes from within.

Gratitude leads to happiness. Instead of focusing on all the things that you don't have, focus on all the blessings that you do have. Start each day off with gratitude. If you have to compare your life with others, compare it to those who have much less than you and would give anything to be in your shoes. You are abundantly blessed; be grateful!

Your attitude determines your happiness. Do you see the glass half empty or half full? Or do you believe it doesn't matter because you can always refill it whenever you want to? Your attitude matters. Make sure to always maintain a good, positive attitude.

Live Your Life Your Way

You have one life to live; live it your way. Don't allow other people's opinions to cause you to live a life that is not your own. Be confident enough to be yourself in a world that will try to persuade you to be someone else. Don't live to please others; find your own purpose in life. Find a path that captures your heart and excites you; then have the courage to follow it to the end.

Never try to be someone else. While it is okay to take certain traits that you admire in another person and make them uniquely your own, you should not try to imitate anyone else. You are a unique human being with distinctive talents. Find your purpose in life and live your life your way.

Don't compare your life to others who you feel have it better than you, who may be better looking than you, or who have more money than you. They are on their path; you are on your path. Comparison and competition do not lead to inner peace.

Defeat and failure are just opinions. There is no such thing as defeat if you don't quit; failure only occurs if you fail to learn from the outcomes of your actions. Failure and defeat only live in your mind; don't let them dictate your actions or attitude. You define your own success. Live your life your way!

Discipline Yourself to Live in the Now

The only time that you can really live your life is in this present moment – the NOW. The past is over and done with. You cannot change what happened in the past, so refuse to allow your mind to dwell on regrets. The future does not exist; don't spend too much time fantasizing about it or planning for it. Focus on the NOW. It is all you really have.

At first, this will take some self-discipline. Living a life of inner peace is living a life of self-discipline. Self-discipline and self-control are vital to your tranquility. Be determined to live your life your way in every moment, no matter what anyone else does or says.

Remember, the man or woman of principle does not forget who he or she is because of what others are. You are not responsible for what others think, say, or do, but you are responsible for your own words and actions. Be mindful and live fully in the present moment. Live in the NOW and don't allow the distractions of life to cause you to get caught up in the past or the future.

Adhere to the 12 Laws of Karma and Inner Peace

Adhering to the 12 Laws of Karma and Inner Peace will help keep you on the right path during your quest for inner peace and tranquility.

Law #1 - The Great Law

This is the law of cause and effect. Everything you do in life will come back to you in some way. What you put out into the Universe will come back to you. The more peaceful you become, the more inner peace you will experience. Don't just develop inner peace in your life and keep it to yourself; share your inner peace and tranquility everywhere you go. The more you share, the more inner peace comes back to you.

Law #2 – The Law of Creation

Things do not happen automatically. Wishing for inner peace won't get you anywhere. If you want inner peace in your life, you have to take action to create it. You are the author of what you create in your life. Your environment is influenced by your actions or your lack of action. You create your own life by your thoughts, words, and actions.

Law #3 – The Law of Humility

You have to be humble enough to recognize that you need to change some things in order to live a life of inner peace. Don't allow your ego to interrupt your journey. If you refuse to acknowledge your mistakes or deny that they have affected your life, you will not be able to correct those mistakes and change the effects that they have had on you. Humble yourself, admit that you need to make some changes in your life, and then take action to develop your inner peace and tranquility.

Law #4 – The Law of Growth

Every change in your life has to begin with you, with your thoughts and actions. Personal growth always starts from within. Accept the things you cannot change, and take control of the things that you can control. For things to be right on the outside, they must first be right on the inside.

Law # 5 – The Law of Responsibility

Everything in your life is your responsibility. You must accept and take responsibility for the life that you have created. Don't allow yourself to develop a victim mentality. If you do not like the results you have been creating in your life, then start making different choices. With better choices come better results. Take ownership of everything in your life; only then will you be able to change the things that you want to change. Taking full responsibility for your life empowers you and puts you in the driver's seat.

Law #6 – The Law of Connection

Everything in your life is connected in one way or another. Everything you think, do, or say has a consequence in your life. Your past, present, and future are all connected. The things you think, say, and do today have their roots in the thoughts, beliefs, and experiences from your past. And your thoughts, beliefs, and actions today will determine your experiences in the future.

Law #7 – The Law of Focus

What you focus on and how you focus matters. You cannot hold two thoughts in your mind at the same time; you can only concentrate on one thing at a time. Develop a laser-like focus and make sure you are focusing on things that help you manifest and maintain your inner peace. Be mindful concerning where your attention flows. Always maintain control of your mind.

Law #8 – The Law of Giving and Hospitality

Your behavior should follow what you truly believe. Don't just talk the talk, but walk the walk. If you want to live a life of inner peace, make it a habit to share that inner peace with others. Help others to cultivate inner peace in their lives, and you will find more inner peace in your life. Give, and it will be given to you!

Law #9 – The Law of Here and Now

Live in the NOW. Living in the NOW has a lot to do with your focus. You can't be living in the NOW if you are constantly thinking of the past or planning for the future. Focus your attention on the present moment because that is where inner peace resides. You only live in the NOW; the past is nothing but memories, and the future does not exist yet. The NOW is the only time you have to experience inner peace, tranquility, and life itself.

Law # 10 – The Law of Change

Everything in life is constantly changing. The past will repeat itself until you have learned your lesson from it and made the appropriate changes in your life. Learn your lessons from your experiences and change whatever needs to be changed to maintain your inner peace.

Law # 11 – The Law of Patience and Reward

You must be patient in order to receive the reward which you are working towards. Living a life of inner peace requires patience, not just with other people and situations, but with yourself. Long-term rewards, such as inner peace, require that you put in the work and not lose your patience with the process. Be patient, take control of your thoughts, words, and actions, and inner peace will follow.

Law # 12 – The Law of Significance and Inspiration

Every thought, every word, and every action is significant in your life and either brings you closer to inner peace or moves you further away. Nothing in life is free. When it comes to your inner peace, you make your choices, and the consequences naturally follow.

~~~~~~~~

Once you integrate all of these principles into your life, you will find it much easier to control your thoughts, words, actions, and emotions. You will not be as concerned with the outcomes of your action, but rather, you will be focused on doing what's right and maintaining your inner peace.

Your habits will begin to change, and along with them, you will see positive changes in your life. You will be more calm and tranquil, no matter what is happening around you or what the circumstances are. Fear and worry will become a thing of the past. You will be at peace with the mortality of your physical body, knowing that you have your life in order and that your essence, who you truly are, will live on.

You will find that you are actively choosing inner peace in every situation, even the most difficult ones. Instead of judging other people, events, and things, you will have a more accepting and non-judgmental spirit. In place of expectations, you will simply accept everyone as they are and everything as it is. You will be at peace.

215

The opinions of others will no longer affect you or upset you. It will become almost impossible to offend you. You will refuse to get pulled into other people's drama or arguments; thus, your relationships will be more peaceful. Your focus will be on your own life, so you will not be concerned with what everyone else is doing.

You will be more selective concerning those you associate with, so you will find yourself spending time with people who help you on your journey of inner peace. Obstacles and conflicts will no longer cause you anger or trigger your emotions. You will refuse to allow anybody or anything to make you feel like a victim because you will always take responsibility for everything in your life.

Your heart will be more open to other people, so you will be more patient and kind. You will look for ways to help others and share your inner peace with them. Since you have taken control of your attitude, you will be happier and grateful for everything in your life.

Your self-confidence will increase, and you will feel free to live your life your way without being concerned about what people think. You will discover your purpose in life. How others live, what they have, how they look, and what they do will no longer concern you, as you no longer compare your life with their lives.

Self-discipline will become a natural part of your life, and you will discipline yourself to stay focused on the present moment. Regrets and daydreaming will become a thing of the past. You will continually build up your karma account.

Only *acting* on the principles in *The Art of Inner Peace* will change your life, and only by continually applying those principles each and every day will you reap long-term benefits. You are in control of an awesome power; you have all the power you need to totally change your life for the better.

In addition, you now have all the tools you need to start living a life of inner peace. It is up to you how you will use them. Inner peace will be yours if you are willing to embrace it and discipline yourself to live it. The choice is yours, as it always was. I hope that you have found *The Art of Inner Peace* helpful for your journey. May you find inner peace and tranquility as you continue on your adventure in this life.

> *No one saves us but ourselves.*
> *No one can and no one may.*
> *We ourselves must walk the path.*
> Buddha

Thoughts to Ponder

My life is my message.
Gandhi

Your daily life is your temple and your religion.
Kahlil Gibran

Knowing is not enough, we must apply.
Willing is not enough, we must do.
Goethe

It is you who must make the effort;
the sages can only teach.
The Dhammapada

No matter how many good words you read and speak of, what good
will they do you if you do not put them into practice and use them?
Buddha

Prepare yourself for you must travel alone.
The master can only indicate to you the road.
Book of the Golden Precepts

All you learn, and all you can read, will be of little use,
if you do not think and reason upon it yourself.
Lord Chesterfield

The words printed here are concepts.
You must go through the experience.
Saint Augustine

I feel again a spark of that ancient flame.
Virgil

Take control of your consistent emotions and begin to
consciously and deliberately reshape your daily experience of life.
Tony Robbins

I know what I have given you.
I do not know what you have received.
Antonio Porchia

217

Thoughts to Ponder

Be yourself, take control of your life.
Emma Bunton

The pen that writes your life story must be held in your own hand.
Irene C. Kassorla

You can influence, direct and control your own environment.
You can make your life what you want it to be.
Napoleon Hill

Freedom is control in your own life.
Willie Nelson

You are in control of your life. Don't ever forget that.
You are what you are because of the conscious
and subconscious choices you have made.
Barbara Hall

Only you can control your future.
Dr. Seuss

Take the power to control your own life.
Take the power to make your life happy.
Susan Polis Schutz

Control your own destiny or someone else will.
Jack Welch

Start living by taking back the control of your life now!
Create a life more in tune with your true desires.
Steven Redhead

Success is hastened or delayed by one's habits.
It is not your passing inspirations or brilliant ideas so much
as your everyday mental habits that control your life.
Paramahansa Yogananda

The test of literature is, I suppose, whether we
ourselves live more intensely for the reading of it.
Elizabeth Drew

Do it Anyway

People are often unreasonable, illogical, and self-centered;
Forgive them anyway.

If you are kind, people may accuse you of selfish, ulterior motives;
Be kind anyway.

If you are successful, you will win some false friends and some true enemies;
Succeed anyway.

If you are honest and frank, people may cheat you;
Be honest and frank anyway.

What you spend years building, someone may destroy overnight;
Build anyway.

If you find serenity and happiness, they may be jealous;
Be happy anyway.

The good you do today, people will often forget tomorrow;
Do good anyway.

Give the world the best you have, and it may never be enough;
Give the world the best you've got anyway.

You see, in the final analysis, it is all between you and God;
It was never between you and them anyway.

Mother Teresa

IF

If you can keep your head when all about you
Are losing theirs and blaming it on you;
If you can trust yourself when all men doubt you,
But make allowance for their doubting too;
If you can wait and not be tired by waiting,
Or, being lied about, don't deal in lies,
Or, being hated, don't give way to hating,
And yet don't look too good, nor talk too wise;

If you can dream - and not make dreams your master;
If you can think - and not make thoughts your aim;
If you can meet with triumph and disaster
And treat those two impostors just the same;
If you can bear to hear the truth you've spoken
Twisted by knaves to make a trap for fools,
Or watch the things you gave your life to broken,
And stoop and build 'em up with worn-out tools;

If you can make one heap of all your winnings
And risk it on one turn of pitch-and-toss,
And lose, and start again at your beginnings
And never breathe a word about your loss;
If you can force your heart and nerve and sinew
To serve your turn long after they are gone,
And so hold on when there is nothing in you
Except the Will which says to them: "Hold on!"

If you can talk with crowds and keep your virtue,
Or walk with kings - nor lose the common touch;
If neither foes nor loving friends can hurt you;
If all men count with you, but none too much;
If you can fill the unforgiving minute
With sixty seconds' worth of distance run -
Yours is the Earth and everything that's in it,
And - which is more - you'll be a Man, my son!

Rudyard Kipling

The Prayer of Saint Francis

Lord, make me an instrument of your peace:
where there is hatred, let me sow love;
where there is injury, pardon;
where there is doubt, faith;
where there is despair, hope;
where there is darkness, light;
where there is sadness, joy.

O divine Master, grant that I may not so much seek
to be consoled as to console,
to be understood as to understand,
to be loved as to love.
For it is in giving that we receive,
it is in pardoning that we are pardoned,
and it is in dying that we are born to eternal life.
Amen.

Six Important Guidelines in Life

1) When you are alone, mind your thoughts.

2) When you are with friends, mind your tongue.

3) When you are angry, mind your temper.

4) When you are with a group, mind your behavior.

5) When you are in trouble, mind your emotions.

6) When God starts blessing you, mind your ego.

(author unknown)

About the Author

Dr. Bohdi Sanders is a multi-award winning and bestselling author of 16 books. His common sense philosophy and worldview have inspired and helped thousands of people worldwide. He has a knack for taking complicated concepts and explaining them in a down-to-earth, easy to understand way which everyone can comprehend and apply to his or her life.

He has degrees in Sociology, Education, Naturopathy, and Holistic Health, and has studied philosophy for most of his life. He is a 5th degree black belt in Shotokan Karate, a father of two, and a proud grandfather of two energetic boys. His work has been recognized internationally and has won multiple national book awards. Some of the recognitions for his writing include:

- Lifetime Achievement Award from *The Elite Black Belt Hall of Fame* for his contributions to the world of martial arts through his writing, along with his martial arts hall of fame induction.
- #1 Amazon Bestseller in 2015 for his book, *Men of the Code*
- #1 Amazon Bestseller in 2013 for his book, *Modern Bushido*
- The Indie Excellence Book Awards: 1st Place Winner 2013
- USA Book News Best Books of 2013: 1st Place Winner 2013
- The Indie Excellence Book Awards: 1st Place Winner 2010
- USA Book News Best Books of 2010: 1st Place Winner 2010

Dr. Sanders resides in beautiful Colorado outside of Rocky Mountain National Park. He can be contacted through email at: WarriorWisdom@comcast.net.

223

Please take a couple
of minutes and review
The Art of Inner Peace

Reader reviews are very important to authors in today's fast-paced world, and I value your opinion. Reviews are the lifeblood of the author. Posting a quick review on Amazon, on Facebook, and other social media really helps independent authors.

If you have enjoyed *The Art of Inner Peace*, please consider taking just a couple of minutes and reviewing it on Amazon, on your social media pages, and elsewhere. Also, please tell your friends about *The Art of Inner Peace,* and let's help others develop and maintain their inner peace as well! Thank you!

Bohdi Sanders

WANT MORE?

Now you can get
daily teachings to
help you stay motivated!

Follow Dr. Bohdi Sanders' teachings on inner peace every single day! Dr. Sanders shares free teachings every day on Facebook and on The Art of Inner Peace website!

The-Art-of-Inner-Peace.com

www.facebook.com/The.Art.of.Inner.Peace

Be sure to sign up for your

FREE
Art of Inner Peace
SUBSCRIPTION

to receive more free motivational teachings, updates, Dr. Sanders' speaking schedule, special discounts on books, and more!

Sign up for your FREE subscription here:
the-art-of-inner-peace.com/Subscribe/

Other Titles by Kaizen Quest

• *__Modern Bushido: Living a Life of Excellence__* by Bohdi Sanders

• *__BUSHIDO: The Way of the Warrior__* by Bohdi Sanders

• *__LEGACY: Through the Eyes of the Warrior__* by Al Dacascos

• *__Men of the Code: Living as a Superior Man__* by Bohdi Sanders

• *__WARRIOR: The Way of Warriorhood__* by Bohdi Sanders

• *__Defensive Living: The Other Side of Self-Defense__* by Bohdi Sanders

• *__Wisdom of the Elders: The Ultimate Quote Book__* by Bohdi Sanders

• *__DEFIANCE: The Dark Side of the Martial Arts__* by Bohdi Sanders

• *__The Warrior Lifestyle__* by Bohdi Sanders

• *__Warrior Wisdom__* by Bohdi Sanders

• *__Secrets of the Soul__* by Bohdi Sanders

• *__Martial Arts Wisdom: Quotes, Maxims, Stories__* by Bohdi Sanders

• *__As a Man Thinketh__* by James Allen

• *__The Mastery of Destiny__* by James Allen